"One of the major voids in our pr... *How to Become a More Effective Leader*, my good friend Johnny Hunt vividly explains how you can effectively influence others to live abundantly in a purposeful, Christlike manner. This is a book for our time!"

—**Steve Gaines,** PhD, pastor, Bellevue Baptist Church, Memphis, TN

"Johnny Hunt, having earned the title of the pastor's pastor, relates from his vast practical experience the essential elements of godly leadership. Rather than repeating cliches and platitudes, he describes and details the important process of answering the call to leadership in today's culture. The characteristics put forth are thoughtfully enumerated; the path to true *godly* leadership is plainly described. God will use this book and its author to inspire and instruct the leadership of tomorrow, something for which our world is hungry."

—**Sonny Perdue,** governor of Georgia, 2003–2011

"Johnny Hunt has been an effective leader for decades. In *How to Become a More Effective Leader*, he shares his personal insights and wisdom for this important assignment. Many will be blessed by his godly and practical counsel."

—**Daniel L. Akin,** president, Southeastern Baptist
Theological Seminary, Wake Forest, NC

"One of the best books I've read on leadership with a strong emphasis on vision and influence. A profound, refreshing book that only a person who walks the talk could have written. Johnny has given us a classic on leadership that will inspire the rookie leader and veteran leader alike. It is amazing that so much wisdom is packed into so few pages."

—**Steve Cannon,** owner/president, Steve Cannon
Insurance & Financial Services Agency

"As a church member, accountability partner, Sunday school teacher, and in leadership in several positions under Pastor Hunt's ministry for thirty-plus years, I personally learned to be a better leader having witnessed Pastor Hunt live before me the principles found in this book and then applying them to my life. Whether one leads in a secular workplace or in a church-related position, one can become a more effective leader by applying one or all of the principles covered in this well-written and well-lived book."

—**Dr. John D. Peacock,** DDS, FAGD, FPFA, general dentist,
teacher, president of Georgia Baptist Mobile Health Ministry

HOW TO BECOME A MORE EFFECTIVE LEADER

JOHNNY HUNT

HARVEST HOUSE PUBLISHERS
EUGENE. OREGON

Bible notifications may be found at the end of the book

Cover design by Charles Brock

Cover Photo © Oksana Kumer / Adobe Stock; Tawng / Depositphotos

Interior design by KUHN Design Group

For bulk, special sales, or ministry purchases, please call 1-800-547-8979.
Email: Customerservice@hhpbooks.com

M This logo is a federally registered trademark of the Hawkins Children's LLC. Harvest House Publishers, Inc., is the exclusive licensee of this trademark.

How to Become a More Effective Leader
Copyright © 2022 by Johnny Hunt
Published by Harvest House Publishers
Eugene, Oregon 97408
www.harvesthousepublishers.com

ISBN 978-0-7369-8181-1 (pbk)
ISBN 978-0-7369-8182-8 (eBook)

Library of Congress Control Number: 2021949790

Printed in the United States of America

22 23 24 25 26 27 28 29 30 / BP / 10 9 8 7 6 5 4 3 2 1

The inspiration and motivation for this book has been the Timothy+Barnabas Ministry that just completed 27 years of instruction and encouragement. When I began this ministry, it was with the desire to help those coming behind me as well as to be a blessing to those around me. I have always believed that one of a pastor's greatest needs is not so much to learn another lesson but to be encouraged in the ones they already know. This ministry could not have been blessed as it has been without the ones who went before me. I'm eternally grateful for all those who have done the same for me.

Contents

Introduction:

It Ain't Easy

P eople are dying for leadership.

Often, they just need somebody to believe in them. Who doesn't need someone to believe in them? Sadly, though, most men and women have no one who believes in them. They have nobody who builds them up and equips them to succeed.

What can happen, though, when somebody faithfully encourages and believes in them? The result is nothing less than astonishing. And when that somebody is a *leader*, mind-blowing things can happen.

Everything rises and falls on leadership.

For more than four decades now, the Lord has placed me in varying kinds of leadership roles. I've pastored small, medium, large, and mega churches. I've served as president of the nation's largest Christian denomination. And today I serve as the VP of Evangelism and Leadership with the North American Mission Board of the Southern Baptist Convention, working with tens of thousands of leaders all over the United States.

I've worked closely on significant projects with the amazing leaders of huge corporations, both domestic and multinational. I've partnered with leaders at nearly all levels of government. I have met with, worked with, and been mutually encouraged by remarkable leaders from around the globe. And wherever I've led, whatever we've tried to accomplish, however large or small the challenge seemed, I've learned one thing repeatedly:

Leadership ain't easy.

Leaders Begin with Themselves

It's been said that the largest room we leaders own is the room of self-improvement. If I'm going to lead an organization to its greatest days, then the greatest development must take place not in my subordinates but in me. As we start thinking as leaders, we must always begin with ourselves. We find most problems by looking in the mirror instead of out the window at others.

Is that easy? No.

Too many leaders resemble the hamster continually running a wheel at top speed, only to end up at the same place every evening. Someone has said that the average leader's life consists of twenty years of having his parents ask where he's going, seven years of his professor asking where he's going, forty years of his organization asking where he's going, and at his funeral, mourners wondering the same thing.

Only when we start *thinking* differently can we start *behaving* differently. When we start thinking purposefully, we start living purposefully. When we start thinking missionally, we start working like missionaries. When we start thinking like Christian leaders, we start acting like Christian leaders...and everything changes.

Godly leaders make things happen. A leader is like a rock hitting a pond, creating the first ripple. When a leader sparks change, he rocks the boat, which causes some ripples—and many people don't like ripples. Often, though, many will buy into what you're doing, jump right in with you, and create second, third, fourth, and even scores of other ripples.

Leaders are the primary shapers of strategy and direction for an organization. I believe, under God, that it is my responsibility to provide direction and strategies for our staff and our people. I have others around me who embrace the declared vision, encourage it, and enhance it; but the main impetus must come from me, the leader. Leaders shape an organization's core values.

Leaders also invite. They invite others into the vision, to the mission, to the task at hand. They don't try to do it alone because they see that as both foolish and futile.

Leaders cannot be copycats. While you can teach what you know, you reproduce only who you are. If you don't like what you're producing as a leader, then maybe the problem is who you are or what you have become.

Your followers may simply be mirroring you. What you criticize in them may be the same thing they criticize in you.

Leaders lead, and when they don't, our problems grow massive. If you don't lead, your organization loses. Your people lose. You lose. We must be very careful to lead how we should lead. If you're called to lead, then lead well. And if you're not called to lead, then leave.

What kind of leaders do we need today? We need leaders who are honest, trustworthy, and godly. We need leaders with vision. We want leaders who sense God's call on their life, with Christlike character, who serve out of their giftedness and strengths. We want leaders who serve others, love others, encourage others. We want leaders committed to pray, who inspire others, who effectively direct the energies and resources of their people. We want leaders who love to build strong teams, celebrate victories, delegate authority, and develop effective strategies. We want leaders who accept responsibility for outcomes.

My greatest joy in life is finding out what God wants me to do and then doing it. What joy we find in obedience and serving the Lord!

God has called me to lead. And I believe He has called you too.

Troubleshooting for Christian Leaders

"Why *Christian* leadership?" someone may rightly ask. "Leadership is leadership. The principles of effectively leading people apply equally, anywhere." Well…yes and no. In one way, you're right. In another way, not as much.

On the one hand, effective leadership looks much the same in whatever context you find it. Good leaders who identify themselves as Buddhists, secularists, or atheists can take the sound insights of great leadership experts such as Ken Blanchard, Barbara Corcoran, and John Maxwell and apply them just as successfully as any good Christian leader. In this sense, leadership is leadership. This explains why I continue to read and recommend books and articles on leadership by practitioners and experts from all walks of life. It's also why in this book I approvingly cite the excellent work of many gifted leaders and writers, regardless of their faith commitments (if any). So yes, leadership is leadership.

On the other hand, Christians believe that Christ is lord over all of life, even over leadership roles and functions. In the Scripture, we see kingdoms rise and then fall when godless leaders take control. Over the years, I have seen far too many Christian leaders fail to consciously apply major biblical truth to their work lives. They may indeed devour good secular books on things like decision making, emotional intelligence, or conflict resolution, but they also overlook many of the crucial things God has to say on those same issues. As a consequence, their leadership differs very little, if at all, from their secular counterparts.

I would like to say to such leaders that you can find a lot of helpful counsel on these leadership topics in many general trade books, and I will give you some good examples of what I mean. But just imagine the power you could experience, and the difference it would make in your organization, if you used these helpful techniques and strategies in the context of what God's Word says about how He wants you to function. Imagine what a difference-maker you could be if you consciously and intentionally moved beyond being a good leader to becoming a great Christian leader!

Again, this book is specifically for Christian leaders—not necessarily leaders of Christian organizations, but leaders who belong to Christ, who follow Christ, who love Christ, and who want to honor Christ. When we forget about or neglect God's wisdom on leadership, we leave unimaginable power, grace, and enablement sitting unused on the table. Why would any of us choose to do that?

Where Do Today's Leaders Itch?

I have written *How to Become a More Effective Leader* to help Christian leaders improve their leadership skills, to learn how to more effectively serve the wonderful people God has called them to lead. I have benefitted tremendously through the years by reading countless books and articles on leadership from experts in the field, by learning directly from amazing leaders who mentored me, helped me, and encouraged me, and by taking careful note of what did and didn't work in the many arenas where God has called me to lead. I also know that our mistakes and failures can teach us at least as much as our wins and successes, and I've had plenty of the former too.

As I began to write this manuscript, I wanted to make sure that I scratched where leaders were itching. I didn't want to write yet another leadership book covering essentially the same terrain already described by so many others. So, I took a survey. My longtime friend, colleague, and associate Jim Law helped me to develop and distribute a simple, eight-item questionnaire designed to identify where Christian leaders today say they struggle the most in their leadership roles.

While the first five questions asked respondents to rank some statement about their experience of leadership, from "strongly agree" to "strongly disagree," the final three items asked open-ended questions about the main challenges they face in leading their organizations. We sent the survey to more than 5,000 Christian leaders, whether corporate leaders or pastors or others, and received back more than 250 telling responses. I will reproduce the full results of the survey in an appendix, but here let me give you some highlights.

Question 1: "I feel very frustrated about some aspects of leading my organization."

Almost 58 percent of respondents agreed with the statement, while more than 14 percent strongly agreed with it. Only about 14 percent either disagreed or strongly disagreed.

Question 2: "I do not struggle in any area of my leadership."

Only about 5.4 percent of respondents agreed or strongly agreed with the statement, while a whopping 88 percent disagreed or strongly disagreed.

Question 3: "The people in my organization follow my lead without hesitation."

About 44 percent of respondents agreed or strongly agreed with the statement, while a bit over 26 percent disagreed or strongly disagreed. A sizeable group of more than 30 percent neither agreed nor disagreed.

Question 4: "I need outside help to troubleshoot some key leadership issues in my organization."

It didn't surprise me that most respondents said they could use some troubleshooting help in their leadership (more than 60 percent) and that only about 14 percent said they didn't need such help. I believe this speaks to a huge need.

Question 5: "I could use a mentor to help me improve my leadership."

Surveys often ask essentially the same question in different ways, and sometimes a slight change in wording can produce very different results. To this question, a whopping 86.4 percent of respondents said they could use a leadership mentor, with more than 26 percent of those individuals saying they strongly agreed they needed a mentor. Less than 3 percent of all respondents disagreed with the statement, and only .4 percent strongly disagreed with it. Christian leaders today seem to overwhelmingly desire the help of a seasoned mentor!

The first open-ended survey question asked, "Where do you think you most need to grow in your leadership?" Almost 17 percent of respondents named "personal/leader development" as their key area of needed growth, while nearly 16 percent identified "vision" as their biggest need. Other top responses included "personal development," "delegation," and "administration."

The second open-ended question asked, "What one thing would best equip you to become a more effective leader?" The "mentors/seasoned counsel" category received more responses than any other, identified by nearly 30 percent of respondents. "Personal development" was chosen by almost 17 percent or respondents, and "spiritual practices/resources" by more than 15 percent. "Additional human resources," "leadership training," and "time management" followed close behind.

The final open-ended survey question asked, "What is the most difficult leadership task you face?" About 18 percent of respondents named "personal challenges," 13.4 percent identified both "motivating people" and "the daily grind," and almost 13 percent named "handling conflict." Other top responses included "building an effective team," "dealing with challenging times," and "moving toward the vision."

As you will see from this book's table of contents, I took these responses to heart as I worked on *How to Become a More Effective Leader*. I desperately want to give you the help you need, where you may require it most, because so much is at stake for all of us whom God has called to lead.

God Calls You to Lead

I know that leadership ain't easy. We face enormous challenges that continually morph and change. What worked before COVID might not work any longer. Zoom meetings don't look like in-person meetings once did, nor do they always achieve the same results (not that many of our in-person meetings accomplished much, anyway). Leadership is not easy—and yet, God has called us to lead.

I want you to thrive wherever God has called you to lead. I want you to experience the thrill and power of serving men and women who need your leadership, who long to attain some glorious result or reach some significant milepost or destination they have never seen as possible for them. I want you to become the leader that God designed you to be.

No, it ain't easy. It will take hard work, trial and error, lots of help, the counsel of trustworthy advisers and mentors, and most of all, joyful reliance on your faithful Savior, Jesus Christ. To be called to lead is awesome, but for God to call you to become a great Christian leader is divine. There's nothing like it!

I invite you to join me as together we strive to become the godly, effective leaders our Lord calls each of us to be. The future rises and falls on it.

PART ONE

PERSONAL **QUALITIES** OF A CHRISTIAN LEADER

1

Visionary

A young man sat in my office one day and said, "I have one major fear in life."

"What is that?" I asked.

"I fear that I'm going to die with my dream in my heart," he answered. "I want to get it out. I want to live my God-given dream."

Can you relate to that young man? If you're like most leaders I meet, I believe you do. I wonder, what would your organization look like if the Lord gave you a God-inspired vision? It's an important question, because a clear vision is foundational to all effective leadership.

What Vision Is

Many leaders today are suffering a crisis of purpose. They are good, dedicated people with quite a dilemma. They desire to serve God but struggle to specify how and in what way.

What do you want to do? What do you really feel called to do? What do you want to do with your life? That's where vision comes into the picture.

Vision sees what could be. Someone once said, "If you don't see it before you see it, you'll never see it." Visionary leaders are able to see something in the future. They see where they would like to take their people, and they see it in very specific terms.

When I was twenty-three years old, I pastored a rural church on the borderline of North and South Carolina. I used to imagine seeing people leaving their houses, getting in their cars, and coming into the house of

God. In my leadership, I always envision reaching people, helping people, touching people. If you don't see it before you see it, you'll never see it. Think about where you are right now. Do you feel discouraged? Scared? Frustrated? Tired? You can start to develop the long view you need by remembering that if you don't see it before you see it, you'll never see it. Try to envision what God wants to do in your leadership. Does that encourage you?

Sometimes my own vision is really big. In the early days at First Baptist Church Woodstock, my vision was so big that I could share it with very few. It scared the socks off of them. Behind closed doors, I had to deal with barriers, even among staff. They didn't see the vision as clearly as I did. I'm also a big risk taker and can get out on the edge without losing sleep. Even if that's not how you're wired, once you have a vision, you'll find yourself willing and able to take risks.

Again, vision sees what could be. If you feel comfortable where you are, if things have been going very well for a long time, it's easy to get complacent, to play it safe. A leader's vision can become limited. Maybe the leader has a chance to touch a much bigger arena, but his organization won't benefit from it (although God's kingdom might), so rather than think bigger, he stays in the same place. That leader is not a kingdom leader, but a comfortable, organizational leader. If you haven't run into that yet, you will.

Or maybe God's already got you beyond where you thought you could go, but He appears to want to take you even farther. God's vision for you and your organization often becomes larger and clearer over time.

What do you feel called to do? What do you want to do with your life? Where do you want to make a genuine, positive contribution? Henry Kaiser is widely quoted as saying, "Determine what you want more than anything else in life—and who can determine that, but you and your heart with God? Write down how you intend to obtain it and permit nothing to deter you from pursuing it."

Once you have a vision, that vision never fundamentally changes. It may get clearer or it may enlarge, but your vision remains essentially the same. The mission refers to getting out there and accomplishing the vision using goals and strategies that change over time.

Nobody can give you your vision. A lot of people will try to give you their vision, but you can't take their vision. You might be able to encourage their vision, enhance their vision, enlarge their vision, embrace their vision, but you can't give them their vision, and they can't give you theirs. A genuine vision comes to you only from God.

What Vision Does

Where there's no vision, Scripture says, the people perish (Proverbs 29:18). The underlying Hebrew really means that without a prophetic revelation, the people cast off all restraint. We need to know from God how the Lord wants us to lead His people.

Leadership is the ability to inspire other people to work together as a team under your direction to obtain a common objective. I want to help people to reach dreams that they may think lie beyond them. Good leaders challenge their people for their best. Effective leaders want their people to accomplish more than they ever thought possible and a God-inspired vision can help them to do just that.

Although the leader is the vision caster for the organization, the leader doesn't have to have all the answers ahead of time. Sometimes, the vision begins with little more than a dream, an idea, and others come along and help fill in the blanks.

This happened at Woodstock with an outreach called Live Out Loud. I had the initial vision, and then I gave it to a team, who carried it out successfully. I told them after it became reality, "It doesn't even resemble the vision that I cast." This is why all leaders must have good people around them. When you have the opportunity to call people to serve on your staff, call better people than yourself.

A sound, God-endorsed vision also will keep you clean. I have a conviction that one of the major reasons why Joseph did not get in bed with Potiphar's wife (Genesis 39:6-20) was the vision God gave him in his teen years (Genesis 37:5-11). Joseph knew that if he went to bed with her, he wouldn't go on with God. He was driven by his vision.

What does God want to do in you and in your organization? Ask Him about it. Meditate over it. Start writing down some ideas. Often, such a vision becomes larger and clearer over time.

How to Get and Develop Your Vision

Do you have a vision for your leadership and your organization, even if in initial form? Forget about any barriers to it for a moment, because there will always be barriers. And forget about finances. Don't say, "Boy, if I just had the money." Just for a moment, refuse to put up any walls where a God-given vision couldn't become a reality in your life. Begin by saying, "No barriers, no financial restraints. What is my vision? What would I really like to see God do with me and my leadership in this organization?"

Let your mind soar. Open your mind to fresh ways and ideas that enlarge your skills, your knowledge, your wisdom, and your faith. Open your mind and heart to God's ways. God may want to do something with you and your team that maybe He has not done with anyone else. Some of the greatest thoughts have yet to be thunk. God may lead you to do something that no one else has done. Dare to dream! Get God's vision for you and your organization as you spend time with Him and He speaks into your life.

I hope that through this chapter God will help you to see and refine a vision for your leadership, and then encourage you to embrace it as God's mission for you as you lead your organization. And how, specifically, do you get and develop a God-inspired vision for you and your organization? Let me suggest six steps to get you started.

1. Take Time to Reflect

The missing ingredient in the life of most leaders is time to reflect. What got you to where you are? When do you sit down and really think through everything? Realize it will take more to get you where you want to go. I don't know where you want to go, but I know it will take more than what you have now. That's how it is with every leader who has a God-sized vision.

Set aside enough margin to reflect on what you're doing—somewhere you can think, where you can pray, where you can look out the window without an agenda. Ask the Lord, "Am I being intentional enough?"

I'll never forget the summer when God convicted me that I needed to be more intentional about my leadership. I had to quit doing stuff just because it was right or good. I had to make sure that I was being extremely intentional about what God had called me to do.

You know what I hear from many leaders? "How can I take time to reflect? I don't even take my vacation time!" If that's you, shame on you for what you're doing to yourself, your family, and your organization. If

God speaks into your life and you fail to listen and obey Him, it not only hurts you, it hurts the people you lead. When you listen to God for His guidance in your leadership, it's a huge win for everyone.

2. Where Are You?

Whenever I visit an unfamiliar mall, I generally go to the directory map first to see where I am. I look for the icon that says "You are here." But that isn't where I want to stay, is it? I'm looking for a specific store. I came to the mall with intentionality, but I will have trouble getting where I want to go if I don't first know where I am.

As a leader looking to develop vision, you must analyze where you are before you can determine where you and your organization ought to go. Who is a part of your team? What do you and your team do well? What do you do poorly? What are you not doing at all? What are your assets? What are your liabilities? How would you describe your current community, market, audience, and potential? How does your history help or hurt your future hopes? Who do you count as allies? What are your own strengths and weaknesses as a leader? In other words, where are you right now, as you read?

Remember that you're on a journey. You're "here," and for the time being, that's good. Your vision, however, will want to take you "there," regardless of where you serve. Pray that God would give you a vision for that community, that region, that audience, that industry, or that whatever-it-may-be, to really make a difference wherever you're called to serve. And begin by getting a full understanding of where you are, the place from where you must start.

Is your organization plateaued or declining? Is it underperforming? Is it asleep? Does it need a radical overhaul just to survive? If you chose the word *plateau* just now, are you being honest? If you can't be candid about where you are—where *here* is—I can't help you to dream about *there*. Without understanding your *here*, you can't build any genuine passion about where you want to go.

Understand that growth in most organizations is basically circular. Maybe your summer's down, but then fall comes, and you say, "We're growing." No, you're not. It's just people coming back from vacation. That's not growth. One good metric is to see where your organization is today and where it was last year at the same time.

We don't generally measure growth from week to week but from year to year. Then we can see whether we're up or down. How about the year before? Look at the past five years and ask, "Where are we? Are our finances growing?" Many times, we discover we've flat lined. I've been there. In fact, I've lived there as long as I want to. I don't want to live there ever again.

Take an honest look at the directory map. Maybe you thought you were closer to *there*, when in reality, you're still *here*. Be ruthlessly honest. What does your *here* look like?

3. Where Do You Want to Be?

The directory map is important, but don't stare at it all your life. Get a picture of where you are, but then begin to develop another picture, this time of where you want to go. *Here* is a good place, but there's a better place: *there*. Where would you like to see your people? What are you asking from God regarding your people?

When I'm out walking in the morning, I like to ask myself, "What am I really believing God for? What am I asking Him to do?" Asking such questions often leads me to a renewed belief in Jesus Christ and His global mission, as well as a renewed belief that my God really can do anything. And so, I begin to ask Him specifically for some things. I remind myself, if He owns the cattle on a thousand hills, He owns everything. I count it a privilege to ask Him for this and to believe that He is a God who can provide it. How exciting to see what He is doing and what He's going to do! I focus my mind on the work God has called me to do.

Some leaders think their big break in life will be the next big job opening that comes along. That becomes their *there*. But your *there* ought to be what can God do right where He has called you.

Did God call you where you are now? What is the *there* for that place? Where do you want to take the group that lives and works where God has planted you?

4. Vision Is Not a Destination, but a Journey

Don't panic over your vision. Do not fret over it, asking, "Oh, what am I going to do?" Just live with it each day while enjoying the journey.

Nevertheless, you do need a vision that you would like to see happen, a vision that brings you and your people to greater days ahead, days when you can have a greater impact. Don't be satisfied with "good enough." Reach for the stars!

When God gives you that vision, know how to own it. Make it yours. This becomes your vision, and you take it and own it by faith. If you believe that your vision came from God, then by faith believe it and by faith act upon it—"I'm going to trust God to supply the needs."

Intentionally do something with it. Sometimes when God puts something in our hearts, we mostly talk about it. We talk about it week in, week out, month in, month out. We run into a friend and tell him or her about it. We see the same friend six months later and we're still talking about it… but doing nothing. A genuine vision from God requires that we intentionally do something with it, act on it, purposefully move in that direction. If we don't, we're really saying, "It's a cool idea, but I don't think it's a God-given vision."

5. Always Be in Transition from Here to There

Don't ever get satisfied where you are. Don't ever think you've arrived. Always look to transition from one thing to the next. Yes, live in the moment, but continue to ask yourself, "What's next?" Such an attitude keeps everything alive and exciting—just the way it should be.

6. Once You Get There, Know that It Becomes Another Here

Once I get *there*, I often begin to think, *You know where I'd like to see our group? I'd like to see us over there, with this many people or that many branches or this kind of sales or these kinds of products.* When I came to Woodstock, I'm not sure I even understood what I was asking the Lord for, but I did ask Him for a ministry upon which the sun would never set. So far, so good.

Now what do you do?

You begin to say, "I want more people in those nations." There's never a moment that I'm alive, whether I'm asleep, resting, or away, but that somebody is serving in Christ's name somewhere around the world, 24/7, because of Woodstock. It's exciting once you get there! But once you get there, then it becomes your present day *here*. Once again, you have to visualize the next *there*, and set out on the new journey.

If you're a Christian leader, there's never a time when you rest on your laurels, when you can say, "We've been so busy and things have gone so well that we've just kicked back. We feel like we've done such a great job."

Have you ever listened to how leaders tend to answer questions about their organizations? "So, how are things going at your place?" someone asks.

"Well, compared to the other companies in our industry…" we start to say. But whoever told you that's the way to evaluate yourself misled you. Don't compare yourself to the organizations around you. Compare yourself to the God-given vision and dream and potential that the Lord has placed inside you.

I wish God would give us the heart of John Knox. I wish we would all come to the place he did when he said, "God, give me Scotland, or I die." Can you imagine? "I'd rather die than not reach my God-given goal!" Are you consumed by passion to make a difference in your corner of the world?

Would life be easier if your organization didn't try to reach beyond itself? Could it survive on half its current budget? All it would have to do is to eliminate certain key divisions. I did that as a pastor, saving hundreds of thousands of dollars by eliminating an expensive ministry. I've cut my staff in half and eliminated a few million dollars. But if you recognize that you have only one life to live, why would you opt for mere survival?

Vision is the foundation of all leadership. You need to hammer this out for yourself and your organization. What would God have you do? For what are you going to trust God? How may He want to get you out on the edge? Understand, it's not always fun! Change is not easy for anyone.

Through the years I've found myself saying, "It's going to take an act of God to change *that* organization." I've got to the point now that I'm willing to say, "It may take an act of God to change *me*," and it normally does. I'm not easy to change, and neither are other people or organizations. But when you begin to make this realization, it can make a huge difference.

What if you were to spend a summer asking God to speak into your life? What if you saw some major things that need to change? What if it takes months for God to work you over so He can get you "there"?

"But I want my organization to buy in the moment they hear the vision!" you say. Or maybe you already have tried to introduce your vision to your organization but saw tepid response. So, you think, *This isn't working*.

To that I would probably respond, "You haven't given it enough time yet. Why don't you just hang in there and see what happens?" At the same time, you can try a number of things to get buy-in.

How to Cast Your Vision to Get Buy-In

In the early days, I publicly stated my personal vision: I would like to take as many people to heaven with me as I can. When you own a vision, you share it, but it always remains yours and does not depend on the behavior of those around you.

Although I stated my vision at one church, it never bought in. At the end of the day, however, the question is not whether they buy in, but whether you've really bought in enough yourself to pursue it. So, I stuck to my vision: I want to win people to Christ.

When I went to Woodstock, local people said, "I'm not going there; it's not evangelistic. They don't do any outreach or anything." To which my simple mind prompted me to reply, "That's why we need *you*." Evangelism became a front burner issue at Woodstock, in part by me modeling it. I modeled evangelism before my people. It's true that whatever is important to you as the leader becomes important to the people you lead. You'll never lead them to do what's important to you if you don't follow it in your own life.

My friend Jimmy Draper is in his mid-80s and still going strong. He recently wrote *Don't Quit Before You Finish*, a book of about eighty chapters, each chapter about four pages long—which I mention in case you're looking for quick bits of wisdom. Jimmy came to me in my early thirties and said, "If God continues to bless your life, bring the next generation with you." His statement haunted me. Through that statement, the Timothy+Barnabas ministry was born. I saw then, and still see today, that nobody will make a great leader who wants to do it all alone or get all the credit for doing it. Bring others along with you.

How do you effectively cast the vision you develop? How do you get it out before your people to influence their thinking and behavior?

I've found that announcements don't cut it, mainly because people generally don't read or listen to announcements. I know for sure that church people don't read bulletins, regardless of how slick those bulletins might be.

For some time at Woodstock, we put out a fine-looking magazine each

Sunday. We spent $70,000 a year producing it. It was *slick*. I felt so proud of it and I wanted everyone else to feel as proud of it as I did.

One day, however, as my senior staff sat around a table, I said, "Let's get honest before God. Jesus is watching. If you tell a lie, we pray you get right here around the table. How many of you read the bulletin?"

Not a single hand went up.

Then I addressed the directors. "How many of you are reading it?"

None of them read it, either.

The magazine looked great, but our people weren't reading it. So, we canned it and used the money formerly spent on it to help cast the vision in a more effective way.

As a church leader, I learned that if the vision was worth airtime on the Lord's day, it made sense to make it part of my sermons. When I preached on servanthood, for example, right in the middle of that sermon, I spotlighted several major talking points about the vision.

I've also used video testimonies. I've shown locations around the world where we ministered. Is there a chance some still won't get it? Sure. So, we find multiple avenues to get the message out in various forms.

Visuals can be very effective. When people came to Woodstock during one series of Sundays, for example, instead of seeing the orchestra in its normal place, they saw on the platform a hair salon, a dentist's office, a doctor's room, and a house being painted. We didn't immediately explain the significance of any of them. We just went right into a song.

Many observers probably thought, *What's going on here?* We had someone give a testimony, with a video to support it, leading right into the sermon. And then I cast the vision once more. We wanted our people to "get" that we had some big things going on.

Once you have embraced your God-given vision, get creative in broadcasting that vision. Show people what they must do. Let them in on your dreams and goals. Make sure they know—and remind yourself—that all of them, together, are a huge part of what is required to bring the corporate vision to pass.

I love to speak publicly from my heart about the dreams God is birthing in me. I might say something like, "There's an available piece of land that seems ideal for us. It would give us room to enhance a certain project. Being able to purchase it right now seems utterly impossible, but I want you to join me in praying about this, to see if it is indeed the Lord's will for us." You may not lead a church, so vision casting may look very different for you. The key is to let your people know that all of you embark on this journey together, not in boardrooms and insider meetings. And if God chooses to make a way, then you celebrate the success together.

Many leaders inexplicably withhold this kind of visionary information, afraid they'll only discourage their people. They get shy about declaring big dreams in public that may sound too grandiose and out of the realm of reality.

In fact, though, the God who gives the vision will establish it with His provision—but only as we allow Him to fulfill His purpose of letting the group embrace the effort. Remember, it's all about what we can do together under God's supply, empowerment, and direction, not what we leaders can do ourselves.

Don't shirk your big responsibilities as a leader by staying good at the small stuff. You're needed for more—for championing the overall vision to your people. By effectively casting this vision, you'll see it embraced, enhanced, and enlarged. You'll become the leader your people need. And isn't that what really matters?

If you've become too ingrown and individual with your vision, be courageous enough to change this about your leadership style. Share the vision—and see the joyful results increase.

A Transforming Vision Begins with a Transformed Leader

Every transformative organization begins with a transformed leader. To keep leading well, you must keep growing personally.

Transformation is an ongoing process. It never stops. God sets leaders aside for Himself and wants to continually work in them.

Transformation takes place first in the mind. The Bible talks repeatedly about being transformed by the renewing of your mind (Romans 12:2). Your thinking must always be challenged and stretched.

One day I told my staff, "If you were in charge, what would you do more of, or less of, to reach our community?" Once they opened up, the meeting got extremely enlightening. But you can't do that if you have a group of yes-men around you. They will not challenge your thinking or stretch your mindset.

If you want to keep growing as a leader, build a safe haven for your staff or your key people to offer diverse thoughts. Whoever they are, invite them to challenge and stretch your thinking. You need to hear them, even if you don't agree with them. I've told staff members, "That's a great idea, but I don't feel we ought to go that way right now. Let's remember it for future use, though."

The bottom line is that being a change agent in the lives of others and in your organization starts with being changed yourself. How is God changing you? Any new things in your life? The change must start with you. God can't work through you until He first works in you.

Let's see how this works from a purely human perspective. What got you to where you are? You have skills, abilities, personality traits, background and experience that have contributed to your success.

Consider your intellect. You can't be a dummy and lead an organization (we've tried). You must be able to learn new things, think through issues, process challenges. You don't, of course, have to be the most brilliant person in the room. You may believe you need to be a genius to make it, but it's just not true. While intellect is important—it helps to know something about finances, leadership, building projects, giving wise counsel, etc.—it's less important than you might suppose.

Besides intellect, we all have certain abilities. Maybe you're a great organizer or administrator. Frankly, if I didn't have an assistant, I'd never know where I'm supposed to go next. Your abilities got you noticed and you caught someone's eye because of them.

Most leaders also have charisma, the ability to attract others. I've never known a single successful leader, however, who got along on charisma alone—at least, not for long.

Is education the key for a successful leader? Some organizations won't hire you unless you have a doctoral degree, and yet, many of those leaders quickly come and go. My late friend John Bisagno never graduated from college. Yet, many say that the books he wrote thirty years ago had the power back then that Rick Warren's have today. While I thank God for education, I've never known someone to make it just on education.

How about experience? It's interesting to watch my employees evaluate new staff members. Some of them doubt education means nearly as much as experience. You may hear someone say about a young person who just spent seven years in school, "Well, she has no experience at all." Really? I think that's an insult to a woman who just graduated with an MBA. The debate goes back and forth, but here's the point: Neither education nor experience by themselves are enough to get you down the road.

May I say something to you? The things that got you *here* are not necessarily what you need to get you *there*. It will take more to get you there than what got you here.

Going forward always requires additional growth. You need to keep reading, praying, seeking the Lord, reflecting, going for long walks, thinking about everything you're doing. Ask yourself, "How can I do a better job? How can I empower those around me? How can I better connect with our people?" Continually review everything in your life.

The plain fact is that going from *here* to *there* requires a different kind of growth. Squeeze as much as you can out of what you have, but at some point, you'll get most of what you're squeezing. That means you must explore some new areas of growth. In particular, make the transition from talent growth to transactional growth, which refers to becoming and doing something of a different kind than before. *Trans* means "beyond," and transactional growth refers to what others can accomplish, guided and inspired by you, the leader.

Why do we have so many underperforming organizations across America? We have them because too many of us leaders are trying to accomplish the work by ourselves. My hands can touch only so much. I can engage only so many—but if I multiply myself through others, it's just amazing what we can do.

I tell people that every organization is designed for the size it is. You must break that whole design…but until you change your thinking, it won't happen.

This small, almost subtle shift in thinking from doing to leading can have a profound impact on your organization. As a leader, it can never be about what you alone can get done. It's always about what you can lead others to do and what they can accomplish. The best leading always comes out of being. When you've been with people a few years and have earned their respect, it's amazing how willingly they will join you and follow you.

Where Do You Think God Wants to Take You?

Do you have a vision for your organization's future? If so, what is it?

However great your vision may be, it is nothing in your life until it becomes your mission. People can die with a vision in their hearts. Someone can say at age twenty, "I've always had a vision of doing *this*," and at age forty they're still saying the same thing. They're not moving toward it in any way at all.

What is achievable is never automatic. Do you know what some of your buddies will say when they hear you've reached some God-given vision? "Shoot, who couldn't grow an organization where he is?" In other words, they think it's automatic. An important Greek word accurately describes such a statement: *baloney*. In Hebrew, the term is *hogwash*. Reaching a God-given vision is not automatic anywhere. In chapter 7, we'll talk about how to generate goals to help your vision become a reality. But understand that you won't automatically get there just because you have a vision.

Nothing is more important than leadership. We need minds broad enough to try to think through what it means to be a good leader so that we can bring our people to a wonderful, God-endorsed place that they never imagined they could reach.

2

Influential

T he key to successful leadership," insists Ken Blanchard, "is influence, not authority."[1] As the co-author of *The One Minute Manager*, a potent little book that has sold over thirteen million copies since its release in 1982, Blanchard knows a bit about leadership. His more than sixty books on leadership and business topics have sold more than eighteen million copies in more than twenty-five languages worldwide.

Blanchard is not alone, of course, in singling out influence as the *sine qua non* of leadership. My friend John Maxwell, one of the world's leading authorities on leadership, has said even more concisely, "Leadership is influence."[2] He has also said, "The greater the impact you want to make, the greater your influence needs to be."[3]

Do you want to be an effective leader? If you want to lead well, you must learn how to build, develop, and increase your influence. You have no other choice.

Key Word: Relationship

Influencers are more concerned about the wants of others than their own desires. In order to influence others, you must really value them. You have to value people more than the tasks they perform or the functions they serve.

When you influence people, you influence your greatest resource. Your greatest resource as a leader is not the material assets you have, but the people you lead. Resources can be depleted; they come and they go. Your leadership depends on how well you influence your people.

When the apostle Paul spoke of the desperately poor Macedonians giving to God's work, he wrote that not only did they give as he had hoped, "but they first gave themselves to the Lord, and then to us" (2 Corinthians 8:5). When you influence people, you influence your greatest resource.

All of us have been powerfully influenced by other individuals. In fact, the Lord can use anyone to influence us. You don't have to be a specially gifted relationship guru.

I often talk about my friend A.J. Joyner. Back when I was a young hellion who didn't yet know Jesus, I remember walking into church one day and seeing A.J. I couldn't believe that he was there. I was just a scalper, a tough, skinny little kid hanging out in the pool hall, where you either learned to fight or you just got whopped a whole lot. At least, you learned to talk like you could fight.

Alfred Joyner was one mean dude. Nobody messed with the Joyner brothers. We all knew who they were—and what they were fully capable of doing.

But when I popped into church that day, there he was. I couldn't take my eyes off him. He was singing. I mean, what was happening? After the service, Alfred hugged me and told me he loved me. Back in the day, men didn't do that. Word soon begin to spread: "Have you seen Alfred Joyner? God changed his life."

Now, I was nonreligious at the time. I didn't know the right spiritual language or the difference between the Virgin Mary and Jezebel. Once I got saved, Alfred and I became best friends. We ate together every Sunday night after church, during which time he shared his knowledge with me and encouraged me. He drove a truck for a major freight company. To this day, Alfred will come and see me, and what a joy it is to be able to stand up and say, "Hey, I'm glad to have the man who discipled me here this morning."

I can still see and hear him pray. When he prays, he acts like nobody else is in the room and he's just talking to Jesus. We're all supposed to be like that, I know, but it doesn't always happen. A.J. Joyner greatly influenced me, and he still does.

An influencer is a people lifter, a people builder.

"How are you doing today?"

"I'm better now, because I got to spend some time with A.J. He really lifted me up."

The key word in influencing is relationship. Influencers intentionally connect with others. Those being led know that the ones leading them really care about them.

A good number of my buddies have thought about starting a little school for preachers, like the Timothy+Barnabas ministry that I've been doing for twenty-seven years. These friends have said to me, "I'm going to do one of these schools. We'll print really nice brochures, send out emails, get it all set up." But after the initial event, they call me and say, "Hardly anybody came. What's your secret to getting people there?"

I tell them I try to build relationships with anyone who expresses an interest in coming. I personally answer their emails. I personally return their calls. I'm not a platform man who says, "When you get a chance, come and hear me," and leaves it at that.

I don't know when we began to think we've gotten so big and important that we don't have to connect personally with those we want to lead. I've chosen not to do that.

Does it take a while to get all these notes written and calls made? Certainly. And sometimes you don't even get a quick voicemail or a brief email in return. But I've noticed that, in the South, most of those who come to Timothy+Barnabas do so because they feel some connection to me because of all the ways I've tried to help them throughout the year.

Influence connects with others before it tries to take them somewhere. I had been connecting for years with many younger leaders before we established Timothy+Barnabas. We built the platform through prior relationships we had formed, not by fancy brochures inviting them to attend.

"It is one of the most beautiful compensations of this life," wrote Ralph Waldo Emerson, "that no man can sincerely try to help another without helping himself."[4] If you think that by pouring yourself into others, you will eventually become exhausted, you're wrong. The Bible says, "God shall supply all your need according to His riches in glory by Christ Jesus" (Philippians 4:19). In the original language, the word translated *supply* basically means, "He keeps giving without any depletion."

Everybody has influence somewhere. You influence your wife and children, your friends, neighbors, and coworkers, and you're influenced by them. But this works well only when you love those you lead.

Someone once told a dynamic, influential leader, "You've never met a man you couldn't love."

"Maybe," the man replied, "but a couple of them came real close." But he loved them anyway, and so he was able to lead them someplace wonderful. Influencers help others to succeed, and in the process, they themselves succeed.

Characteristics of Influencers

As a leader, you have both the privilege and the ability to influence those you lead. But first, you must believe that that you can influence those you lead.

What does it take to become an effective influencer? What personal characteristics do potent influencers share? Let me list a few of what I consider to be the most important ones, in alphabetical order.

Accessible

Influencing takes time, patience, and effort. To be accessible requires a willingness to return calls, answer emails and texts, and keep appointments. You're not one of the untouchables. Some have said, "If you want to touch more people, you cannot be as available." They usually mean you should spend most of your time writing and thinking before speaking publicly. While I understand the sentiment, you'll have a hard time finding that approach in the Bible. In Scripture, we see Jesus going through Samaria to reach a solitary woman, who then touches a whole town (John 4). We see Him stopping in the crowd to speak and heal Bartimaeus; He would never pass through Jericho again (Mark 10). He expresses genuine concern about a woman with an issue of blood (Matthew 9). Have you noticed how He's in the people business? Jesus was the ultimate influencer. By remaining accessible to people, He influenced tax collectors, fishermen, religious leaders. If I'm trying to teach leadership, I don't want to misrepresent the leader I'm following, and that's Jesus.

Admonisher

The word *admonish* means "to put into the mind." You often can't effectively admonish those you lead without going the second mile with them. Someone once said, "You cannot influence from your comfort zone.

You've got to transition to be a second miler. The neat thing about a second miler is that not many people are out there on the road with you."

Directive

An influencer directs the energies and resources of his or her people. Colleagues, associates, and others begin to put their energies where the leader directs them to put them. Whatever is a big deal to the leader becomes a big deal to them.

Encourager

Influencers encourage others, knowing that encouragement fuels enthusiasm. *Encouragement* simply means "courage in." What's discouragement? Courage out. In a depressing time in your life, you need to sit down and think about what's discouraging you. What's taking out your courage? Then you must think about what puts courage in. If you can encourage a discouraged associate, you get to influence everybody your associate will ever encourage. That's just good stewardship.

Genuine

Influence is about being genuine. In 2 Timothy 1:5, Paul calls Timothy "unfeigned" (KJV), or "sincere." What you see is what you get. Leaders don't pretend to be one thing in public while being something very different in private.

Grateful

Influencers are grateful for others' influence in them. As a result, they become gracious and generous. Somebody cared enough to pour into your life. Will you do the same for others?

Humble

Since the essence of influence is others, influence requires humility. You cannot be a servant leader without humility. Ask God to cleanse you and plead in His name to fill you to overflowing with His Spirit. You could pray, "Lord, please clothe me in humility. May I be the greatest foot washer wherever I serve." I hope that no one will ever hear me declare what I won't do; but I can tell you that I've been able to delegate some things that I no longer have to do. I pray I'll never get to the point where I think I'm a big shot, too big to do *that* disgusting thing.

Information Sharers

When God brings good influences into my life, I don't mind sharing them with others. If God brings good influences into your life, make sure you don't try to keep them to yourself.

Initiator

Influencers realize that for their followers to walk five miles, they first must commit to taking the first step. The way to measure your influence is not by whether those you lead make it the first mile, but whether they take the first step. Leaders sometimes tell me, "Boy, I feel like I need some theological education, but I just can't go to seminary right now, given my family's financial situation."

"Take a class," I tell them.

One guy told me, "If I go to seminary now, at my age, do you know how old I'll be when I finish?"

"Well," I replied, "how old will you be in four years if you don't go?" Influencers help others to take that first step.

Inspiring

If you're a godly, gifted, Christlike leader, you will inspire others. You won't be able to help it.

Integrity

A leader can be trusted at all points; everything in the picture frame is right and true. Integrity is developed in the small moments of life, where the leader consistently does the right things. Jesus had something to say about being faithful in the "little" areas (Luke 19:17). Integrity speaks of who we are, not of what we do. Leaders with integrity don't leave their followers wondering about their motives. The men and women following them never feel like hogs assembled for a feeding, like one hog that watched a farmer filling his trough to the brim. The hog turned to another hog and asked, "Have you ever wondered why he's being so good to us?" A person of integrity influences others because he wants to bring something to the table that will benefit them, not put them on the table to benefit himself. Integrity builds trust. Integrity gives, it doesn't take, and you're never more like Jesus than when you're giving.

Involved

My generation posed this question: "Should a leader be close to his people or away from them? If you get too close to the people, maybe they won't listen to you." My generation did not believe in spending lots of quality time with the people. I have not chosen to go that route. A talk I've presented on many seminary campuses carries the title, "The Shepherd and the Sheep." One of my key points is that at the end of the day, a shepherd ought to smell like his sheep. In the biblical context, a shepherd cares for, feeds, ministers to, and loves his sheep. He even names them. He knows them so well that he checks to make sure flies haven't laid eggs in their hair or nose. He knows *so* much about them. I used to do senior adult choir tours every year. Did I fly to the venues and leave my people on their buses? Nope. I climbed on the bus and rode along, and some incredible stories came out of that time. To hear folks talk about what they did before they retired, I never knew that I led so many important people.

A second, related question often comes up here. If the organization grows and you add staff, should you be involved with the staff? If you get too close to them, will they do what you want them to do? I would like to think that if I'm around my staff members, they'll respect me more the better they get to know me. I don't want anybody to say, "I thought he would be like this, but really, he's *El Jerko*. He's not a very good Christian. He's ugly to people."

Longevity

This is a must. It takes a long time to turn a ship around. If I had a word to share with you as a leader, it would be this: Never take a position unless you intend to stay there for life. Anyone who takes a position seeing it merely as a steppingstone to somewhere else may demonstrate less than pure motives. Now, do I still pastor at Lavonia Baptist? No. I wept when God began to show me it was time to leave. I wanted to stay. I begged Him, "God, if you are going to pull me away, please give me at least one more year in this area." He wouldn't do it. Same thing when

I went to Falls Baptist. I had a dream, but that church had no dream receivers. I can still remember what I tried to get them to embrace. They didn't. I really believed I would retire at Longleaf Baptist, where I had a wonderful ministry for five-and-a-half years. And then God sent me to Woodstock, where I stayed for thirty-three years. I thought I was going to retire there, since I had reached an age where nobody wants you anymore and you have no choice but to stay where you are. But then, in 2019, I became VP of Evangelism and Leadership at the North American Mission Board.

Longevity is a must. When you stay someplace for a long time, there's so much you don't have to figure out anymore, because you've all been together for so long that you know each other deeply. To stay somewhere a long time, to build a team, to build leadership that lasts—that's when your influence grows powerful.

Prompt

Influencers are not procrastinators. Procrastinators basically don't want to influence anyone. If they did, they wouldn't put things off.

Believe in Them

If you want to influence people, you must believe in them. Influencers have a commitment to connect with others on a deeper level than most. The reason? Their heart is in it.

I have an eleven-year-old granddaughter, Hope, with cerebral palsy. She certainly loves her mom and daddy, and I think she loves her papa. Every time she walks in our house, I'm excited to see her.

Like many children with special needs, Hope has trouble connecting the dots, leaving her often frustrated. An evangelist in my former church is a brilliant college graduate who also has cerebral palsy. He has explained to me where all the frustration comes from. He helped me to better understand my granddaughter, even though it takes him a long time to tell me.

"Long before I am able to tell you what I'm thinking," he said, "it's here, in my brain, but I can't get it here, to my mouth. As a little kid, that builds frustration."

A woman we call Miss Janet cares for Hope. When everything goes wrong for Hope, she has meltdowns. But Miss Janet loves her and cares for her. Hope knows that Miss Janet believes in her. And when someone knows that you believe in them, they will do anything and everything to avoid disappointing you.

Have you ever done something and immediately thought, *Why did I do that?* While we've all been there, some just seem to have more of a talent for doing so. When you've led for a long time, many of the people you have believed in and helped will make some really dumb decisions. All of us are just one decision from stupid. What then? I've heard it said this way: "A real friend is the person who walks in when everyone else walks out."

Who is that person in your life? In whose life are you that person?

I'm thinking of a certain leader who had to leave ministry for a time. One night when I got up to speak, this man introduced me. He was back in ministry, seven years removed from leaving our City of Refuge. He couldn't introduce me without crying because he immediately went back to where we first connected. "Pastor Johnny," he said, "I don't know if I told you, but my son surrendered to preach." At that moment, God helped me to realize that I didn't attempt to help only this person. God had in mind saving this man's whole family.

What might have happened had we not believed in that man? Maybe his sons and daughters would have said, "If that's the way a church treats a man of God, then we don't want to ever have anything do to with church again." We helped restore their belief in the body of Christ.

Do we feel comfortable in that although we don't shoot our wounded, we do pass them by? I don't want to think about how many times I've missed the opportunity to be a good Samaritan.

As a leader, you have to believe in people now. Everybody wants to believe in people after they amount to something. Jesus believed in Simon Peter when he was cussing, swearing, and cutting off people's ears. I've known some people who got saved but still carry their knife.

Everybody loves winners. We need some people who love losers—hellbound losers, just like we were.

You must learn to love people before they amount to something. Look for things to praise in them. Identify with their failures (which should be easy, since you can do that just by listing yours).

Odus Scruggs believed in me long before I started believing in myself. He paid for my college education, loved me, and told me he had looked for a young preacher like me his whole life. I was with him the night he died, decades later.

Odus saw someone he believed in. He treated me like he loved me. He saw something, or the becoming of somebody, that I could not see. He invested in my present and in my future. He made me feel special. He invited me into his home. He introduced me to his extended family. He wanted everybody to know us. He saw in me, evidently, what Jesus saw in Simon Peter—that is, what I could become. He taught me much from his humility and generosity.

Odus paid for my college at Gardner-Webb and bought me my first nice suit. I'd never had a nice pair of shoes in my life, but he bought me a pair of Florsheims and my first pair of Hush Puppies. He regularly took me out to eat and bought my children clothes—they always had new Easter dresses or little boots that he bought them. Odus had no idea what his influence was going to do. I wonder sometimes, did Jesus let him in on it? Or is that going to be what I get to tell him when I get to the other side?

Odus was a big giver. I've never known anyone so generous. I was his pastor for a time, and whenever he shook hands with me, he normally had at least 220 dollars in it. He told me, "I've never missed anything I've given away." It reminds me of what Martin Luther once said: "I have held many things in my hands, and I have lost them all; but whatever I have placed in God's hands, that I still possess."[5] I spend more time thinking about this than almost anything else. I look for opportunities to believe in others because of Odus.

I remember Adrian Rogers saying, in essence, "Walk slowly in crowds; be friendly and personal with your people; greet them after speaking engagements; don't be in a hurry. Invest in others by showing more interest in their story than in your own."

To this day, on my way to engagements, I pray that God would let me serve the ones I'm about to meet. If the group sends someone to pick me up at an airport, I pray, "God, let me say something or do something to encourage him, to build him up and show that I care." I once spoke for a whole week on the campus of Southeastern Seminary. A man later said to me, "Pastor, I worked in the office that sent us to pick up the preachers who spoke. I would watch how you treated the van driver." Today he's a nationally known preacher. I'm glad I did that with him! Those you lead watch you in the most unexpected of places.

Although everyone needs someone to believe in them, most people have no one like that. Do you know who believes in you? And who in your sphere of influence needs you to believe in them?

Seven Ways to Influence Teams

Teams work best when they know the leader believes in them. Not only can you influence individuals, but you can also influence whole teams. Ask yourself the following seven questions:

1. Do I add value to others?
2. Do I add value to the organization?
3. Am I quick to give away the credit when things go right? Or do I have to get the credit?
4. Is our team consistently adding new members?
5. Do I use my bench players as much as I could?
6. Do many people on the team consistently make important decisions? This gets really cool when you're working with somebody that you believe has really good leadership potential, and so you ask him or her, "What do you think I ought to do? I have these options. Help me make a good decision."
7. Does our team emphasize creating victories more than producing stars? Does the team get us moving in a good direction?

Mark Cortes is a great, dear brother to me. He served the same church his entire ministry. He once told me, "In order to influence an organization, you must move with the movers." There's a price to pay for growth, and commitment is the price. Are you willing to pay the price by believing in your teams and in your team members?

Three Ways to Make an Appeal

Many leaders think that getting people to buy into their influence is difficult or complex, but it really isn't. The process of persuasion starts with your integrity and positive character traits. After that, it quickly moves to one of three strategies, according to the Center for Creative Leadership.[6]

Leaders have told me, "I talked to so and so, but I've just not been able to get him on board. I haven't been able to influence him." But don't give up! Maybe you've tried only one approach. There are at least three major ways of trying to influence others.

First is the *logical*. You appeal to the thinkers. This appeal taps into their head—their intellectual and rational positions. Objectively and logically explain your reasoning in a clear and compelling way. They may want to meet you for lunch and say, "Explain to me why you want me involved." Offer factual, detailed evidence that your proposal is feasible, without overstating or being unrealistic. Demonstrate clearly and logically why your idea is the best possible option, showing that you have carefully considered other possibilities. Explain individual benefits, such as gaining more visibility, learning new skills, or improving the work in a way that makes the job easier or more interesting. Speak to the head.

Second, you can develop an *emotional appeal*. You appeal to the feelers, tapping into the person's heart. Engage their emotional motivator. When you hit them where they feel, they step up to the plate.

As a pastor, I never wanted to know what or how much individuals in my church gave. Others do want to know. One man came to me and said, "Pastor Johnny, we have a group of businessmen in the church who hardly ever give anything, week by week."

"Okay," I said.

"But *you* can make an appeal," he continued. "It's outrageous what they give when they respond to your appeals."

So, I called a meeting with these men. "I don't know what you do," I said. "I'm just told that when Pastor Johnny makes a personal appeal to you, you guys step up to the plate." They all smiled, as if saying, "Yes sir, we love Preacher Johnny."

"With that in mind," I continued, "I have a great need and I'm gonna ask y'all to lead out." And they did.

What was I doing? I tapped into something I'd learned. Logical appeals did not move these men, but emotional ones did. Someone might say, "I wouldn't do that." That's okay; I will. Somebody called me one day and said, "Someone in our church played the lottery and won a large amount. They've come by and want to give it to us. Would *you* take it?"

"Absolutely," I said.

"Well, we think it's wrong," they replied.

"Listen," I said. "God owns everything, and the devil has had it long enough. Bring it over here. We'll use it."

You don't have to agree with me; that's all right. But just for the record's sake, while you're acting all spiritual and saying you wouldn't take it, you don't know where the money comes from regarding the people who do give. I just want to tell you that.

The point is, I simply tapped into the human heart. I connected to individual goals and values. Maybe we talk about raising funds to shut down sex trafficking, and maybe some people give who have never given before. Another time, we'll talk about helping people with addictions, and a mom and dad out there have an addicted son. Such work helps set them free. We describe these tasks with enthusiasm, linking the request to a clear, appealing vision, something the person can fully support. You appeal to the person's self-image. You appeal to the individual's heart.

The third approach has really helped me. You make a *cooperative appeal*, a request to the doers. This appeal taps into a person's hands. Some individuals in your sphere of influence want to do something. You tap into these doers' sense of service to accomplish something worthwhile.

Sometimes, you involve these doers in physical work, giving them ownership of some project. I once stood up at Woodstock and said, "We have 325 Haitian kids we want to support. If you have a passion for these kids, the ministry is here today."

I had told the ministry, "We will get support for all of these 325 kids in one morning. I have only one problem: I have two worship services. I'll have to save some of those children for the second service, because the first service will want to claim them all." I had been at Woodstock for about twenty-five years.

My good friend Tim, who represented the ministry, told me, "Pastor, I need to tell you something. One thing I love about you is that you flat out believe God. But listen to this. I don't want to set you up for heartbreak. It ain't going to happen. If you get about 100 on Sunday, you'll be as strong as anybody."

"No," I answered, "I'm going to get every one of them, just like I told you."

I placed the majority of these kids in my first service, the biggest one. Afterwards, our people were standing in line, with every one of them saying, "Where's my kid?"

Three Cautions about Influence

You need to be aware of a few potential problems with your influence. I can think of at least three major ones.

1. Abuse of Influence

The former governor of Georgia attended Woodstock for eight years. We're personal friends; we talk on a regular basis. I have his mobile number and personal email address. People sometimes come to me and say, "Hey, I hear you're close with the governor. Could you give me his mobile number?"

"No. But give me your contact information and I'll get word to him."

Do you see the problem? That information isn't mine. I can't abuse that relationship or my influence without losing either or both. Neither can you.

2. Thinking You Deserve Your Influence

Never begin to think that you deserve the influence you have; that's entitlement. Whatever influence I have, God has given to me. I pray that I'll remain humble and grateful for it. I pray that it won't puff me up. Our head ought to remain smaller than our hands, mainly because we keep our forehead glued to the floor in gratitude to God. Realize that you need to be a good steward of the influence God grants you.

3. Don't Use Your Influence for Self-Promotion

Beware of trying to use your influence to promote yourself or to mark yourself as somehow a cut above others. That's a sure way to become selfish and self-centered (and to lose your influence). You really can be snared by your own success! Most leaders who fall formerly seemed bigger than life. Often these leaders felt as if they didn't have to answer to anybody. But all of us will have to answer to God (Luke 16:2; Romans 14:12; 2 Corinthians 5:10; Hebrews 4:13; 1 Peter 4:5).

Exponential Leadership

Martha Graham is famously known for saying, "Some men have thousands of reasons why they cannot do what they want to, when all they need is one reason why they can." Influencers can give followers that one reason. They can do so because influencers refuse to leave the world as they found it.

Do you realize that your leadership influence can become exponential? No one knows where your influence may lead the men and women who follow you. Not only do you influence men and women directly, you also influence the people those men and women will influence. It's what we call exponential leadership.

Your influence builds legacy. By the grace of God, you are able to end this life with a lasting legacy for Jesus, in part because of all those you have influenced for good. Influencing does not happen overnight! It's a long process that takes place over a lifetime.

When you influence others, you enlarge them, expand them, enhance them, empower them, equip them, exalt them, edify them, enrich them, encourage them, and engage them. No more noble occupation in the world exists than to assist another human being's success.

Somebody has influenced you enough so that you felt inspired and impacted through their investment. Influencers challenged you to step up to the plate, and now it's your turn to issue the same challenge to others. You are a potent influencer—if you will wisely use the influence you have been given.

3

Confident Decision Maker

Untold numbers of Christian leaders struggle with a trio of highly connected challenges that keep them from leading well. I know this not only because of countless conversations I've had with frustrated leaders over the years, but also because of the survey results we obtained for this book. In part of the survey, we asked leaders three open-ended questions. Their responses repeatedly named this same set of challenges: confidence, decision making, and boldness.

When we asked, "What is the most difficult leadership task you face?," we heard:

- "Leading with confidence: I often feel less sure of myself."

- "Decision making."

- "Not knowing how to handle a situation."

When we asked, "What one thing would best equip you to become a more effective leader," we heard:

- "Confidence (in general, in myself, in my calling)."

- "Developing my own courage and vision to lead."

- "Leading with boldness and assurance."

The third question brought this trio of challenges to the surface most clearly. When we asked, "Where do you think you most need to grow in your leadership," we heard:

- "Making tough decisions."

- "To be more assertive without being a jerk."

- "I need more confidence in myself and in my ability to lead."

- "Being more bold in leading. I often just go with the flow, when I perceive another 'flow' might be a better trip."

- "I lack confidence and I fear being shut down when presenting new ideas."

- "Overcoming fear of what others think."

- "Confidence in the leadership role God has given me."

Do you see yourself in any of these responses? If so, you're not alone. Countless Christian leaders struggle with the Three Banditos of lack of confidence, tentative decision making, and shortage of boldness. These three thieves often travel together. When leaders struggle to lead confidently, they strain to make decisions, especially hard ones—precisely when they need boldness the most.

I can confidently tell you this: If you don't arrest these three thieves and learn to better deal with them, they will continue to hold your leadership hostage.

Becoming More Confident

Daniel Harkavy has led an executive coaching company called Building Champions for almost a quarter of a century. He and his team have coached thousands of leaders over that period, including men and women from huge corporations such as Nike, Daimler, Chick-fil-A, and many others. Harkavy is a committed Christian who also has served his community as a member of several nonprofit boards. He knows leadership inside and out, from both a for-profit and nonprofit perspective.

Harkavy has coached many leaders who expressed a desire for certainty regarding all aspects of their leadership. He pushes back against that desire.

In his most recent book, *The 7 Perspectives of Effective Leaders*, he writes, "Given the speed and pace with which things change, confidence is a much better target than certainty."[7]

But how does a leader gain that confidence? And how can leaders project personal confidence to the men and women they lead so that the vast majority want to become followers?

Make Sure You're a Leader

If you have any doubt that you're a leader, you shouldn't expect much confidence to follow. So, how can you know that you're really a leader? Test yourself against the following nine characteristics of genuine leaders.

1. You have a divine compulsion to lead.

You sense a heavenly calling, a divine pull to accomplish something extraordinary with a group of motivated men and women. Christian leaders are fueled by their personal devotion to Christ and their unwavering commitment to biblical truth.

The undeniable call of God on your life to lead is the only thing that will give you staying power. If God calls you somewhere and all hell breaks loose, it will be all right, because you know that God called you to be part of that hell-raising organization until you can get it straight. Stay there. God will take care of it. Never stop using the well-worn proverb, "Where God guides, God provides." If God has guided you there, God will provide for you there.

2. You have an undeniable inclination for Christian leadership.

You have a strong, unfading desire to lead others to wonderful destinations, under the lordship of Christ.

3. You think like a leader.

Making mundane, micro-level decisions does not fulfill you. You see farther, you see first, you fly higher. In whatever context you find yourself, you end up leading in some way.

4. Others easily discern your potent influence.

Less than a year after I was saved at age twenty, the pastor at Longleaf

Baptist Church in Wilmington asked me to speak on something called Baptist Men's Day. I was just a kid, fresh out of the pool hall, an untrained layman. After I spoke, several people came up to me and said, "Johnny Hunt, you sound like a preacher."

I didn't know it, but I already was one; I just didn't yet see or understand my calling. Still, I had this divine compulsion that others recognized and endorsed.

5. You have an ability to change the way people think.

Because of your leadership, people do what they said they'd never do—and they follow you, smiling. God has given you the ability to change the way others think. You have significant influence with them.

6. Other leaders feel attracted to you.

Did you know that leaders feed off of each other? They're like sharks smelling blood in the water, except the feeding frenzy is life-giving and soul-building.

7. You have the resolve to stand for what is right.

You have an internal strength that comes from the conviction of your calling. You can't help it! You are courageous. All great leaders have courage and can become as bold as a lion, which comes from a clear conscience, a divine call, and the strong desire to live out that calling.

8. You take reasonable risks, and you accept the heat that goes with them.

Daniel Harkavy would call these "strategic bets," new initiatives that add to or differ from how your organization currently operates. "Strategic bets grounded in current reality and anchored to vision enable you to move into an offensive position,"[8] he says.

9. You love leading.

You love being a leader and you can't imagine doing anything else.

Christian leaders have the right to lead because of who they are, not because of what they do. If you ever have to tell your people you're the leader, you're not.

Jesus was the leader. Do you know what the leader can do? He can get in a boat in a storm and go to sleep in the back of the boat. You can sleep if you really are in charge.

Quick Tips on Building Confidence

A steady flow of books, articles, and Internet chatter provides an avalanche of practical advice on how to build your confidence.

Brian Tracy's book *The Power of Self-Confidence: Become Unstoppable, Irresistible, and Unafraid in Every Area of Your Life* encourages readers to understand their true potential, gain a proper mindset, let go of destructive emotional baggage, beware of people-pleasing, use their mistakes to push them forward, stop overthinking, live on purpose, and similar counsel.[9] What's not to like in that list?

Or, if you're in a hurry, you could read *5 Weeks to Self-Confidence* by Lynn Matti.[10] She advises her readers to confront their inner critic, build their self-esteem, set goals, know their beliefs and values, improve their communication, along with similar guidance.

Do you need even more bite-sized chunks? Then maybe Barrie Davenport's *Confidence Hacks: 99 Small Actions to Massively Boost Your Confidence* would be more to your liking.[11]

If you'd rather not shell out any money, you could scan the Internet and identify scores of memes, lists, articles, and posters, most of them offering decent (if pretty obvious) advice.[12]

My point is that if you need to build your confidence, you can do so. Start with what God says in His Word, put His wisdom into practice, and then fill in with the helpful tidbits lying all around you. God wants you confident in your leadership, so get to work.

Better Decision Making

Daniel Harkavy makes a strong point that many of us miss. While most everyone these days identifies "influence" as the key to effective leadership, Harkavy states that influence makes up only half of the secret sauce for creating great leaders. The other key, he insists, is sound decision making. He describes one leader who had great influence but poor decision making, and another leader who consistently made great decisions but had no influence. Both came up short. And so Harkavy claims, "Your leadership effectiveness will be determined by just two things: *the decisions you make* and *the influence you have.*"[13]

Don't Delegate Your Decision-Making Responsibilities

Leaders must lead. That may seem simple and obvious, but all leaders must lead, even when they get tired.

Do you ever get fatigued? Sometimes I feel emotionally down. And when I get tired, I droop emotionally, mentally, and spiritually, which can affect me in all areas. And yet, I still must make some major decisions.

So, what happens when I feel dog tired and not at my best? "Johnny, what do you think we ought to do here?" someone may ask. Because I'm so tired, I may answer, "Whatever. Go ahead and make the decision." Do you know this is exactly how some people will try to hijack your leadership? They may think, *If he won't lead, I'll step up to the plate.*

While delegating some decisions may be a good choice (when it honors Christ), if I delegate some decisions to others because I'm not willing to step up and do what I need to do, or I'm not at my best, then sooner or later (and probably sooner), my organization will land in hot water. And so will I.

Leaders must lead, a truth that powerfully hit home with me a few years ago when I realized I'd given others some things to do that God had never given me permission to give away. As the leader, I have no right to delegate my key responsibilities. It's my duty to lead, and that means making critical decisions that no one else should be making.

Three Areas Where You Must Make the Key Decisions

Regardless of the type of organization you lead, at least three areas require your personal attention.

1. Lead the direction of your organization.

As the leader, you must set the direction of your organization. That's your responsibility. You're the leader. So long as you're in that position, that's part of your calling. It doesn't mean you become a dictator; it's just leading.

Adrian Rogers once asked me, "Have you ever read the book *A Communist Manifesto*?" I thought, *No! I don't even feel inspired to read it.* He said, "I'll give you the gist of it. The few people who formed the very first communist party sat around a table one day and came up with rules that would help them to take communism to the world. That was their plan, to take over the whole world. Rule number one was, 'Our cause is greater than anyone around this table.'"

How often do we refuse to lead because we allow some individual to be more important than the cause? That's not good decision making. That's not leading. Leaders lead, especially when it comes to keeping the main thing the main thing.

2. Lead by hiring key personnel.

I'm always part of the process of hiring key staff members. I don't interfere with the hires my top-level staff members make, but I never delegate to others the hiring of any top-level staff. Still, I get help.

I don't hire key staff persons without my wife present at the interview. She does none of the interviewing—she just sits there and listens—but I've learned that she sees things I don't see. She also sees things I don't want to see.

Suppose I interview a man so gifted that I want him to serve with me now. I feel so enamored by what he can do that any red flags don't concern me—but they do concern my wife. She's a prophet, with a prophet's black and white perspective. She cuts to the chase.

I once got really pumped about hiring a certain candidate. After the interview, my wife and I dropped him off at his hotel. I felt a little afraid of asking for her opinion, but I knew I needed it. "What do you think?" I asked.

"Did you hear what I heard?" she answered. And I thought, *Oh Lord, here it comes.* She listed four or five red flags. I had noticed them too, but I didn't want to pay attention to them. When you think you've found your person, sometimes you believe you can just ignore the details.

"If you call that man to serve on your staff," Janet continued, "every time you're with him, money will be the issue."

"I disagree," I said. "I think you're pushing the envelope on that one." I hired him against her counsel.

One day, the guy said to me, "Hey, I hear you're a runner."

"Yeah," I replied.

"May I jog with you?"

"Sure," I said.

One of the first times we ran together, he asked, "What do you think about my salary?" From then on, the money issue came up every time we got together. Soon, I started finding reasons not to be with him; I just wanted him to do his job. Before long, we parted ways.

Janet never said anything; she didn't have to.

When your organization gets ready to make major hiring calls, you need to make them. Be wise about it, however. Give those you trust the right to speak into your leadership. That's just good decision making.

3. Lead in key financial areas.

One year when our organization was flatlined, I brought in my eight senior staff members and said, "We need this amount in our budget in order to begin an important new initiative. We need to get our budgets in line. Here's how much money I need to come out of your departmental budgets."

When they came back, each of them said, "I can't cut this," "This is mine," and "This is off-limits." We weren't anywhere close to the required number.

"This ain't enough," I said. "Here's the number I need. Now, go back and make some real cuts."

When they returned the next time, it looked as though each of them had been praying for their friends to do some chopping. Nobody wanted to give up anything.

"I've given you two runs at this," I said, "and you've brought back budgets that didn't cut nearly enough. I'm sending you back one final time. And if I don't have enough when you return, I'm going to take what I need from each of you. I'll take it from wherever I want." You can do that when you're the leader.

"And when I take it," I continued, "some of you are going to say, 'No, not from *that* area! Take it from *here*!' Which just means you were deceptive, and now I have to question whether I have the right person on my team."

When they returned the third time, we had more than enough money for the new initiative. Everything we needed was there.

Yes, you may have finance people and a business administrator, but when your income falls short, no board member will call any of your staff. They'll say to you, "You're the leader. Where's the money? How do you plan to get it?"

Although I've never signed a check, I lead the way in finances. I don't make the smallest decisions for my senior leaders. I do, however, direct our overall operation. That means I make the key financial decisions for the benefit of the whole organization.

Get Your People on Your Team

Earn the right to be followed. You earn the respect of your people by loving them, caring for them, and letting them see how you respond.

When you love and care for your people and they genuinely believe that you're there for them and are not trying to cheat them out of anything, somehow or another, God begins to bless. You get momentum on your side. You can take a parked locomotive engine, put a two by four in front of it, start it up, and it won't move. But get that baby going, get its momentum up, and it will blast through a brick wall.

Motivate your people to follow you by encouraging them. Many are diamonds in the rough, just waiting for somebody to come along who believes in them, who wants to pull their great potential out of them.

These days, I try to celebrate more with my people, to applaud their victories. I'm learning to slow down long enough to get excited over the great thing they just did and enthusiastically commend them for it. Do you think that motivates them?

Decision making becomes a lot easier when you work to get your people on your team. Once they're solidly with you, they won't often say, "I disagree with you on that." It's amazing what motivated men and women will do for you and with you if you can just get a little momentum on your side.

Decision Making Comes with a Cost

When you agree to lead an organization that has waited a long time for someone like you, the people often celebrate your arrival. What a great day! They love you! They compliment you! Every time they do so, it's like putting a quarter in your pocket.

But then, you start making decisions. "I've taken a look at this situation, and we need to make a change." Will that decision cost you? It probably will, maybe a couple of quarters. Then you shake up a little more of the organization, and that costs you too. A few more quarters slip out of your pocket.

If you want to succeed as a leader and gain the support of your people, especially their trust in your decision making, then you must invest your quarters as well as spend them. If you don't, before too long you'll find yourself out of change. You'll have lost a significant amount of influence. I've known John Maxwell to say, "Make sure you have change in your pocket."

I talk to my wife along these lines. We discuss our relationship using the picture of me making deposits into her emotional love bank. I will ask her, "How's my account?" If she replies, "In serious trouble," I'll check my calendar, change things up, and take her away to someplace special. Not only do we enjoy ourselves, but I go from "in trouble" to "flat loaded."

In your decision-making, you must learn how to move from expenditure to investment. In simplest terms, leadership expenditure is you doing it, while investment is you teaching them to do it. When your people begin to feel that, because you've invested in them, they're investing their time and talents in your ideas, you'll quickly fill up your own Fort Knox's worth of credit for the hard decisions.

Tips for Making Better Decisions

Brothers Chip and Dan Heath wrote a great book on decision making titled *Decisive: How to Make Better Choices in Life and Work*.[14] They based their work on a thorough study of academic literature on how individuals tend to make decisions.

It turns out that, in general, most humans are simply bad at making good decisions. There are psychological studies that say biases and other problems can hamper our decision making: We feel overconfident in our judgments, we treasure information that supports our wishes and dismiss information that doesn't, and we allow our short-term emotions to sabotage us.

The Heaths developed a decision-making process designed to reduce the impact of our biases and empower us to make better choices. According to them, four very typical human errors guided their approach:

- We tend to narrow our options (we want *this* or *that*)

- We allow confirmation bias to skew our decisions (we seek out information that agrees with us and devalues information we don't like)

- We allow short-term emotion to adversely affect us

- We get overconfident about our decisions (we think we know more about the future than we really do)

In their book, Chip and Dan use the acronym WRAP to help us defeat our unproductive but very human tendencies. *W* stands for "Widen your options." *R* stands for "Reality-test your assumptions." *A* stands for "Attain distance before deciding." And *P* stands for "Prepare to be wrong."

The Heaths then provide dozens of helpful tips, based on their acronym, to help us make better, healthier decisions. They also suggest that when we invite groups to join us in the decision-making process, we gain confidence, take bigger risks, make bolder choices, and enable everyone to feel better about the decisions we finally make, whether they turn out well or not.

I see a lot to admire in their book, but again, none of it supersedes what God tells us in His Word. It does, however, provide us with a lot of nuts and bolts that can give us a smoother ride.

When all is said and done, I endorse this wise saying I saw recently: "Be decisive. Right or wrong, make a decision. The road of life is paved with flat squirrels who couldn't make a decision."

Boldness: Sometimes Required

Most of us know bold when we see it. We also usually know when we need boldness but lack it. So, how can we become bolder as Christian leaders?

From Where Does Boldness Come?

If you have a genuine interest in this question, I'd like to challenge you to do a biblical word study on the term *bold*. In the New King James Version, the term appears only thirty-five times, so it doesn't require hours of study. I'll give you a head start, providing ten categories that suggest how, when, and why Christian leaders can grow bold.

1. Boldness comes in response to prayer (Psalm 138:3; Acts 4:29-30).

2. Boldness comes with practical righteousness (Proverbs 28:1).

3. Boldness comes with time spent with Jesus (Acts 4:13).

4. Boldness comes when we act in Jesus' name (Acts 9:27-29).

5. Boldness comes in trying times (Acts 13:46).

6. Boldness comes by grace (Romans 15:15).

7. Boldness comes because of our Christian hope (2 Corinthians 3:12).

8. Boldness comes during moments of opposition (2 Corinthians 10:1-2).

9. Boldness comes in Christ, through His Spirit (Ephesians 3:12).

10. Boldness comes to empower effective evangelism (John 7:26; Acts 4:31; 9:27-28; 14:3; 18:26; 19:8; Ephesians 6:19).

To be bold, we must be willing to get uncomfortable. Why is boldness even required, except when we face opposition? Too often, perhaps, we don't want to be bold because we fear the offense of the cross (Galatians 5:10-11). We don't want to risk offending someone. We don't want to create waves. We want the good things boldness often brings without any of the discomfort associated with it.

Times come, however, when Christian leaders need to be both bold and uncompromising—never arrogant, never obnoxious, never belligerent, but "bold as a lion" (Proverbs 28:1).

The Making of Boldness

To become bolder in your leadership, intentionally put yourself in situations where you feel *very* uncomfortable. These episodes should make you sweat more than a little.

While I was never formally discipled, my training certainly was intentional. Nearly every question I had about the Bible, Alfred Joyner answered for me. He was a real man of prayer and a great soul winner. Immediately after I got saved, Alfred started telling me, "Johnny, I'm going to make a visit tonight and I want you to go with me." And that was it. Honestly, that is how I learned to witness.

That first night, he took me to see a guy named Beau. I'll never forget it as long as I live. We met Beau at the door, who said to us, "I'm just on my way out, guys, but good to see you all. My wife's here, though." She was a member of our little church.

"We've come to see you, Beau," Alfred said.

Beau had a folding chair that he turned around and straddled when he heard Alfred's comment. "What can I do for you?" he asked.

"We've been praying for you, Beau," Alfred answered, "and we just wanted to come by and see you. Johnny got saved the other day and I wanted him to tell you what happened."

Alfred hadn't told me I was going to do that. As I look back on it, had he told me, I probably would not have gone with him, or I would have gotten sick or wet my britches. But isn't that what a witness is? You just tell what happened to you. So, that's what I did.

As time went on, Alfred and I did more and more visiting. And day by day, I got more and more bold, just like Alfred.

They say that the older you get, the more you reflect. And today I think, *I'm the man I am because of the investment Alfred Joyner made in me.*

What Boldness Doesn't Look Like

A church once asked me to speak at its missions conference. I had never visited the church, located in an affluent community on the edge of a large city. At a dinner before my talk, I met many individuals from the church who left me very impressed. *Wow*, I thought, *this is quite a church*.

That night, the pastor got up before I spoke and talked about the sacrifice it would take for the church to meet its target. *This is going to really challenge my heart!* I thought. *I'll be able to use this back home!* He described the goal, said that some of his people might have to give up their end-of-year commissions or bonuses, and then closed with this killer: "Some of you need to give up a Starbucks a week."

And I thought, *What did I just hear?*

Let's just put it on the record: giving up one Starbucks a week will change the world. If you can get everybody to give about $5 a week, you could flat turn this world upside down.

Such a "sacrifice" is *ludicrous!* I don't mean to be offensive, but I do mean to be bold. Give up a cup of coffee? For the kingdom of God? *Wow!* I thought.

What Boldness May Look Like

In my early days at Woodstock, I wanted to raise enough money to allow us to use budget dollars to help struggling churches. Eighty-five percent of our churches in the Southern Baptist Convention had never planted a single church, never had a baby. In fact, Woodstock had never planted one, and at the time we were 150 years old. That's a long time to go without having a baby!

Although we prayed about what we ought to do, we never did what we prayed about. By God's grace, I wanted to lead a charge to change all that. As part of a big campaign, I was asked if I would be willing to meet with families and groups. I had never done that because such an approach went against my core. But I did it and it was *awesome*.

We started with those regular givers, because we knew that 75 percent of our people didn't give regularly. It shocked me to learn the number of those in our church who gave under two hundred dollars a year; my grandchildren gave more than they did. We called the Georgia Division of Children and Family Services to find out the average size of a welfare check in our county. I told our people that if they tithed based on the amount of an average welfare check, we would take in more than we did on an average Sunday.

As the campaign continued, I said at one Sunday service, "I'm asking you to give beyond, but some of you can't give beyond because you don't give below."

Is that too bold?

Through the campaign, we saw giving significantly rise through regular tithes and offerings. I knew, however, that the people who already gave had chosen to give more, while the uncommitted remained uncommitted. I knew that even if we reached our goal, we might get the money, but we wouldn't have grown any children—and God's in the business of raising children, not money.

So, I got bold once more.

"We're not going to borrow *any* money for this," I told the church. "I'm putting it all in the budget." Do you have any idea how much your budget increases when you do such a thing? "I need to inform you," I said, "that we're getting ready to be embarrassed as a church. We don't take in nearly enough money to accomplish this, unless those of you who don't give start giving. So, when you get in the car today, ma'am, look at your husband and say, 'We're two of them.' Or husband, you're the spiritual leader. Start the conversation by saying to your wife, 'We need to get our house in order. We need to start supporting the work of the kingdom.'"

We raised enough money through that campaign to meet our budget and yet still have millions of dollars to help struggling churches. Holy boldness, paired with much prayer, good planning, and blessed timing, can sometimes help to turn the tide.

Boldness Beyond the Church

You may not work in a church, so such stories may not resonate with you. You may lead a company, a business, a community organization. Regardless of where you lead, life sometimes requires you to be bold.

I love the famous story of the late Steve Jobs and how he once convinced a great leader to join Apple. Jobs wanted someone who could take Apple to the next level and had set his sights on PepsiCo president John Scully, even though many Apple leaders already had tried and failed to recruit Scully. One day, as Jobs and Scully sat on a balcony overlooking Central Park, Jobs is reported to have asked him, "Do you want to sell sugar water for the rest of your life, or come with me and change the world?"

That's bold! Scully later said that Job's question landed like a punch to his gut. He soon quit his job at PepsiCo and joined Jobs at Apple.

This unforgettable story usually ends here, but since this is a book for Christian leaders, I don't want to leave you thinking of boldness merely as a tool to get what you want. Jobs' boldness got him his man, all right, but his man turned out to be less than ideal. About a decade after Scully arrived at Apple, the company forced him out. Might things have turned out differently had God somehow been involved in the process? Maybe.

What I know is that in October 2011, Steve Jobs died of cancer at age fifty-six. Shortly before his death, he reportedly said, "I reached the pinnacle of success in the business world. In others' eyes my life is an epitome of success. However, aside from work, I have little joy. In the end, wealth is only a fact of life that I am accustomed to. At this moment, lying on the sick bed and recalling my whole life, I realize that all the recognition and wealth that I took so much pride in have paled and become meaningless in the face of impending death."[15]

Is there a real difference between leadership and Christian leadership? I will leave that question for you to answer.

4

Godly

One of the most engaging, innovative, and fun museums in the world opened in Washington, D.C., in late November 2017. Many years in the making, it covers 430,000 square feet of space spread over eight floors, cost $500 million to build, and sits just three blocks from the US Capitol. Its interactive exhibits and cutting-edge technology give visitors an immersive, personal experience as they interact with 4,000 years of history.

"History of what?" you ask. That's maybe the best part. The Museum of the Bible (MOTB) describes itself as a "global, innovative, educational institution whose purpose is to invite all people to engage with the transformative power of the Bible."[16] The MOTB strives to be among the most technologically advanced and engaging museums in the world and, in line with its mission, also sponsors traveling exhibits, supports academic research around the world, and even participates in the Tel Shimron archaeological excavation in Israel.

What would cause someone to go to all the time, expense, and labor to create such a unique institution? In this case, the answer is clear. The primary mover behind the project is Steve Green, the president of Hobby Lobby, the world's largest privately owned arts and crafts retailer. Steve is a committed evangelical Christian with a long-time dream to use his considerable wealth to create a captivating attraction that would draw twenty-first century people from around the world to consider anew the true nature and power of the Bible, God's Word. As MOTB's Chairman of the Board, he and the museum's CEO, Harry Hargrave, provide oversight of and strategic leadership to this exceptional outreach.

Hargrave has an interesting story of his own. He spent more than forty-five years working in finance, marketing, and business operations for large corporations and has directed several foundations and trusts. Harry chose the site of the museum, obtained city approvals for its construction, and oversaw its planning and development. He is also a founding elder of the Park Cities Presbyterian Church in Dallas, Texas, and has been married to the same woman for nearly fifty years.

Both Steve Green and Harry Hargrave have earned their reputations as outstanding leaders over decades of hard work and notable success. But they're not just leaders; they're Christian leaders. They wound up working together on the MOTB project because their deep faith in Jesus compelled them to do so. They love God and want others to know His love too. They put their money and their time where their mouths are. I'd call them godly.

Choose to Be a Godly Leader

Do you want to be a godly leader? Paul told Timothy, "Train yourself to be godly" (1 Timothy 4:7 NIV). Training is never easy, and training yourself doesn't make it any easier. But it is crucial if you want to be an effective Christian leader.

A phenomenal Christian leader of the past, Charles Spurgeon, once spoke some choice words to preachers that equally apply to all Christian leaders. "It is a shocking state of things," he said, "when good people say our minister undoes in the church parlor what he has done in the pulpit. He preaches very well, but his life does not agree with his sermons. God help us so to live that we may be safe examples to our flocks."[17]

Let's walk through several ways for every Christian leader to be a safe example for those they lead. While none of these are deep, we do need to be intentional about each of them.

1. Give your first hour each day to God's Word.

I've been a Christian for forty-nine years. I never owned a Bible until my wife got me one the day after I was converted. Somebody told me to start with the New Testament, so I did. It was all very new to me.

Early on, I formed a real passion for the Gospel of Luke. To this day, it's my favorite Gospel. If you will study Luke, read a chapter a day and get through it in a month, you'll see what Jesus did during His days on earth. If you've ever wondered what a day looked like in the life of Jesus, Luke will tell you.

Luke introduced me to John the Baptist, a man who has always intrigued me. John, basically an Old Testament prophet, ministered in the days of Jesus. Luke says John was strong in the sight of the Lord and drank neither wine nor strong drink. That may not mean a lot to some people, but I had just been converted out of a pool room. In those days, I had spent a lot of time at the Red Fox Saloon, so I knew a lot about alcohol abuse.

When I read about John, I made it my prayer that I would follow his example. I prayed Scripture. And I began to think, *God, I don't want to be mediocre. I want to be strong.* As a testimony to Jesus and His work in my heart, I became a strong layman, a faithful contributor. I became a soul-winner, bringing people to faith in Jesus. The church where I was involved baptized more people the year I got converted than in any given year of its thirty-six-year history before then. God did something amazing in my life.

The word *strong* really got to me. I wanted to be strong back then, and I still do today. Maybe you were blessed to be raised in a good Christian home, but maybe you were a hellion like me. And I was a good hellion; I could raise hell with the best of them. And I did. Nobody ever tried to get me to calm down. Nobody ever called and said, "You're going to the pool-room too much. Why are you still at the Red Fox Saloon?"

When I got saved, though, the people who knew me suddenly got uncomfortable around me. They wanted to calm me down. I think they wanted me to backslide so I could get along with the rest of the church. I'm telling you, if you let somebody get on fire in a church, you'll make a lot of people nervous! They'll get uncomfortable around you. But as a good leader, you ought to make some people uncomfortable.

A man named Bob Harrington greatly influenced me after my conversion. Bob came to faith in Jesus at age thirty in his hometown of Sweet Water, Alabama, and in the '60s and '70s became a well-traveled evangelist. Popular television shows such as *Phil Donahue, Merv Griffin,* and *The Tonight Show* often had him as a guest, in part because of his "one-liners and unconventional religious wit."[18] He toured thirty-eight cities with famed atheist Madalyn Murray O'Hair, debating the Bible. "Many may say Madalyn knows the Scriptures better than I do," he would say, "but I know the author."[19]

I remember the first time I drove from Wilmington to Elon College, North Carolina, outside of Greensboro, to hear Bob preach. I wanted to meet him because God was really using him. Sometime later, this great Christian leader fell away when he forgot about leaders training themselves to be godly, but in those days, God had His hand on him. When he wandered away from the Lord, he slid back and divorced his wife, Joyce. But before then, I used to watch him after I got converted.

I once waited in a long line after Bob spoke, just to get him to sign my Bible. I'd also get up early every Sunday morning to watch his program, "Chaplain of Bourbon Street." He had a little slogan, "It's fun being saved." He wore a red tie, red socks, and used a red Bible. He shared the gospel in a brilliant, hilarious way, and led a lot of people to Jesus.

After Bob got away from the Lord, we didn't hear from him for many, many years. One day, word got out that he had genuinely repented, got right with God, and made every amend he could. But oh, how foolishly he had wasted those years! One day I was preaching and thought I saw Bob in the crowd. I gave an invitation and a man came forward—sure enough, it was Bob Harrington. "Mr. Hunt," he said, "I hear that in my early days I really influenced you."

"Bob," I said, "afterward I can take you to my office. I have a Bible that you signed, my first Bible. You're bigger than life to me. Welcome back."

He started crying and said, "I'm glad for the way God's used you, and that God used me to help you. Is it true that I signed your Bible?"

"Yeah," I answered.

"Would you honor me today by signing my Bible and writing something encouraging in it?" he asked. Later, he showed up at Timothy+Barnabas and sat in the front row. He said nothing the whole time; he just listened.

Bob lived on into his eighties and died of dementia a few years ago. When he died, I was one of the first people that his family called. "Daddy wanted you to be one of the first to know that he'd died," his daughter Rhonda told me. "We went over to the house and opened up all his albums, and the first picture on top of the first album was one with you." It was the photo we had taken in church that day when he rededicated his life to the Lord and I signed his Bible.

Do you want to be a godly leader? I do. I don't want to be known for wandering away for years. The best way to nip wandering in the bud is to prioritize the Word of God in your life. Get up every morning and read your Bible. Have an unhurried quiet time with the Lord.

The Bible is God's inspired Word, written by men whom the Holy Spirit carried along as they wrote. Through His Word, God equips you for His work. You simply cannot live a godly life apart from knowing and following the Bible, God's Word.

2. Develop and keep a prayer journal.

Prayerlessness is idolatry of the self, a very real danger for effective leaders. Pray in the morning over the calendar events of your day, and never lead a meeting without praying beforehand. Pray quickly when you hear about people's needs. The Bible says, "Pray without ceasing" (1 Thessalonians 5:17).

When we don't feel like praying, we need to pray until we do feel like praying. As C.H. Spurgeon said, "If your heart be cold in prayer, do not restrain prayer until your heart warms, but pray your soul unto heat by the help of the ever-blessed Spirit...If the iron be hot then hammer it, and if it be cold, hammer it till you heat it. Never cease in prayer for any reason."[20] If you're desperate to be a godly leader, this is where it starts.

As the former director of retail merchandising at Coca-Cola, Steve Hyland tried to apply this principle of praying intentionally in every aspect of his work life. He prayed for coworkers as needs were identified or expressed. He also enlisted other Christians to join him in intercessory prayer. As individuals came to Steve to share their requests, prayer became more personal as he immediately prayed with them.

Steve often used his commute time to praise and thank God, cast his burdens upon God, and ask for opportunities to share the gospel and minister to others. While at the office, he prayed throughout the day for wisdom (see James 1:5), whether regarding work projects, dealing with challenging situations, or asking for God's guidance in his interactions with coworkers. When you make prayer a part of your DNA, as Steve did, expect to see your effectiveness as a leader grow in ways you can't even imagine.

3. Stay accountable.

You never reach a point when you no longer need someone to hold you accountable to live in a holy way. Godly leaders always open their lives to somebody, realizing that how we live privately is at least as important as how we live publicly. If you don't have a person like that, find him today, someone who can spur you on toward godliness.

Don't pick just anybody. Get to know the person. Discover whether this is someone you can trust, someone you can ask to care for you without pulling any punches. A couple of men in my life check in with me regularly and have permission to ask me anything. They also can ask my wife anything about me, our calendar, and our time together. One of these men is Dr. John Peacock, a long-time successful dentist. Our relationship goes back even before I became a pastor. I asked John recently to describe some of this accountability relationship. Here is what he wrote:

> What impressed me about all these men in our accountability group was an openness and willingness to be vulnerable with each other. We let men ask whatever was needed to make sure each of us was living as close to the Lord as we could and making Him the focus of our life. That was a great influence on me personally, to know other men were praying for me and loving me enough to watch my life and possibly see something about which I might have a blind spot. I have asked for input from these men, and been asked for input, to help make a decision or meet a spiritual challenge. It is awesome to know you have men in your life like this.

> Godly leaders need to be accountable to someone other than their immediate family, someone who can and will hold them accountable as needed. Everyone needs someone they know they can call on for advice and will get honest input, even if they need to be told what they might not want to hear. A leader who answers to no one is in a dangerous position in life.[21]

4. Develop a kingdom mindset.

It will make a huge difference in your leadership if you pray earnestly that God would give you a kingdom mindset. I once tried to get a leader friend engaged in some mission endeavor. "I have to be honest with you," he told me. "Mostly I'm concerned about how many employees I can get to stay on their work tasks. It takes about all the energy I have just to do that."

It's easy to get discouraged in that type of setting, because your measurements are not broad enough. If you broadened your perspective to see how you could have a kingdom impact worldwide, it would take a lot more to discourage you. It's hard work out there, but you can do it when you partner with God. The kingdom is larger than your little corner of it, and none of us can afford to wait to launch out until we have everything else perfectly in order. Just get involved in broader kingdom work at some level.

The opposite problem is equally serious. When we think kingdom work is all about us, we set ourselves up for a fall that comes with pride. Ask God to show you whenever ego starts to take control in your life.

Almost 200 years ago, D.L. Moody said that we must stab the major cities in America in the heart with the gospel. In many cases, unfortunately, we've done the opposite. Someone from the North American Mission Board of the SBC once asked me when I pastored Woodstock, "Would you pray about what city God would have your church to take?" And he challenged me: "Would you lead your church to give?" I took his challenge, and it ended up being the largest single amount we ever gave for any church plant. We prayed through it and felt God wanted us to plant a church in Las Vegas, at that time the fastest growing city in America.

To make a long story short, we did plant a church there, and in less than twenty years, that church was attracting more than 3,100 people to its services. Better yet, can you guess how many churches got planted out of that one church? Seventy-one! That's a lot of kingdom growth that, humanly speaking, stemmed from one key decision.

We leaders must not wait on kingdom business! Get involved with kingdom endeavors, regardless of your job or industry. Most of us have seriously misjudged our capacity for God. We try to look at what we can manage instead of what God can support and manage through us. We forget that while God used the apostle Paul in a staggering way, Paul himself said, "I will not venture to speak of anything except what Christ has accomplished through me to bring the Gentiles to obedience—by word and deed" (Romans 15:18 ESV).

Is your plate already full? Just remember, in the kingdom, it's not your plate.

5. Always remember that time is fleeting.

Almost two billion people in this world have little or no access to the gospel. Thousands die without Christ every day. Jesus is still the only answer for sin. Spreading the gospel to the nations remains God's only plan. Understanding this urgency makes the temporary pleasures of sin pale. Live as if today really is all God gives you.

I love to teach in Turkey, one of the most unevangelized countries in the Middle East. Did you know that far more people are getting saved in Iran than in Turkey? Although Turkey is westernized, it's godless. So, what do we do there? We train Iranians. The largest Iranian church in the world is located in Denizli, Turkey. They are there because they had to flee their own country. Iranian Muslims tried to kill them when they trusted Jesus, so they became refugees. I have pictures on my phone of thirty-year-old ladies and twenty-five-year-old guys who may never again see their families. They can't stay in Turkey indefinitely but are waiting to be assigned to whatever country will take them—often Australia, the United States, or Canada. They have no idea where they may wind up.

I love teaching in that church, because they feel offended if I preach for less than an hour. On one visit I gave an invitation after the message, and about twelve Muslims got saved—but everybody responded. And I do mean *everybody*. The invitation lasted three hours, mainly because all of them feel so broken. I heard it all night long: "I don't know where I'm going to go"; "I don't know if I will ever see my parents again"; "I can't go back to Iran; pray for me."

One man named Farsi had been in an Iranian prison for six years. Every time he got called up to the Muslim ruling council, they said, "Deny Jesus and go home. See your wife and children." And he replied, "I can't deny Jesus." Every time, they put him back in prison. Farsi served as my translator at the Denizli church.

When I first visited Turkey, the believers there introduced me to Farsi like this: "This is the apostle Paul of our network. Give him all the material you have. He can read English." I sent Farsi every lesson and many sermons I wrote and he and I became good friends. My last time in Turkey, I said to him, "So, Farsi, what's going on in your life?"

"Pray for me," he said. "I'm sensing God is leading me back into Iran. I have to get back there and preach the gospel."

We had been trying to get him to the United States, and then to Canada, where his wife and children now live. When I last saw him, he hadn't seen them in eight years. He may be in Iran now, for all I know.

Live with urgency because time is fleeting.

6. Speak with grace.

Leaders must keep a tight rein on their tongues, especially Christian leaders. Careless or hurtful words, spoken in jest or without thinking, can spark fast-moving firestorms that usually prove hard to put out.

Avoid crude jokes. Determine not to talk poorly of others. Use your words to build others up, not tear them down. Talk more about God than yourself. Speak truth and live love. Trust that someone is always listening, because someone always is.

7. Train others.

Everybody needs a Paul in their life, someone who is ahead of them. Everybody needs a Barnabas to encourage them. And everybody needs a Timothy, in whom they can invest. When you mentor someone, you give back some of what you've been given.

If you're a leader anything like nearly every leader I've ever known, you have received so much from others. Who has invested in your life? Who has helped to make you a better leader? What has this person done for you?

If you're a leader who follows Christ, you ought to be mentoring someone. Understand, though, when you invest yourself in another, you also make yourself vulnerable. A mentee watches you. You become their model for leadership.

How can you mentor a promising leader? I hardly ever sit down and individually teach a mentee. I normally have several at a time, and I'm extremely proud of each of them (see chapter 9). We have some incredible conversations. Mentees watch you, seeking a guide and example of both leadership and Christian faith. It should encourage us to fight for godliness, knowing that our mentees will be disappointed (or worse) should we fall.

8. Become a soul-winner.

A few years ago, I had the opportunity to spend a year with a young man who I consider the greatest soul-winner I've ever met. He witnesses to everybody. He never takes a plane ride without talking about Jesus to someone. He shames me. He's a big, strong guy, but very soft spoken as he shares the gospel.

I bought him a gym membership because he leads somebody to Jesus practically every week at the gym. Nearly every week he brings a gym buddy with him to church. He works out with them and is strong as an ox. Even the ripped guys see him as exceptionally strong, and he consistently and humbly shares the gospel with them.

Doing evangelism is basic Christian obedience, but it takes a life of holiness to share the gospel in the power of the Holy Spirit. How important it is for leaders to model evangelism! Faithfully and consistently share the gospel with others, modeling genuine Christian faith as you do so.

9. If you plan to continue to lead, you must continue to learn.

Every month I read one major, good book. For me, that's a requirement. "That's legalism," you may say, but it's really not. When I put a requirement like this on me, it's discipline. If I tried to put it on you, that would be legalism. For me, though, it's necessary.

I do a lot of writing, traveling, and preparing for various events, but I still make time to read. One month it may be a deep theological book by someone like Dr. Al Mohler. Another month it may be something by Jerry Bridges, who wrote for fifty years with the Navigators.

Would it surprise you to hear that when I traveled to some Eastern Bloc countries, which had toiled under communism for decades, I met some of the godliest men and women I've ever known? I met them in Romania, Russia, and the Ukraine. They had no formal theological training at all. *How did you get to be so godly?* I wondered. Ninety percent of the time, I discovered they had received training through the Navigator 270 program. They learned to be godly under conditions we can't even imagine, in large part by reading and learning on their own.

Keep learning! If you intend to keep leading, you must keep learning. Learning sets you apart as a leader. By trying to be the best you can be—not trying better than anyone else but the best version of you—you'll end up being better than most.

10. Clothe yourself in humility.

Godly leaders are characterized by their humility. The more effective they are, the less arrogant they are. A reporter once asked me what most attracted me to the life of Billy Graham. "The greatest men I've ever met," I replied, "have been the humblest men I've ever known."

Arnold Palmer is another example. For twenty years before he died, he hosted a group of pastors every November. We'd go to his place; he'd hang with us. He was always really kind.

One year, I took my friend Dan Dorner, who is a good golfer, as was his father. Two of Dan's sons went to Samford University on golf scholarships. Even so, Dan was like a kid in a candy store. "Dan," I told him, "we're going to meet Arnold Palmer on this trip." As we had breakfast one morning, we looked out onto the putting green and saw Arnold there. "Grab your hat," I told Dan. "We'll go get it signed."

Dan immediately objected. "No, we'd better not bother him." He was acting like a scared puppy, tail tucked between its legs.

"Come on," I said, "he won't mind."

We walked to the putting green and watched Arnold sink putt after putt, one after another. It was really something. "Mr. Palmer," I said at last. "Excuse me."

"Hey, boys," he said as he laid down his club. "How you doing? Good to see you!" He looked at me and said, "I've seen you here before."

I reintroduced myself and added, "This is Dan Dorner. His daddy had the same cancer you had."

"Wow, really?" he said. "How's he doing?" Arnold expressed great interest in both Dan and his father.

I pulled out a pen and said, "Hey, Mr. Palmer, would you sign this hat, one for Dan and one for his dad?"

"Not with that sorry pen, I wouldn't," he answered. But then he reached in and got his own Sharpie and signed the hat. He acted like he had nothing else to do in the world but talk to us. I'll never forget it.

As we walked away, Dan said to me, "I've only seen him on television, and he was always bigger than life. But I have more respect for him now, after meeting him, than I ever did before."

Good leaders are humble leaders. Max DePree had it right when he said, "The first responsibility of a leader is to define reality. The last is to say thank you. In between, the leader is a servant."[22]

11. Cultivate a sense of humor.

I've always had fun as I've served in various leadership capacities. If you lack a sense of humor, you probably won't make it in leadership. I really do have a good time most of the time. Some things just tickle me.

12. Be real and genuine.

All leaders feel tempted at times to exaggerate their successes and downplay their failures. Great leaders may feel that temptation, but they always work to resist it. If you want to be a great leader, you will have to strive to be a person of integrity in all matters and at all times.

You might think that pastors would rise above such temptation, but you would be wrong. Try an experiment. Ask a preacher what he's running in Sunday attendance, and more often than I'd like to admit, he'll give you his Easter attendance, which might double or triple the usual number. Or he might answer without finishing the statement. Someone asks, "What are y'all running up there?" and he'll say "900," but under his breath he'll say, "but last week we counted just 300."

Business or organizational leaders probably have different challenges with integrity than pastors, but they all face the temptation to compromise on their integrity. Do you pad an expense account? Overestimate the cost of doing business while underestimating potential sales, in order to get a tax break on some new initiative? Hide the reason for hiring a buddy rather than a more qualified candidate? Tell your assistant you're leaving for an important meeting, when really you're headed out to the golf course?

If you're going to be a godly leader, pay your bills. Take whatever steps may be necessary to avoid pornography. Be honest with your spouse on all matters. Confess your sins and stand before your people with no hidden areas of disobedience. Be confessed up. I often pray, "God, make me more committed in my private life than I'll ever appear to be in my public life."

13. Be mindful of your physical condition.

The promise of the resurrection gives us no permission to abuse the body God has given us. I know leaders who run themselves ragged, doing so with a self-satisfied smirk that supposedly announces their total commitment to the cause, whatever it may be.

Listen, the Spirit of God dwells in you. Your body is His temple. Godliness cannot be separated from your commitment to take care of yourself and keep up the only frame God has given you.

Did you know that exercise wards off depression? After I got cancer, I fell into a bad place and didn't feel like doing anything. My wife made me exercise. She would declare, "You need to go walking." To this day, when I'm at the beach, I walk an average of five miles every day. I walk fast, just like I talk and eat. I always have. But my wife will have none of that. She talked to me again this week about eating too fast. She remains hopeful.

I consciously work into my regimen some form of exercise—the treadmill in the morning, a long walk outside, or a workout at the gym. I use that time not only to get exercise, but to think through my day. By then I've already begun my day by praying and doing my devotions, so when I go to exercise, I pray through and think through my day.

Take care of yourself! It really will help you to become the godly leader you want to be.

Never Get Over Your Conversion

This is my forty-ninth year of knowing Jesus. I came to faith on a snowy night on January 7, 1973. I reflect on my conversion experience a great deal. You should, too, especially if you want to keep growing as a godly leader.

Think about your own lostness apart from God's intervention. Remember what it was like before you had any peace. Consider deeply God's mercy and grace toward you.

Remember those who shared the gospel with you and let your gratitude for yesterday's grace compel you toward today's obedience. We need more godly leaders serving in all kinds of roles and organizations. Why not commit yourself to being one of them?

PART TWO

PERSONAL COMPETENCIES OF A CHRISTIAN LEADER

5

Manages Time Well

Most leaders think they can do more in a day than is realistic. I've learned this lesson the hard way. Our daily plans often resemble fantasy more than reality. Just because we create a pile of to-do lists doesn't mean we can make it all happen. Frustration lies in that gap between what we thought we could do and what in fact we get done.

One thing's for sure: If you regularly leave the office saying, "I didn't get a cotton-picking thing done," you need to better identify your priorities and really own your schedule. Time is a precious commodity, too valuable to squander.

Take Charge of Your Schedule

If you don't take charge of your schedule, peripheral things will begin to clutter your life, making you miserable. You'll hear yourself saying things like, "There just has to be a better way to make a living."

The frustration you may be feeling right now could be the result of a schedule that has spun out of control. The good news is that you can take charge again. God wants you to enjoy leading wherever He has called you to lead.

Whenever you start acting more reactively than proactively, you know at least four things have happened to you. You know:

- You are unprepared.

- You've made no plans.

- You're not purpose-driven.

- You've become more of a follower than a leader.

If you see yourself in any of those four scenarios, what can you do? You take them and reverse them.

- What does it look like to lead in the place where I serve?

- What do I believe God has called me to do?

- What are my priorities and how, specifically, will I follow them?

- What should my schedule look like?

In this chapter I want to give you some practical, life-tested help to enable you to take charge of your schedule and more effectively manage your time. Before I get to the nuts and bolts, however, let's consider one crucial issue: cramming.

Cramming Decreases Productivity

All leaders have a great deal to do; that's just the nature of the job. We look at our long to-do lists and often think, *I guess I'll have to do twice as much today as I'd like.* But did you know that trying to cram more into your day decreases your productivity? You try to do so much that at the end of the day, even if you checked everything off your list, you probably did none of it well. I'm learning that lesson more and more, even in recent days. I've also learned that refusing to overpack my schedule puts a lot of energy into my life.

When you overpack your schedule, you tend to feel overwhelmed, which leads to procrastination and frustration. You want to take a break; you want to pull away from everything. Studies show that as we feel more overwhelmed, we slow down. And what happens then? We become less productive.

All leaders have the same problem of overreach. Not only do we get less done, but whatever we finish we do with lower quality. We're not as effective as we could be.

We're all better off when we put some margin in our schedules. Do fewer things on your list. Slow down and be more thorough, remembering that a slower place eliminates costly mistakes. Doing something once rather than twice saves time, even when done at a slower pace.

I called my assistant one day after I finished videotaping some teaching for a men's conference. She had worked hard with me to help me develop the material. I kept revising, changing, and editing. After the taping session, I called her to say, "I want to thank you for how much you helped me. The material was just right. I felt relaxed when I delivered it—like I really knew it. And I did the taping just one time; I didn't have to go back and re-record anything." How did we manage that? Simple: We refused to overreach. Since we managed our time well, I didn't feel pressed going in and I didn't feel pressed coming out.

I have found that I need the wisdom of Ecclesiastes 10:10: "If the ax is dull, and one does not sharpen the edge, then he must use more strength; but wisdom brings success." In other words, you're better off to slow down, plan ahead, and be sharp at what you do. If you ignore this wisdom, you chop more and get less wood. Why? When you don't sharpen your ax beforehand, it gets duller and duller as you work harder and longer, which means you get fewer and fewer things done. You're not being productive.

To increase your productivity and reduce your frustration, learn to better manage your time. And recognize that building a more productive day or week starts with an honest evaluation of how you're currently working.

What Are You Doing with Your Time?

What are you actually *doing* as a leader? Have you ever written out what you do, hour by hour?

Every now and then, we've felt that some of our staff members were not being as productive as we expected. And so, we started putting them on an hourly evaluation. We would say, "For the next couple of weeks, write down everything you do with your time, on an hourly basis. If something lasts for three hours, write it down. We want you to tell us exactly what you're doing with your time."

One way to do such a time analysis is to use a daily grid that lays out twenty-four boxes for each hour of the day. In every box, write down what you did with that hour. Some hours will be blocked for sleeping, eating, recreation, etc. Be meticulous about recording exactly what you did with each hour not taken up with sleeping or eating. Over a two-week period, you may feel shocked to see how, in fact, you spent your time.

This exercise works just as well (and may feel even more shocking) if you use it to estimate how you *think* you use your time. Using the same grid, mark out ahead of time the hours you expect to sleep, eat, exercise, shop, whatever. Then take the remaining blocks of time and try to fit in them the tasks you need to accomplish. Very often, leaders realize with alarm that they simply don't have enough hours in a day to finish what they say they need to accomplish. They're trying to do too much. They have more tasks on their to-do lists than they have hours to do them in.

What then? At that point, it's past time for some serious time management improvements.

How To Grab Control of Your Schedule

The best way to regain control of your schedule is to be proactive about what you do. A reactive approach, where you constantly respond to whatever comes up, leads to poor decisions, increased frustration, and exhaustion. So, how can you be proactive and regain control of your schedule?

1. Use a weekly to-do list.

I use such a list and have forever. Every Monday morning, I lay out everything I need to get done for the week.

Choose and then use some system of weekly/daily planning. If you see yourself violating it, ask yourself, "*What* am I doing?" I suggest that you lightly pinch yourself to recall that God has called you to serve Him as a leader. Don't take it for granted and don't diminish its importance by letting your schedule get out of control.

2. Keep your weekly to-do list with you at all times and add to it as things come up.

In my day planner, I check off items as I complete them. If I do something by the end of the day that I didn't have on my list, I write it in so that I have more to check off.

3. Take the last fifteen or twenty minutes of each day to list on the next day's schedule what you need to do, based on your weekly to-do list.

I do this every day before I leave the office. As I get ready to go to bed at night, I plug in my phone, where I keep my day planner. I rehearse the priorities of that day and make sure I did what I was supposed to do. I want to make sure that I didn't miss some biggie. If I have, I move it to the next day so that I can take care of it first thing in the morning.

Next, I look at the following day. I may just glance quickly over the calendar to see what I need to accomplish. This way, I'm ready to start immediately when I arrive at the office the next morning. I always write in my key tasks, even if I do those tasks every week.

4. For your last task each day, identify the unfinished priorities on your weekly to-do list and move them to the next day's to-do list.

Let's say it's November 1. I go into my calendar and look at my thirty-one days in October. I look through what I've done to make sure I didn't miss anything. Inevitably, I see that I've missed a few things. Maybe I forgot to return someone's phone call.

So, I'll call the person and say, "I'm so sorry, but I just looked over my schedule and saw that I planned to call you on October 11. I totally forgot; I beg your forgiveness. How may I help you?" Nine times out of ten, the answer is, "It's okay, I've taken care of it." Even if there is a chance the matter has been forgotten or taken care of, you should still follow up. That's the right thing to do.

5. Keep your door closed.

Keep your office door shut when it needs to be. An open door communicates that it's okay to come in and visit. It also means that you're allowing someone else to dictate your schedule.

When I close my office door, it means I'm studying or working on something that requires my undivided attention. The closed door says, "I don't want any interruptions." My assistant knows this. When my door is open, someone in the hall is welcome to think, *He's free; I'll ask his assistant if I can see visit with him for a few minutes.* When the door is closed, however, it means "He's busy. Don't even ask if you can come in."

Suppose the front desk calls my assistant to say that someone has dropped by, asking to see me. My assistant looks at my appointment book and sees no such meeting on the schedule. My door is closed, which means I'm not to be interrupted. What does my assistant do?

We never lie; that's not permissible. She doesn't say, "I'm sorry, he's not here." My assistant goes out front, meets the individual, and says, "He is here, but he's in an appointment."

Someone may ask, "But you're in your office, alone. How is that an appointment?" If I'm studying, I'm meeting with the Lord and getting into the Word. If I'm engaged with something else that requires my undivided attention, I have an appointment with the clock. *Appointment* means "an agreement to meet at a certain place and time." When I have my door closed, I assure you I've agreed to meet either the Lord or some pressing challenge that I'm trying to solve. I'm not going to drop the Lord or the pressing challenge just to meet with someone who shows up unexpectedly for who knows what reason.

Sometimes the person shows up with a genuine emergency. I say "genuine" because a lot of leaders use the term to describe something other than a real emergency; apparently they use a different dictionary than I do. Don't let someone else define your emergencies for you. When somebody has the same thing going on for two years, it's not an emergency.

My assistant, who has been with me for more than two decades, knows what a real emergency is. She comes back to her desk and may tell me, "I think you might want to deal with this issue; it seems important." She'll tell me the nature of the issue, and at that point I may choose to leave what I'm doing to address the unexpected situation or to continue whatever I had been doing.

More times than not, it's just something minor that would pull me away from my priority, my main task. You can't allow these kinds of interruptions. If you let it be known that nearly anyone can come in to see you whenever they drop by, you can bet your priority times won't remain a priority for long. The drop-ins will become your priority instead of whatever you had set as the priority.

Nobody can make these decisions for you. All of this may sound elementary, but I can pretty much guarantee that someone reading these words right now is struggling in these areas.

6. First thing in the morning, check to see if you have received any
critical emails overnight that need your immediate attention.

Respond only to the critical emails, no others. You're starting your day, you're moving, and you must deal exclusively with your priorities.

7. Turn off your email, forward your phone, and start to work on your
top priorities listed from the night before.

Let's talk about death by email. Email is the most abused form of management time in the workplace today. That's certainly true in my life. There's no easier way to waste time than to get lost trying to respond to emails. I would count myself blessed if one hundred of the emails I responded to last year could be categorized as critical.

That little email *ding* has interrupted more valuable work than any other factor in the office. It not only interrupts, it distracts. We finally had to lay the hammer down on staff members responding to those incessant little *dings* during our meetings. We have a lot going on in our staff meetings. We're talking about some major point, then *ding*!

Last time I checked, my staff works for me. If I instruct them to do something and they don't want to do it, all I need to do is find somebody else who will accept my authority and leadership. If you have trouble with that, it's all right. I'm all right with you having trouble with it. But in fact, my staff answers to me.

If I say, "Turn off that phone in this meeting," they can't call a board member to get a different opinion. So many workplaces suffer from death by email. Turn off your email *ding* indicator when you need to get work done!

Also, forward your calls. Just set your phone so you can say, "Forward to my assistant" when working on top priorities. Because of the addictive nature of our hearts toward our phones, if you're sitting there trying to get important work done, your phone will get you off track quicker than anything else.

Above all, never work on lesser tasks when priorities remain on your to-do list. Tackle your priorities first. Finish the more important things before moving to other tasks. Ask yourself, "Am I using the best time of my day for my main priorities?"

If every day you get at least one of your priority items done, you've not had a bad day. It's better to leave at the end of the day saying, "I accomplished something," rather than, "What a frustrating day!"

Understand that some of your days will get interrupted. When that happens, remind yourself that you have other days coming up when you can get those tasks knocked out. That's not bad at all. Remember, it's your schedule, so act like it. Look for every opportunity to take charge of your schedule and protect the priorities that you set, the ones that you believe need to get done first.

8. When you finish your top priorities, reward yourself.

My reward isn't a second cup of coffee (though if it's yours, that's fine); it's calling my mentees. Maybe I've had quite the morning. It's been tough, but I've accomplished a lot. I might call one of my mentees and say to him, "Round up the other two slugs. Come on down to my office and I'll take you over to Starbucks."

Before my mentees arrive, I sit out in the sun for a minute to catch my breath. Once they show up, I know they're going to pick at me. It's going to be light-hearted and it's going to pull me back to the good equilibrium that I need to engage the rest of my day. They encourage me. They may think I'm trying to answer their questions, but really, they're encouraging me, especially if they buy my coffee (and I don't believe they ever have).

Here's another thing I do. When I finish a major project—let's say it's 11:30 a.m. and I started on it at maybe 5 or 7—I always take a little break. I never jump immediately into something else. I may take a break by telling myself, "I think I'll catch my breath here." I may go for a short walk. Whatever looks like a reward to me that day, I do.

9. Take the next fifteen to twenty minutes to respond to emails.

After you've accomplished a priority task, take a short amount of time to turn on your email and see what's come in. Most won't require an immediate reply, but others may. Discipline yourself to keep this review time short—don't get caught in an email black hole.

10. Turn off your emails again and start working, if possible, on your second-tier priorities.

If you've already finished your top priority items, you can start moving on down the line. Don't skip around or flit back and forth between action items. Try to finish whatever you start.

11. Make lunch appointments.

Manley Beasley taught me, "Don't waste your mealtimes." If a man says to me, "I need to see you this week," I may reply, "Where do you work? Can we meet halfway, or maybe you can come here? Let's grab some lunch." I know I'm going to eat; that's pretty much a given. I do a lot of meetings over breakfast and lunch, and sometimes when it's couples, we meet over dinner.

12. Fill your afternoon with block times for appointments and meetings.

Use your afternoon to return phone calls, do more email correspondence, have scheduled meetings with individuals in your office, or lead regular meetings. Do everyday tasks and activities in designated blocks of time so they don't interfere with your priority tasks.

Time Management Is a Team Sport

Did you know that good time management is a team sport? Your team includes you and those working with you, or whoever God has brought into your life to help you accomplish the work He has given you. Your staff can give you more time by better managing time with you.

I often say, "Hey, we need to meet and go through our schedules, to make sure we're all on the same page." Not long ago I said to a top colleague, "Can we meet now?" but his schedule was tied up serving some important clients. We waited to tackle the issue, because I couldn't handle it without him. Later, we made a schedule, went over it, and he laid out everything. We walked through it and he helped me to manage my time better.

Use your staff to help you with time management. At times a colleague may say to me, "I really need to meet with you. A couple of things came up and they're both pretty important. You'll want to know about them."

I might reply, "Can you drive me to the airport?" That's about a forty-five-minute drive for us. We'll chat in the car, and if we don't finish, I'll say, "Call me on your way home while I'm waiting for the plane, and we'll finish up then."

Let's Not Crucify Each Other's Time

Since time management is a team sport, it means that those of us on the team can crucify each other's time. I know *crucify* is a serious word, but so is the value of the team's time. Let me list four ways we often do that.

1. Coming Unprepared to Staff Meetings

Coming to a staff meeting ill prepared can mean extra phone calls, time-consuming efforts to get clarity, or a blizzard of emails that could have been avoided. Make sure your staff members come to meetings ready to discuss whatever you've prioritized as the key issue. If not, everyone shows up talking about trivial things, until you finally say, "By the way, here's the big issue I want to discuss." No. Start with your biggie. Get the top priority out of the way; deal with the hard things first.

2. Failing to Schedule Appointments

I may say to my assistant, "This lady says she needs to run this issue by me. Let's go ahead and schedule Tuesday afternoon. Tell her I can see her at 1:45, and that I have about a thirty-minute window."

At the end of our half-hour meeting, my assistant knocks on the door, opens it, and very kindly says, "I'm sorry, but your next appointment's here." If you don't do something similar, that half hour turns into two hours—"So, how have you been doing, Johnny? How are those grand-kids of yours? And how 'bout them Falcons?" While I love such conversa-tion, everyone who comes in to see me knows that they're on the clock. A half hour means a half hour.

"I can't believe you do that," someone says. But listen, the last time I checked, I have only one life. I believe people are dying and going to hell; that's one of my burdens. I don't have a lot of time to waste.

3. Sending Poorly Articulated Messages

Poorly articulated phone messages can crucify your time. Try to be very clear on what you need from someone. Poorly written emails can cause similar problems. May I offer you three brief but clearly defined rules of engagement?

First, if you and your team are engaging one another through email, demand that everyone clearly gives *details* and *appropriate times*. Second, make sure your staff knows when you're not available so that they know to protect that time. Third, communicate with great clarity so nothing is left open to question. If you fail here, a second (longer) conversation will almost always ensue.

4. Lacking Respect for Your Time

When someone calls the office and says, "May I speak with Johnny?" my assistant may say, "I'm sorry, he's in a meeting." About 99.99 percent of the time, that's all she needs to say. No one goes any further. The person understands I'm unavailable.

But then she may say, "He's got a break at noon and afterwards has scheduled a lunch. He may be able to call you before that lunch. He's already told me that he's returning calls this afternoon at about 1:30. What would be a good time to call you? We just need to make a time appointment."

I'm not being a stickler. I don't mean that I never move outside this framework. I'm not legalistic about it. I just have some clear guidelines that I believe help me to accomplish a lot.

Simple Ways to Lose Control of Your Schedule

It's all too easy for most leaders to be reactive and so lose control of their schedules. Let me list five of the worst schedule-wreckers.

1. Respond to every email or text, regardless of priority.

This is a great way to be reactive and lose control of your schedule. It's human nature that we assume we must respond immediately to whatever calls for our attention. Sometimes we do this because it makes us feel special. We somehow feel unimportant if we are not always at the center of everyone else's problem-solving.

Let me warn you: This is the single most counter-productive thing you can do. It'll always keep you on the downside of accomplishing the major tasks you need to get done. Before too long, you'll find yourself saying, "I feel like I never catch up." Does that sound even a little familiar to you? Just a little uncomfortable?

I've heard it said, "Be mindful that when you die, most likely there will be something in your inbox." I like my desk to look neat at the end of the day, even though I never really get completely caught up. I just pace myself. If I have to leave some things undone, I'll try to work them out later in the context of my priorities. I always ask myself, "Where do these things fit in among everything else I need to get done?"

2. Work on several tasks at the same time.

When you try doing several things at once, you're basically saying that none of your tasks have priority over any others.

3. Jump from task to task all day long, failing to finish any.

Don't start a lot of fires without actually cooking something.

4. Start, quit, and restart several tasks each day.

How many times today did you start and restart various tasks?

5. Respond to every request the moment you receive it.

Refuse to cave in to the tyranny of the urgent.

Six Benefits of Effective Time Management

Better time management returns control of your life to you. It allows you to achieve the most important things you feel called to do. It gives you an increased sense of calm and, in short, helps you to become a much better leader. In my own life as a leader, better time management also delivers six benefits that continue to greatly improve my life.

1. Increased Margin

It's harder to keep margin at certain times than at others, but with that margin in place, I know I'm going to accomplish more than I would otherwise. I know that every day cannot be typical. That's just a fact. No one can plan with certainty—as in, "Here's the way my day is going to go." Surprises happen. Emergencies blow in.

You can be in the middle of a productive day and suddenly hear that a family member or close friend has died unexpectedly. You probably didn't account for "brokenness" or "tears" on your schedule. How many times do we plan for life to go a certain way, but it goes in the opposite direction? It's amazing how one event can turn your day inside out, disrupt your week, your month, your life. That's why you can't cookie cut every day to look just like every other day.

You need enough margin in your schedule to address emergencies. Every day, you need to leave a little time for chaos, to deal with what I call The Reality Factor. Times will come when you say, "This day didn't make sense," or "This week was a total loss." If during one of those weeks I'm dealing with someone who knows nothing about the situation, I usually say to them, "This is not normal, okay? This is not typical."

If one day God allows me to do more publishing, I want to do a video series or two in which I can give men and women some good, solid leadership training. In order to do that, of course, I'll need some margin in my life.

2. More Time for Family

By taking on too much for several years, I violated time with my family. Often, they just got the leftovers. One night, my wife took me to the theater. I didn't think she could see me in the dark, and I fell asleep. I foolishly thought I could fake it. I was just so tired. Today, every Friday night I date my wife, with few exceptions. I don't know of anyone in my life, apart from Jesus, who deserves my best more than my wife does. If you really want more time with your family, then get serious about improving your time management.

3. More Time for Personal Pursuits

I like to speed walk and to exercise. I used to run more than I do now. I once studied the history of the marathon, because one of our missionaries wrote me from the Greek town where it all started. History tells us that in 490 BC a Greek soldier ran twenty-six miles, nonstop, to announce a Greek victory over the Persians (sadly, the man collapsed and died after delivering his news; I guess he had no margin). That's how marathons got started. I don't have any battle results that I need to announce, so I don't run all that fast a pace. If you ever happen to see me actually *running* twenty-six miles, you know that somebody is either chasing me with a gun or hunting me down with a bow and arrow. But I do like to speed walk and exercise.

4. Less Stress

Would you like to have less stress? I would. My doctor told me he'd like me to have less stress, too, because apparently the stress is causing deterioration in my main arteries. Eventually it will affect my heart. I'd like to avoid that, if possible. Time management can be a lifesaver.

5. Improved Mood

You're happier, more content. Who wouldn't want that? By the way, do you think people can't read your curt demeanor when they know you're in a hurry? The men and women in our lives are all supposed to be important to us. We also have many important things to do, some critical tasks to finish. If we don't get a handle on our schedules, how can we treat all of these important people and tasks as important? Better time management puts us and everyone around us in a better mood.

6. More Energy and Fun

A friend watched how weary I grew over the last few years, especially over a certain period. "I just called somebody," he told me. "You know what I told him? We were talking about you and I said, 'The old Johnny is back.'"

Because I'm paying attention to time management, I'm no longer pushing through, straining to get to the end of each day. I'm able to listen more intently, slow down, I have more energy and am told I'm a lot more fun to be around. I tell you, it's awesome!

After I preached a few sermons following that difficult time, most of the emails I received had words to the effect of "our old pastor's back!" While it encouraged me to hear the news, I admit that it pained me for them to have to say such a thing. What a shame. But it was absolutely true!

You're Not Indispensable

Please, learn to manage your time more effectively as a leader. Get control of your schedule. Know how you're spending your hours, days, and weeks, and then make whatever changes may be required to get a life outside of your time in the leader's chair.

I'm sorry to break this to you, but you're really not more indispensable to your organization than Moses was to Israel. Moses, the uber-leader, had allowed his schedule to spin out of control after the nation's exodus from Egypt. He felt captive to the constant demands of leadership and he lost his joy. He carried on, dutiful as ever, but when his father-in-law Jethro saw how Moses exhausted himself by failing to manage his time well, he said to him, "The thing that you do is not good. Both you and these people who are with you will surely wear yourselves out. For this thing is too much for you; you are not able to perform it by yourself" (Exodus 18:17-18). Jethro then gave Moses some excellent advice about delegation and controlling his schedule, Moses took it, and the whole nation could finally breathe a big sigh of relief. Scripture doesn't tell us, but I'll bet Moses smiled a lot more from that day forward!

Wouldn't you like to smile more? You can. When you get control of your schedule, you put joy back into your life as you accomplish more. Don't wait another day!

6

Delegates Well

Your value as a leader depends not only on what you can do but even more on what you can get done through others.

Thank God for the principle and process of delegation! If you want to continue to lead well, you need to draw around yourself a staff of able individuals, assigning to them appropriate tasks.

Do you know where many leaders get stuck? They say, "If you want it done right, you need to do it yourself." But if you take that approach, you can't possibly do what you need to accomplish. Effective leaders have no real choice but to empower and develop other leaders. Learn to delegate to others the tasks appropriate to their level of ability, while you continue to do what only you can do.

Empowering the Entrusted

As leaders, we can't afford to try growing our organizations through our own talents alone. We do that through the talents of others. I don't know of anything that helps build an organization more than establishing good relationships with those you lead.

If you get to really know your people, they will bankrupt heaven and earth to serve you wherever you most need them. When you make it a point to be relational, men and women will stand in line waiting to partner with you. After you've been there awhile, your phone will ring constantly with people asking, "How can I help you?" Let them help you. If you don't let them, after a while, they'll quit calling.

Always think about how to build relationships with others, working to find out how you can best serve together. Ask God why He brought these specific people into your organization for such a time as this.

When your transactions with others become more important than your own ability to accomplish tasks, you make your team broader and stronger. While your own ability may allow you to continue to prop up your organization, it's the accomplishments of others that will propel your organization to new heights.

Utilize the Strengths of Your People

I had one employee who used to be a successful coach. The man had unbelievable passion. When he spoke to you, he often got so dramatic that you'd think you were in a huddle wearing a helmet. He got fired up and passionate about whatever he was doing.

I put him in charge of organizing a big event and right before it took place he told me, "Here's what I want you to make a big deal over. Here's where we need to celebrate our people. Here's where we need to challenge our people."

I smiled and said to him, "I like what you're asking me to do, but I disagree with you on one point."

"What's that?" he asked.

"*I* don't need to be the one doing this," I answered. "*You* need to do it. You're at the top of your game, son."

Do you think hearing something like that causes a person to lift his chin? I told him, "When you were telling me how to do this, I thought, *I want the people to hear it the way* you *say it, not the way I regurgitate what you say*." Empowering him to do the job lifted him up and made him feel better about what God had called him to do. It encouraged him to believe that he worked for someone who believed he could do it.

Too often we magnify people's weaknesses instead of harnessing their strengths. Let's tell them instead, "Here's your strength—do that."

Another time we developed a special presentation for maybe a dozen guests, featuring some important officials from our county. We put together an attractive program. It would have been so easy for me to go in there and be in charge—but no, one of my key leaders had spearheaded the charge. Why wouldn't I give him the responsibility to lead? We also had a young man in his early twenties who was helping with our design work. I said to both of them, "Why don't you guys lead it?" So, rather than me getting up at the end of the meeting to thank our guests and salute everyone for a job well done, I just sat there. I didn't have one little thing to do with the morning. They did it all behind the scenes, and they got acknowledged for their work publicly.

If you want to build a winning team, then treat your people like winners and give them multiple opportunities to shine. When you cross the goal line, make sure you're not always the one carrying the ball. Give your leaders lots of opportunities to score.

Winners always want to be significant players. They want to move from success to significance. Great leaders don't try to put in what was left out, but to draw out what was put in. You have some great people, so draw out what's already there. They have it to give, if only you will learn how to draw it out of them.

What to Look For

You can't delegate important tasks or initiatives to just anyone. What should you look for in those who have the potential to lead? Let me suggest several characteristics.

1. Vision-Driven

Is the person you're considering vision-driven or status quo? When I interview someone for a position, I take care that I don't tell him the wonderful story of our organization and then say, "How'd you like to be a part of it?" What is he going to say, *no*? That's not how we handle it.

Instead, I go into the interview assuming that the person already knows a little about us. I ask, "What value do you think you can bring to us? What is your personal vision for this or that division?" I want the person to tell me what he's bringing to the table. I want to hear her speak into what we're already doing. Then I ask, "What is your philosophy of getting employees more committed? How does that relate to you spending time with them or investing in them? How do you plan to go about working relationships within the company?" Be careful in the interview process! Don't merely tell the candidate what you have to offer. See if she or he has a vision for what you're doing, and especially if they have any good ideas about how to expand that vision.

2. Energetic

Is the person energetic? I like to be around people who have energy for what they do. I like to hire people with the will to create positive change. We need some real energy for whatever we want to accomplish!

3. Proven Character

I'm big on tapping character. I tend to select people based more on their character and commitment and less on their giftedness. Don't put people in positions where their character can't sustain them. And don't put somebody you just met in a place of major responsibility.

Proverbs 14:29 says, "He who is impulsive exalts folly." I've learned that the hard way. At first you may think, *This person would be great for this spot.* But a deficit in character can cause disaster. Be careful about delegating an important task to someone you don't know well. Take time to get to know them! I want to empower the entrusted, but first I must know who I can trust.

4. Teachable

Many folks just aren't teachable. Some think they already know it all, while others feel they know enough to get by. I want people who can grow. I like delegating responsibility to people who can grow with me and who want to do so. I ask myself, "Can this person walk into the future with me? Can this person grow with me?" I've learned that you can outgrow people who serve with you (and that some people working with you can outgrow you).

Have you heard of "leading from the middle of the pack"? Someone may say, "I believe I have greater vision than my leader does." You normally lose people like that. They start thinking, *Should I really stay in a place that holds me back?* If you continue to grow yourself and keep moving up, however, they can continue to grow too. Lifters and winners add great value to your team. Give them places where they can grow.

I once had a leader who required more of his staff than probably anyone else in our organization. One day, he told his people, "I want you to read this new book on leadership over the next two weeks. Then we'll discuss it as a group."

I know that sometimes his staff thought, *Man, where does he think I'm going to get all this time?* It was his way of trying to grow his team, to keep them sharp. They grumbled at times; don't most of us tend to be a little lazy? But when all was said and done, they thanked God for him, for they had become what they were because he had raised the bar.

Most People Are Underchallenged

A woman once said to me, "I've been in church for twenty years. I'd never attempted to win anybody to Christ. Why is it that now, at this point in my life since we came under this ministry, I've led both my mother and my brother-in-law to the Lord?" I'll tell you why: She had been underchallenged her whole life. No one had ever asked her to evangelize anyone.

As leaders, it's our responsibility to lovingly challenge our people. Most of us do not expect enough from them. Do you want to lead more effectively? Then determine now to stretch your people by frequently laying out some appropriate challenges.

Over the years I've tried to think of many ways to challenge staff, employees, volunteers, and members of my congregation. I want to give them ownership because I know human beings do not pay for what they don't own. In the church world, many times a pastor will build a big, new facility…and be gone within a year. Oh, he had been *so* excited and worked *so* hard to get the thing built! But he ended up leaving because he encountered huge challenges about debt servicing or some other contentious issue related to the new building.

At Woodstock, we had hundreds of people involved in the building process, probably 300 on the building committee alone. We took everybody from our preschool and said, "Tell us how you want your part of the building designed." What right does a committee of five have to design a part of the building where none of them work? We did the same thing with students, senior adults, and many others. It worked extremely well.

When I'm on a seminary campus and students start feeling at liberty to ask difficult questions, it's not unusual for a young man to ask, "Do you think it's wrong to want to do a great work for God?" No, I don't. Nehemiah literally said with his own lips, "I am doing a great work [for God], so that I cannot come down" (Nehemiah 6:3). I want to do a great work for God!

You may rightfully ask, "Why do you believe most people are under-challenged?" Lack of vision, for one thing. I get a fire in my belly over something I believe God wants us to do. While I don't intend to talk about it continually, I just do. Without a vision, leaders can't challenge anyone, and therefore don't know how to fully incorporate the resources at their disposal. Never forget that people are the greatest resource you have.

A second reason why our people are under-challenged is far worse than lack of vision. A high degree of self-centeredness exists among leaders, even Christian leaders. We get so entangled with our own egos and power that we have a hard time seeing the value in others, or we fear to empower them because we worry that they may steal some of our glory.

How, though, can I believe that God will give me an organization that matches my vision if I don't lead by example? We need more modeling of what our people should be. Our followers see the envisioned future better when we emulate it than through our exhortation of it. Every leader needs to do more show than tell. Whatever is important to you becomes important to them. If your vision and mission are important to you, then how are your people seeing you work for both?

Take your staff, employees, and others on this journey with you. When you spend years equipping, training, and pouring into them, pleading with them to join you in the mission—and they get it—eventually they will start coming to you. They will even ask *you* to join *them*. That's the ultimate success!

I urge you, don't do anything alone. Always think *others*. Continually challenge your staff because that's when you'll get to plan your greatest celebrations.

Focus on People, Not Numbers

One of my pastor friends came to see me one day and said, "I really believe that when I get to about 1,000 in attendance, I won't be dealing with all the junk I have now." And I thought, *I'm way beyond that and I still have lots of junk.* Does it surprise you to learn that my friend is no longer at that church?

When you set your mind on a number instead of people, you're in trouble. As Jesus is my witness, I've never thought, *Oh God, give me a big church.* Numbers do not drive me.

A leading medical doctor in our area once called me. "I'd like to have lunch with you and ask you some questions about your church," he said. When we met, he asked, "What do you tell people who want to know how your church got so large?"

"I preach the Word and love our people and encourage and mobilize them to be faithful to the Great Commission," I said. "And we've just grown. God blessed. As a result, here's where we are today."

He started implementing the same basic approach and God began to bless him. When he gave excellent care to one person, that individual would tell a neighbor, "Boy, I just loved the bedside manners of Dr. Smith." Before he knew it, he had another patient. And today he has a group of probably forty doctors who work for him. "But that was never my goal," he insists. "Never, *ever* was that my goal. I just wanted to take care of the patients God sent to me."

I believe that if you focus on the people you have, develop them, and genuinely and purely desire to empower them, they become the entrusted. And you can delegate important tasks to those you trust.

Know When and When Not to Delegate

There's a difference between taking charge and allowing others to be in charge. Wise leaders delegate when they can, but they also know when they can't. Learn how to spot the reliable people in your organization and then empower them to do key jobs.

We all know that you can ask some people to do a job and then you can forget it; it's as good as done. Others, however, you need to check up on, even for the same job.

So, who do you empower the most? You delegate to the person who, when asked to do a job, not only does it but does it well. That's how you grow as a leader. It's just good delegation to allow competent people to take charge of specific situations.

The same thing is true when you bring people on staff to serve you. Turn them loose! Allow your people to be the experts you hired them to be.

And know this: When you turn them loose and they do a good job, they'll get lots of recognition. Those who used to give you all the credit will now say, "That was a smart move to bring on so-and-so. I've never seen someone do as much in that position as she has!"

Insecure leaders who hear observers praising others don't smile; they have a stroke. Insecure leaders can't give praise because they need all of it. You must be secure to brag on other people, and all good leaders are secure.

Empowerment's Key Attitudes

What are the key attitudes you must have if you're going to lead and develop other leaders in your organization? This is simple stuff, but potent.

1. Believe in your people.

You cannot lead anyone you don't believe in. When a leader says to me, "Please pray for me. I hope God will open another door for me because I am leading the sorriest people," I feel obligated to point out that the problem might not be the people, but the leader. That individual won't lead anyone anywhere with such a rotten attitude. You must believe in your people.

If you had seen me when I was nineteen years old, you would have seen a worn cue stick in my left hand, a cigarette between my fingers, a bottle of beer in my right hand, and God's name in vain on my lips. I was a hoodlum. But Jesus looked at me and said, "He'll make a great pastor. I could save that man, fill him with the Holy Ghost."

Jesus believed in Peter. Jesus saw in Peter what no one else had ever seen. He saw Peter for what he could be. Peter's *now* did not alter Jesus' view of Peter's *then*.

Later, Jesus bid Peter to walk on water. When the apostle panicked and started to sink, Jesus rescued him from drowning and the two of them climbed into the boat. Do you think Jesus knew what would happen? Surely He did. And yet, He bid Peter come anyway. Peter may have sunk, he may have screamed and cried for deliverance, but thank God for a man who's willing to get out of the boat and go!

Do you realize that God will call you to some faith adventures on the water? That's part of God using you to lead. That will also help your prayer life as a leader. The posture of your prayer will have a lot to do with the desperation of your heart. God will bid you to do some "impossible" things to show you that you can't do it without Him.

2. Correct your people when they go off course.

Jesus also corrected Peter. All of us need correction, including you and me and your young leaders. Jesus took Peter aside and rebuked him when the brash apostle suggested Jesus didn't really have to go to the cross (Matthew 16:22). Simon was trying to declare, "You don't need to die," when that was the very purpose for which Jesus came. And so, Jesus replied to Simon, "Get behind me, Satan. You are an offense to Me, for you are not mindful of the things of God" (verse 17). What a strong rebuke! And yet, God chooses to use men like that. God will use a man who sometimes isn't even mindful of the things of God.

Do you believe that when God called you, He knew you were going to mess up? I love a saying I heard recently: "When God put a calling on your life, He already factored in your stupidity." Aren't you glad?

Does the Lord know in advance our coming gaffes? Or do you think Jesus says, "Good Lord, I missed it again. If only I had known Johnny was going to do *that*, I never would have called him in the first place"? It consoles my soul to know that whatever I'm struggling with, Jesus knew about it long before He called me. That's why Jesus did not say to Peter, "Had I known you were going to try to convince me not to go to the cross, I'd never have called you in the first place." Instead, He said, "Peter, I want you to be part of building my kingdom—but you need to get your mind on the things of God."

3. Turn your hindsight into foresight.

I've been out there long enough to be able to confidently say, "What God did in this person's life, He can do in somebody else's life." Encourage your people to learn from mistakes and turn them into springboards for success. I'm grateful I did a lot of stupid stuff in the past because I can laugh about it now and use it in my life to get better.

Focus 80 percent of your attention on what people do right and only 20 percent of your attention correcting what's wrong. Some people do a lot of things right. I want to make sure that I don't miss that.

The older you get, the more reflective you'll become. And the more reflective you get, the more forgiving you'll be. Senior adults tend to be more forgiving than almost anyone. Why? They've watched their children screw up. They've watched their grandchildren screw up. And they've had to forgive and work through some deep issues. A lot of times, it's easy for leaders to make harsh judgments because we don't have skin in the game.

We haven't established good relationships with our people and so we find it easy to take off the gloves and tear them to pieces.

4. Where there's no faith in the future, there's no power in the present.

I often get phone calls that sound something like this:

"Hey, Johnny, pray for me."

"Certainly. Any particular way I can pray?"

"I'm forty-nine years old and thinking I need to make a move. I want you to pray for me because I need to move *now*, or it's going to be too late."

"What do you mean, it's going to be too late?"

"Man, I'm forty-nine years old! I mean, who wants anybody in their fifties?"

If you view yourself in that way, you'll portray that poor image to anyone considering you. If you feel that way, it'll be hard for anybody to get pumped about you.

If God allows me, in these latter days I want to write about how to remain valuable for the kingdom. Proverbs 19:20 says, "Listen to counsel and receive instruction, that you may be wise in your latter days." I feel I have as much to offer to the kingdom of God today as I ever have. Without faith in the future, however, neither I nor you nor your people will have any power in the present.

5. Allow people to play to their strengths.

Too often we want our people to play to our strengths. We want them to play a role that is not conducive for them. That won't work. Don't expect everyone to be like you. But when you put a person in their sweet spot, man, what joy they have in serving!

If you were to ask me what one thing I did poorly in my early days of leadership, I'd say, "I saw in most of those who I wanted to serve alongside me what I thought I saw in myself." That's not the best approach. Leaders need people different from themselves, who have strengths in areas where they're weak. Acknowledge your weaknesses and build a strong, diverse team around you. And remember that support cannot be taken, only given.

Empowerment's Key Actions

What key actions can leaders take if they want to develop others to whom they can delegate important tasks and initiatives? How can they empower the entrusted?

1. Listen to others.

Listen to your staff, listen to your leaders, listen to your employees, listen to your customers. Hear what they dream about. This will help you to know how you can empower them to fulfill those dreams.

2. Don't assume you're irreplaceable.

This statement means more to me with every passing day. Don't try to be irreplaceable. If you can't be replaced, then you can't be promoted. So, delegate to others. Everybody is replaceable. *Everybody*.

3. Lead by example.

Demonstrate what you expect from others. If you spend a lot of time with certain people, let them be influenced more by what they see in your life than by what they hear from your mouth.

4. Eliminate confusion by providing a clear vision.

Winston Churchill once wrote in a memorandum, "It is essential that you should beforehand give the decisions which allow your lieutenants to act effectively."[23] As a leader, you know where you're headed and why, so communicate this information to others. In so doing, you will allow them to focus on the right direction and help you in the process.

5. Don't demand loyalty; earn it.

I really struggle when someone who works for me says, "Tell these people that they need to follow me and listen to me. Tell them that when I speak, I'm speaking as you." This gets it all wrong. You don't demand loyalty, you earn it. The surest way not to get your rights is to demand them. Loyalty is a two-way street: You can't have it if you don't give it. When you're loyal to your people, they will be loyal to you.

The Don'ts of Empowerment

If you really want to empower your people so that you can effectively delegate to them, watch out for several common pitfalls.

1. Don't assume too much power and control.

When you take too much control, you'll discourage those who work for you. They will sense that you don't trust them, or you will come across as a control freak.

2. Don't operate on the basis of my way or the highway.

If someone asks, "How can I pray for you?" tell them to pray that God will give you wisdom, as in James 3:17. Wise individuals can be easily entreated. A wise person is not hard to get along with. A wise leader never says, "It's my way or the highway." Strive to build unity instead.

3. Don't intervene when others can work it out for themselves.

Imagine that you see some conflict among your employees. You think, *That person's not behaving properly.* Should you intervene? Proverbs 26:17 would tell you, "He who passes by and meddles in a quarrel not his own is like one who takes a dog by the ears." Step in too soon and you are liable to get bit.

4. Don't withhold information.

Information is a means of empowerment. Keep your people abreast of what's going on. Tell them, "I want you to be fully aware of what I'm aware of."

5. Don't be indecisive.

I've made some wrong decisions, but by and large, I hardly ever get to a place where I can't make a decision. I like the axiom: "Be decisive. Right or wrong, make a decision. The road of life is paved with flat squirrels who couldn't make a decision."

6. Don't be afraid of mistakes.

Life is full of mistakes, so accept that mistakes will happen. You'll make some mistakes, just like your people. Own them. Provide a good example for those watching.

7. Don't expect everyone to produce at the same level.

Your people will have differing work ethics. Everyone will not function in the same way. Be careful! Remember the parable of the talents (Matthew 25:14-30). Managers live in a micro world while leaders live in a macro world. See the bigger picture.

The Do's of Empowerment

There are also many positive steps you can take to empower your people.

1. See your team members as allies, not enemies.

Sometimes we grow suspicious of teammates, with very little reason. Sometimes we have reason to be concerned, but we should never assume the worst.

2. Encourage others to step forward and assume leadership roles.

Why are you doing what you're doing? Are these the right tasks for you to take on? Could someone else do them? Should someone else be doing them?

You may say, "I don't have anyone to help me." Have you ever tried asking? In the early days, people would come to me and say, "Pastor, we need some volunteers. Please announce it this Sunday."

You don't enlist good people from announcements. You enlist good people through lunch appointments, where you sit across the table and tell them what you have observed in their life and how they could come alongside and help you. Let them know how important the task is, and then solicit their support. More times than not, you will build a great team.

3. Operate from the philosophy that everyone will prosper or no one will.

We're in this together!

4. Do whatever benefits the whole team.

See number 3. Also, remember that if you're standing alone at the end of a successful project or outreach, you haven't really been successful.

5. Encourage cooperation.

Iron sharpens iron (Proverbs 27:17). Friction can be a good thing when it means everyone is bringing their contribution to the table.

6. Learn to let go.

Give ownership. Don't hold everything so tightly.

7. Learn the hot buttons for each of your team members.

How can you get this critical information if you don't strive to get to know your people? But once you know it, you've got to use it responsibly.

8. Push decision making to the lowest level feasible.

You can give more to some people than to others; know who they are. Some things, only you can do. You must be able to decipher what you cannot task others to do. Some calls, only you can make.

9. Know when to back off.

Give people space. Don't overwhelm them. Give them time to prove themselves.

10. Give credit where credit is due.

Never praise yourself but always be quick to praise others. Acknowledge the accomplishments of others but don't give praise where it's not deserved unless you want to affirm mediocrity and noncommitment. Appreciation throws gas on an already burning fire, but it doesn't do much for a flickering flame about to fizzle.

Delegation = A Voice

I don't use an authoritarian approach in my leadership because I believe it overlooks two essential elements, the first one basic to human nature and the second one necessary for leading people.

People want a voice in the direction of their job and their calling. I want to hear from my people. I don't want merely to announce to them, with no input, "Here's what we're going to do." As the leader, I recognize that I don't need to make all the important decisions, nor do I need to accomplish every important task. One great way to give voice to my people is to delegate certain responsibilities to them.

How can you help yourself or your people if you raise up leaders but prevent them from leading? The purpose of selecting and training leaders is to turn them loose to lead, entrusting them with the deposit of wisdom and responsibility you've invested in them. This means taking your hands off the wheel that turns every gear in your organization, giving others time in the driver's seat. Although it may go against your controlling tendencies, you're in for the ride of your life when you sit back and watch what God can do through others.

7

Executes Well

Nobody becomes known for what they said they wanted to be. People and organizations go down in history not because of their fabulous mission statements, but because of what they accomplish.

Whatever your vision is, it must become your mission, something that you begin to work toward. And to fulfill your mission, you must create strategies, set goals, develop plans, and identify steps to get to wherever you want to be. In other words, the best vision, mission, strategies, goals, plans, and steps will get you exactly nowhere unless you intentionally execute whatever you've thought through and put down on paper.

Overview of a Successful Journey

In this chapter I'll frequently employ terms such as "vision," "mission," "strategy," "goals," "plans," and "steps." Let's begin with a quick summary of how I use these terms and how the activities they describe work together to help you lead your people to the enticing destination you all long to reach. Notice that these terms move from a macro level to a micro level.

1. Vision

This is where everything starts. Vision provides a compelling picture of where you want you and your people to go. A vision doesn't normally change much over time, if at all. It equips you to work with the end in mind, to live with the end in view. Your vision may not reflect conventional wisdom, but it embodies what you believe the Lord has in mind for you, your people, and your organization.

2. Mission

The vision that you set as the leader requires a commitment to act. That commitment to act is your mission. One can have a vision and do nothing about it. No one ever does anything with a vision until that vision becomes the mission.

Do you remember back when everybody scurried around writing their mission statements? Many of those mission statements were very pretty. The trouble is, you can write all you want to, but until you do something, it won't make any difference.

3. Strategy

Your strategy is a global plan of action designed to help you achieve your overall aim. While your vision tends to remain the same over time, the strategy you employ to help get you there may change quite a bit. A bad economy, shifting demographics, cultural trends, and the like may all prompt you to adjust your strategies.

4. Goals

Goals are specific, measurable targets to shoot for in line with your vision and following the strategy you are employing. Unless you put in place (and carefully follow!) a goals program that includes measurable outcomes, your vision will drift.

5. Plans

Plans are detailed blueprints or stratagems that lay out how to meet each of your goals. They identify specific activities along with the people assigned to carry them out.

6. Steps

Your steps identify the order in which you intend to execute your plans. Step One occurs before Step Two, Step Two before Step Three, and so on. If you try to accomplish Step Three before you finish Step Two, you probably will waste a lot of time and effort and may put your goals in jeopardy.

It's Godly to Plan for the Future

There's nothing unspiritual about being serious enough to plan for your future.

Jesus said that no man builds a tower if he doesn't first sit down and plan what it will cost him. Otherwise, if he can't finish the project, observers will ridicule him for his lack of foresight. Jesus also said that no one goes to war without considering the strengths and weaknesses of his opponent and of his own forces. Otherwise, if he doesn't carefully count the cost of his battle plans, it might be the last time he ever goes to war (Luke 14:28-32). God expects us to plan wisely.

In this regard, I love a trio of verses from Proverbs 16, all of which include different terms that say essentially the same thing. Each verse throws a dart at the same board and hits the same bullseye:

- The preparations of the heart belong to man, but the answer of the tongue is from the LORD (16:1).

- A man's heart plans his way, but the LORD directs his steps (16:9).

- The lot is cast into the lap, but its every decision is from the LORD (16:33).

What do these verses tell us?

We are wise to make prayer-fueled plans but we're not God; we must leave room for divine intervention. None of us has perfect faith, not on this earth. So, we make plans, taking care to ask wise associates for their counsel (Proverbs 11:14; 15:22; 24:6), and then the Lord directs our steps. We don't skip making plans altogether; that's not wise (Proverbs 21:5). We do our research, we speak with advisors, we pray a lot, probably we fast, and then we start thinking through and writing down our plans. And we pray: "God, I really believe this is what You want me to do, but if I've taken a wrong turn somewhere, please step in and redirect my path."

It's not more "spiritual" to skip planning and go wherever the wind takes you, presuming that you'll wind up wherever God wanted you.

There is a story about a man who once said to the evangelist D.L. Moody, "I don't like your style of evangelism."

"Which do you use?" Moody asked.

"Well, I don't have one," the man replied.

"I like mine better," Moody declared.

Having a plan is better than having no plan. Some people may not like your plan, but they never seem to have a better one. So, go with yours.

At the judgment seat of Christ (2 Corinthians 5:10), I believe that Jesus will evaluate us based on what we did with whatever He gave us. And remember, He has declared that to whom much is given, much is required (Luke 12:48). I doubt anyone will stand before the Lord on that day and say, "Before You say anything, Jesus, if I had to do it all over again, I wouldn't have given You everything I gave." Who would say such a thing? Too many of us are far more likely to say, "I wish that I'd served You more, Jesus. Now that I see You face to face, I recognize how pitiful my service has been." Developing a strategy and making plans to accomplish your mission and reach your vision simply makes sense.

Shortly after I went to Woodstock, I learned that as many as 117,000 people lived within a five-mile radius of the church. I thought and prayed and then shared with our people a workable plan for knocking on each door in this swath of 45,000 houses, trying to give every one of those tens of thousands of people an encounter with the love of Christ. Such a big plan couldn't happen over a single weekend. We didn't ask folks to meet at the church one Saturday morning and then try to figure out what to do from there. Carrying out our God-sized mission took a great deal of preparation and planning. But if we were to obey Jesus' call to take the gospel to those within our "Jerusalem" (see Acts 1:8)—that is, our nearest circle of influence—how could we leave it to happenstance and just hope that neighborhood doors would automatically open?

Consider your own situation. Do you need to change how you operate? Have you let yourself become too dependent on letting things work themselves out, shooting in the dark, and hoping for success?

Plan for the future. Show your people what they must do.

What's Your Strategy?

You need a clear and specific approach to help you execute well, and that something is an overall strategy. Think of strategy as a global plan of action designed to help you achieve your major aims. It's a general plan for reaching your long-term goals in the middle of uncertain conditions.

I've always called strategy the "vehicle" to get us where we need to go. Sometimes the vehicle gets low on gas, sometimes it's just not the right model to get us to our desired destination. When we began our trip, maybe we needed a fuel-efficient economy car to get us across a desert. But once we made it through the heat, we see that the car that got us *here* can't get us over the mountain *there*. So, we switch vehicles. Once we reach the summit and glimpse in the distance the fabulous spot on the beach where we wanted to go originally, we recognize we need to change vehicles again. Our vision hasn't changed; our mission hasn't changed; but the strategies we use to get us *there* must change along the way.

Set Your Goals

A set of specific, measurable goals designed to achieve your mission is where the rubber meets the road. What goals do you have, calculated to get you to your desired destination as pictured by your vision? A leader must have a vision, but that vision must be reached through goals that work toward achieving the vision.

Effective goal setting focuses the leader's vision by spelling out what specific actions the organization will take to accomplish that vision. These goals will often take you out of your comfort zone. You probably also have some employees with very small vision, who have a hard time getting out of their comfort zones. They prefer a more predictable life.

Fulfillment of your vision is the primary benefit of goal setting. Goals simplify the decision-making process. Setting goals to achieve your mission helps you to avoid getting sidetracked with nonessentials.

Goal setting is not easy! It takes constant review and a willingness to change whenever appropriate. Remember, while goals change, vision doesn't. Strategy may change—the *how* in how are we going to get there? But the destination always remains the same. The leaders who rise above their peers do so not because of their vision, but because they successfully implement targeted goals. Without specific, measurable goals, your vision will remain wishful thinking.

Setting goals involves writing down what specifically it will take to accomplish the vision. What's the budget? Timeline? Staff required? Resources? What else? Write out your goals in detail, which helps to crystallize your thoughts and encourages you to make your ideas concrete.

State your goals positively. Goals need the motivational force of a positive mental image that allows you to picture yourself in the future, doing what you want to do or being what you want to become. Appropriate goals help you to think through the key question, *What would I like to do in my life?*

I write out every goal, as specifically as I can. These specifics force me to analyze the various resources I might need, including the required money, time, and personnel. When you write out your goals, sometimes you'll see that one goal conflicts with another. Writing down your goals forces you to establish your priorities. You must prioritize your values to determine which goal is most important.

I also have life goals that help me to stay on track in both my personal and professional lives. When I get an invitation to do this or that, sometimes my wife will say, "That's a wonderful opportunity, but it has nothing to do with what you say are the priorities of your life." To which I might reply under my breath, "I wish you hadn't looked. I wanted to do that." Specific goals produce persistence.

Make Your Plans

Break down your vision into smaller, more bite-sized plans so that you know precisely what you are to accomplish in each area every month. Suppose I lead a division of a service company that regularly attracts about sixty customers a month. I might say, "With all the neighborhoods around us, I think we could easily grow to one hundred customers every month." That's an increase of forty customers per month, achieved over twelve months.

I won't shoot for two hundred customers—that might not be realistic for us, and we might not have the staff to accommodate such growth— but I'll still believe God for an increase of forty. Our plans allow us to take specific actions designed to achieve that result, making sure that we measure our actual growth over the year.

After the first thirty days of implementing our specific plans, where am I in a month? It would be cool if we had four new customers, wouldn't it?

Identify Your Steps

The best of plans sometimes fail because they neglect to spell out three very important details:

- In what order do we tackle these detailed plans?

- Who is going to do what?

- By when should this be finished?

Consider the scenario above, with the service company. Let's say you developed three distinct plans to increase your customer base, from sixty to one hundred a month. One of those plans focuses on direct mail appeals, another on targeted Internet advertising, and the third on improved customer service leading to new referrals. They all sound great, right? But you're a small company with limited personnel and resources. You cannot possibly execute all three plans at the same time. If you tried, you would either execute all of them poorly or run out of time and money before any of them had a chance to work. So, what do you do?

First, you prioritize them: Maybe you decide to tackle the customer service initiative first, then direct mail, then Internet advertising. Bill and Felicia will head up the first and will have it up and running by September 15. If that goes well, Sue and Jerry will oversee the direct mail project, starting by October 30. And finally, Bill and Sue will tackle the Internet marketing piece, getting ready to roll it out by December 10. If something unexpected happens, or schedule conflicts arise, you regroup and set new targets.

The SMART Thing to Do

Make sure you have a way to measure your goals, because measurement makes a huge difference. I use a five-letter acrostic to help me in this area. I want to make S-M-A-R-T decisions.

1. Specific

For what specific things will you ask God? You may not reach those goals, but they can still be a source of encouragement. As you go into it and seek to do the will of God, your creativity improves. Target those specific goals.

Suppose I want to mentor a particular leader, but I look at my calendar and say, "I just can't add anything else to my plate." The Lord might let me know, "Good. What can you eliminate from your plate?" Or alternatively, what am I doing right now that I could combine with mentoring that leader and so accomplish both things at the same time?

Some of your people will echo the objection: "I know the boss keeps challenging me on this, but I don't have time to do anything else." The question is not whether they have time to do it; the question is how they've prioritized their time. In general, we find time to do everything that we consider important.

2. Measurable

If you can't measure it, you can't monitor it. Make sure you measure these outcomes against the established vision.

3. Attainable

Is your debt too large, or is your income too small? It all depends on how you look at it.

Ask the Holy Spirit to give you wisdom. He will direct you to commit to the goals you could never obtain in your own strength, but which you can obtain with His power and help. In 1 Corinthians 15:10 the apostle Paul wrote, "By the grace of God I am what I am, and His grace toward me was not in vain; but I labored more abundantly than they all." So then, who labored, Jesus or Paul? Yes. Both.

The Christian life is not lazy river rafting, especially for leaders. You don't get in the inner tube, get in the flow, and God carries you there. No. You swim against the tide in the power of the Holy Spirit of God.

Paul also wrote, "Therefore, my beloved, as you have always obeyed, not as in my presence only, but now much more in my absence, work out your own salvation with fear and trembling" (Philippians 2:12). The Greek scholar A.T. Robertson says that *fear and trembling* in that passage refers to self-distrust. I do not trust myself to get *there*. I tremble at that idea. Getting your organization to line up behind your God-given, biblical vision is not always easy. No one ever said it would be.

4. Realistic

You need realistic goals to reach a realistic vision and mission. Be realistic in how long it will take to develop leaders and train them. A leader comes to me every now and then and says, "I've been in this organization for about a year. It's not really what they told me it was. I'm going to give them six more months, and if it doesn't change, I'm gone."

I'd say, "Leave tomorrow. If you're not going to dig in your heels and give what it takes, then go ahead and leave now." You're telling God how long you're giving Him to change the people?

Who's in charge?

5. Tangible

These measurable goals are tangible, not outrageous. While some accomplishments are intangible, you should always set tangible goals. The groups I've led did not always meet their financial goals, but those goals were tangible. We knew when we hit them, or didn't.

Constantly Review

If you want to realize your vision, you must frequently review your goals so you can adjust to changing situations. Setting goals is not a one-time exercise, but an ongoing discipline.

The same thing is true of goals set by division leaders and other direct reports. Insist on performance reviews of core leaders twice a year. I do a staff evaluation every year. I'll have periodic staff meetings to review the individual visions set by these leaders, and then we'll meet to see where they are and let them own the situation, wherever they may be. I'll ask, "Do you think what is happening is good, or not?"

We'll hear some success stories and also learn of folks who are struggling. I believe these meetings encourage everyone present. Meet with your people regularly to challenge them, see where they are, talk about some misses and discuss their wins.

Don't Make Your Goals Dependent on Others

Set your goals as the leader on your own behavior, not on hoped-for behavior from others. I have hoped that some people would do what I felt confident they were capable of doing, but they didn't perform up to their ability. Their miss, however, didn't change what we did.

If you predicate what you do on somebody else's behavior, you'll hurt yourself if you and your organization don't get *there*. Again, base your goals on your behavior rather than on hoped for behavior from others. Base them on your performance, not on the performance of those who work for you or who serve with you. Always base your goals on things under your control.

And don't forget, God has an interesting way of encouraging you. When somebody doesn't reach your expectations, someone else will exceed them enough to make you wonder, *How did that person* do *that?* It's a good, blessed balance.

Division Leaders Need Their Own Goals

I can't set goals for other leaders. They must set their own, based on our organizational vision and mission.

You might consider giving every manager or director within your organization thirty days to write a clear, compelling, and concise description of how they plan to meet their goals. Remind them of the three great *C*s.

- Can you do this with clarity?

- Is it concise?

- Is it compelling? Does it draw me in so that I want to be a part of it?

I don't want everyone living out *my* vision. I want my division leaders to feel they're living out our common vision in their own way, appropriate to their own sphere. Also, because I want everyone in the organization to feel ownership, each division leader must have something to present to their people. They must be able to answer the question, "What are you believing God for this year, in three years, in five years? What does that look like?"

After your direct reports create their own individualized vision for their part of the organization, you meet with them individually to see how they did. Look closely at the words they use, to see if they convey what the writer believes they convey. I want to hear what they think, because I've had the opportunity to review all of their goals and strategies.

This process will tell you if the person has vision or not. If it's unclear, I'll go back and say, "This is a lot of ink, but what do you mean?" If I can't see it, then how in heaven could they sell it to someone else? What are they going to contribute? What are they going to do with what they receive? What do they wish to accomplish? When do they wish to accomplish it?

Their goals must be just as clear and compelling as their vision. A leader without a goal is like a ship's captain without reference points. The clearer the leader's goals, the sharper his or her vision focus, and vice versa. Don't hammer anyone with what you think they ought to do; they've told you what they think they ought to do. But you could ask them, "How many new leaders will you train this year? You can't continue to grow your division unless you're constantly training leaders. If you're going to expand, you must have more leaders. What will you do to grow more leaders?"

On Taking Time Off

After I've spoken at a conference or meeting, attendees often have said to me, "You talk about developing people and growing organizations, but the bottom line is, you must be so busy that you don't have a life."

In fact, I take off more time than most leaders I know.

"How can you do it?" someone wonders aloud. That's easy: When you get old, you work smarter. Somebody else does most of the work. Remember, leadership is not about how much you can accomplish through your own gifts and abilities, but about how much you can accomplish as a team, through your people.

I've said it already, but we misjudge our capacity for God. God can do so much more through all of us. Much of this is about learning to use our hours wisely.

The Book Execution

Have you read the 2002 book *Execution*? It was a #1 *New York Times* bestseller and was updated in 2009. "The discipline of getting things done was what differentiated companies that succeeded from those that just muddled through or failed,"[24] the authors wrote after the worldwide recession of 2008. In this book, Larry Bossidy, the former chairman and CEO of Honeywell International, and Ram Charan, a business theorist, provide outstanding guidance from a purely business perspective on the necessity and power of execution.

The authors insist that the main reason companies fall short of their promises is lack of execution. The best way for organizations to succeed, they claim, is by creating a system of getting things done through questioning, analysis, and follow-through. A business succeeds by meshing strategy with reality and by aligning people with goals. Bossidy and Charan highlight what they call the three core processes of every business: the people process, the strategy, and the operating plan (getting things done on time). In the book, they also make three major points about execution:

1. Execution is a discipline integral to strategy.

2. Execution is the major job of every business leader.

3. Execution must be a core element of an organization's culture.

If you find yourself always talking about what you intend to do, but never manage to execute it, you might find their book extremely helpful. You simply must come to a point of execution, or all your work on vision and mission will come to nothing.

In *Execution*, Bossidy and Charan list seven essential behaviors for every corporate or organizational leader. I believe you will see a good deal of overlap between their "essential behaviors" and what I've chosen to highlight in *How to Become a More Effective Leader*.

1. Know your people and your business.

2. Insist on realism.

3. Identify clear goals and priorities.

4. Follow through.

5. Reward the doers.

6. Expand people's capabilities.

7. Know yourself (perhaps the most critical of the seven behaviors, they say).

If you need help with execution, find a book like *Execution* and study it. More importantly, put its insights into practice in your leadership and organization. Let the wisdom of others, gained over many years and tested in real life, help you to get to wherever you believe God wants you to be. What do you have to lose?

Bottom Line: The Commitment to Act

Why do so many leaders fear to set goals? For one thing, effective goal setting is hard work. It takes determination and commitment. Second, and perhaps more telling, leaders must deal with the fear of defeat. They think, *What if I announce I want to do all of this and we can't do any of it?* The fear of defeat, of failure, prompts them to stay where they are.

Frankly, I'd rather aim at something and miss it than never have tried. Strong Christian character often gets created through temporary defeats. Great leaders will tell you that one of the best lessons comes by failing and realizing what wouldn't work. "Well, I got that out of the way," they'll say, and so they go on.

I've attempted many things that did not work. Learn to accept defeat as a needed lesson. Can you own your failures and learn from them? Can you overcome the fear of ridicule?

In the early days of Woodstock, we needed "only" a million dollars to buy a great piece of property. One woman said to me, "I'm on the board at the bank. I went ahead and checked, and all we have to do is get the trustees to sign, and we'll get our million dollars to buy the land."

So, the meeting's done, right? Not exactly. Time out. I did something fairly stupid. I had prayed and fasted about the will of God for that property, and I sensed God telling me that our people could give the money rather than borrow it. This would be an opportunity for them to encounter God and know who He is. He would show Himself strong on our behalf, and the episode would help us in the future to become who we eventually became.

I don't have perfect faith, but that's what I felt I heard God say. Even though I was new at Woodstock, I said, "We're not borrowing the money. The people are going to give it."

That brought up a major problem, however. The previous year, the church had taken in less than $250,000, total. We needed a million bucks in thirty days, or we would lose our option on the land. Another buyer already had lined up to purchase it. In other words, in thirty days we needed four times more than what we had taken in over the entire previous year.

"I believe I heard from God," I declared.

After the meeting and I got in our car, my wife Janet looked at me and said, "Wow. You're really confident about this, aren't you?"

"Man, I hope so," I said. "I'm serious as God."

As I said, I do not have perfect faith, but I felt I had heard from the Lord. I believed it and I felt we were supposed to go for it. I thought I would have been disobedient to do otherwise.

Sure enough, the ridicule started coming. I went to eat at a local restaurant and the people there snickered, "You've got them out on a limb, haven't you?" And they made fun of me.

Later I called one of my ministry friends who had been in it a long time. John Morgan at Sagemont Baptist Church in Houston had raised a gazillion dollars over the years. "John," I said, "you need to help me and pray for me."

"What are they saying, Johnny?" he asked.

"They said, 'You've got them out on a limb.'"

"Well," he replied, "that's where you belong. That's where the fruit is."

Oh, that's good, I thought. *I can't wait to go back to that restaurant and eat tomorrow.*

But it all felt very scary.

One Sunday night not long afterward, as I was preaching, a guy raised his hand. What does it mean when a guy raises his hand while you're preaching? He's feeling blessed, right? Until he starts looking urgent. So, I stopped. It had never happened before or since.

"Do you have a question?" I asked.

He stood up and couldn't speak for weeping.

"I've been robbing God," he said. "I've been stealing from the Lord. Can you get the ushers to pass the offering plate so I can get obedient?"

Since when do you need to ask a Baptist preacher to get the offering plates? Come on!

We got the offering plates out. Before we could pass them out, another man stood up, and then another, and another, and another, all of them with the same story.

"Thank you, Mike," one said. "I was sitting here thinking the same thing."

God came that night. By the time we left church, we had a million dollars in hand. We bought the property and that's when our Woodstock journey really started.

I think God says to all Christian leaders, regardless of where they're leading, "Give Me an opportunity to show who I am. Stand back and see the salvation of the Lord. Watch Me rescue you."

A million dollars in one night, back in the early '80s? I can look back on the story now, tell you what I learned, and shout the victory. But at the time, I felt as scared as a long tail cat in a room full of rocking chairs. I thought, *Oh, Lord!* It's easy to stand up and say God owns the cattle on a thousand hills, but when is the last time you asked Him to sell one of them? That was a powerful testimony to me of what God can do.

Watch God Come

Can you see now how all these pieces work together, from strategies and goals and plans and steps, all designed to help you fulfill your mission and reach your vision?

Is it a lot of work? Sure, it is. Will you fail along the way? No doubt. Will people ridicule you for following what you believe to be God's calling? Without question.

But how much of all that will you remember when God comes? Get to work until He comes. And then tell your own story.

8

Emotionally Intelligent

A young man I used to mentor called me one day, clearly focused on a single issue.

"I have a BA in expository preaching," he said. "I have a master's degree in expository preaching and I'm going to get a doctorate in expository preaching." And then he stopped talking.

I remained silent.

"I…thought you'd respond," he said.

"You didn't ask me to," I answered.

"Well, please respond."

"I wouldn't get a doctorate in expository preaching," I declared.

"Why not?"

"I don't know of many preachers getting fired because of their preaching," I answered, "but a bunch of them are getting fired for their lack of leadership. Go get a doctorate in leadership and learn how to relate well with your people."

Do you know that you can't even spell leadership without relationship? If no one has taught you the good relational skills you need as a Christian leader yet, then immediately put that pursuit near the top of your priorities. Don't delay. Take some classes, read some books, get a mentor or two who really knows people. If you want to succeed as a leader, you must develop your relational skills.

Somehow or another, God has allowed me to develop a lot of strong relationships over the years. It may have started for me in the pool room where God made me street smart, but wherever it began, I learned quickly that I could not lead well without building strong relationships.

To succeed as a leader, you need to gain a strong sense of how to relate to every person in your organization, regardless of their background, past, or personality. God wants to use you to touch them, no matter what kind of organization you lead. A sure way to fail as a leader is to have no clue about how to relate well to the men and women you've been tasked to lead.

Your Greatest Resource

Because I travel a lot, I speak to many groups of various kinds. Often, before I visit some organization, the senior leader takes me to dinner and unloads on me.

"I'll tell you this," the leader may say, "I just don't know what it's going to take with our people. They're the laziest, most noncommitted bunch you've ever seen."

When I later engage with the group and meet some of the people, however, I inevitably walk away thinking, *That leader has no clue. That's one of the finest groups of men and women I've been with in a long time. The vision, the dream they have—it's just amazing.*

How did we leaders get like this? How did we come to the place where we can't see the treasure trove God has presented to us in the amazing individuals whom He calls us to serve? Why do we struggle to see the enormous difference we could make with the men and women already in our organizations?

While I don't know the answer to that question, I do know that we must never lose sight of the truth: The greatest organizational resource we'll ever have is our people. It's people, people, people, *people*! You don't need money, you need people. People have money. Money follows people. When you focus on money, the money eventually dries up. You need to get, engage, develop, and keep people.

A man with a high position in our state once wanted to have dinner with my wife and me. He was a member of Woodstock. "You know," he said, "I've had this position for what, five years? You've asked very little of me, and my wife and I were talking. What can we do for you? While I'm in this position, what can we do for you that you would really like for us to do?"

"I'll get back with you on that, partner," I replied. "We'll come up with something."

Your greatest resource as a leader is your people. Your relationships, not the money you have or the other resources you may control, are your most valuable treasure. The best way to effectively lead any organization, by far, is to get to know how your people tick. For that, you need to improve your people skills, or as the parlance goes today, increase your emotional intelligence (EQ).

EQ for Leaders

Researchers Peter Salavoy and John Mayer coined the term "emotional intelligence" for a 1990 article they published in the journal *Imagination, Cognition, and Personality*.[25] Author Daniel Goleman popularized the term a few years later in his best-selling book, *Emotional Intelligence*.[26] Since then, the concept has taken on a life of its own, spawning further books, articles, seminars, workshops, and entire organizations.

The Institute for Health and Human Potential describes emotional intelligence as the ability to "recognize, understand and manage our emotions" along with the ability to "recognize, understand and influence the emotions of others."[27] A very helpful book, *Emotional Intelligence for the Modern Leader*, written by executive coach and keynote speaker Christopher Connors, provides not only insight into how leaders may increase their EQ in order to lead their organizations more effectively, but also includes various tools, exercises, and assessments to help these lessons "stick."

In the introduction to his book, Connors claims that "EQ is the predictor that distinguishes outstanding performers and leaders from the average. More than any other skill, EQ helps you build transformative relationships throughout your organization, whatever your role may be."[28] He promises that his approach "will teach you how to apply this dynamic skill set to transform the way you lead—and the way you see yourself. Wise, practical leaders understand how to use EQ to grow their business, boost their career prospects, and create future successful leaders."[29]

While Connors does not approach his subject from a Christian perspective, the counsel he gives on how to boost your relational skills mostly rings true and dovetails with much of what we've already discussed in *How*

to Become a More Effective Leader. Connors says, rightly, that the best organizations and leaders thrive on traits like self-awareness, empathy, adapt-
ability, and motivation.

Connors begins his book with a chapter called "Resonant Leaders" in
which he presents short profiles of four highly successful leaders, providing his readers with four examples of "emotionally intelligent leadership
in action."[30] I know that at least two of these leaders, Tyler Perry and Brad
Stevens, publicly identify themselves as Christians.

Perry is an actor, screenwriter, director, and producer, best known for
his "Madea" character (and the thirteen films the character has spawned).
In 2015 he bought Fort McPherson, a former military base outside of
Atlanta, and on its 330 acres built a film studio featuring 50,000 square
feet of permanent sets (including a replica of the White House) and twelve
sound stages. The highly successful Marvel film *Black Panther* was filmed
at The Tyler Perry Studios. Perry is the first African American to own out-
right a major film studio. Connors writes that Perry's "destiny has been
to lift others up."[31]

Perry himself has said, "I've never chased money. It's always been about
what I can do to motivate and inspire people."[32] He added, "You're not truly
successful unless your success is having a positive impact on the world."[33]

Brad Stevens became one of the youngest head coaches in the history
of the National Basketball Association in 2013 when he left a highly successful coaching stint at Butler University to coach the famed Boston Celtics of the NBA. He was thirty-six years old. In 2021 he left his post as the
Celtics head coach to become the team's president of basketball Operations, replacing the retiring Danny Ainge. Stevens, a protégé of UCLA
coaching legend John Wooden (also a committed Christian), has said,
"The best leaders lead by serving others."[34] Connors points to the career of
Stevens to say to his readers, "Lead by example, but part of that leadership
should be conscious acts of serving and understanding the needs of your
employees so you can set them up for success."[35]

A leader's EQ depends on four key components, according to Connors: self-awareness, self-management, motivation, empathy, and social
skill. The most difficult of these to master, he claims, is self-awareness.
To better understand themselves, Connors says leaders must gain a deep
understanding of their personal values, of what makes them passionate, of

their purpose in life, of their mission (their definition of success), and their goals. The secret, he writes, is a "willingness to get to know yourself better than you've ever dared. You must be willing to go deep."[36]

In Connor's system, "social skill" is a composite of several core components of EQ. When these components come together in an integrated way, leaders gain the "confidence and assuredness to influence and engage others in an impactful way. To make this work, you must connect on a transformative and not a transactional level."[37] In other words, the needs and wants of employees must come first. "In order to have 'raving fans,'" Connors declares, "we first need to inspire, create energy, and stir the positive emotions of the people we lead."[38] Three "foundational activities" can help make this possible: goal setting, making time for personal development, and reflection.

Those leaders who want to create emotionally intelligent organizations, Connors insists, must have leaders who are empathetic, adaptable, operate with a positive outlook, and believe in people. They are passionate about the organizational culture they help to create and, above all, are positive, people-first, receptive to others, and ready for new ideas. Their "people first" orientation leads to widespread camaraderie and frequent celebrations of success.

If you believe that you need to improve your EQ, an accessible book like *Emotional Intelligence for the Modern Leader* may provide you with some basic help, especially through its tools, exercises, and assessments. Do not approach any tool like this, however, with the hope that it will solve all your relationship deficits. The best way to learn how to improve your relationships is to dig deep into the Scripture, which has oceans of counsel and divine wisdom on this issue, grasp what it says, and then actually put into practice in your daily life whatever you find there. Mentors can have a profound effect, as well. When you carefully observe how a master relationship-builder cares for, loves, and leads other human beings created in God's image, you'll gain far more than a raft of books or any PhD can ever give you.

Understand and Satisfy People's Basic Needs

I once asked my senior team, "Are you sensing fulfillment in what you're doing here? Do you feel we're providing the resources you need to adequately allow you to do what you've been called to do? Is there real joy for you in what you're doing?"

I could only trust that they would be honest with me. Leaders must know what makes their people tick and how to meet their basic needs. If the best leaders are people first, then we need to make sure we're doing all we can to know our people well—their needs, their hopes, their dreams, their desires—and do what we can to set them up for success.

Your people need to know what's expected of them, at every level. And you need to know what you must provide for them to meet those expectations. Your secretary needs to know what's expected of her. The same with your key staff. And by the way, those expectations can change. Good leaders embrace change. I encourage my people to embrace change so that they don't feel intimidated when it starts to take place.

Many times, my top assistant and I sit down and I say, "Things have started changing around here. We need to address the situation differently." He may reply, "Am I still fitting the bill? Are you satisfied with my performance? Do you feel good about me, given the new realities?" I want him to ask the same questions of me.

All of us need to know what's expected of us and must feel reassured that we will be provided with the appropriate resources to do our jobs. If your people need developmental opportunities, provide them. If they think there is a great opportunity out there for them to help them grow, make it available. If they want to attend some great leadership conference, try to make it happen. Make the necessary resources available, if possible, to give them access to books that will keep them sharp.

Your people need you to give them both critical feedback and affirmation. Oftentimes I may say, "We just pulled off an excellent thing. Let's celebrate it this week, but first, let's talk about what the celebration might look like." Affirm them in what they are doing well. Frankly, some people need more affirmation than others.

A contract person once worked for me who would walk around the building after he had taken on a project, pull members of my staff aside and say, "What does Johnny think about what I helped him do?" He needed affirmation, a pat on the back. He needed to hear me say, "Hey, that was an awesome job!" Then he was all smiles. But until he heard from me, he felt anxious.

Others can just do their jobs and keep right on going without a word from you. Still, they need to know that what they do matters to us. It doesn't take long to text, email, or, better yet, send a handwritten note to say, "I want to thank you. You're knocking the socks off this project!"

The fastest growing division in our organization one year had a new leader. This young man really shined, and I let him know it on many occasions. I told him that it was a great day when God chose to give him to us. It was remarkable how the Lord blessed that division. I learned, however, that I had to take care where I said such things; three of my peers soon tried to hire him away from me. One came after him his first year with us. Another called and offered him a gazillion dollars. Do you know why he didn't take the job? "I can't," he said. "Thank you for being so generous, but God called me here."

All of us want to be on a winning team. Most of us know that it costs something to be on a winning team and we're glad to continue doing the things that helped us win in the first place. Winning teams have productive, team-oriented players.

Do everything you can to help your people become winners, to really soar in the area where God has called you all to make a difference. But don't forget: Without first meeting the basic needs of your people, you will get no stellar performances.

Eight Guidelines for Developing Your Leader EQ

Over the course of my career, I've learned a great deal about how to lift up the people I lead and help them to find fulfillment in whatever God may have called them to do. The following eight principles have risen to the top. My good friend Gordon MacDonald shared this outline.

1. Make key relationships a top priority.

Put the people you value most into your calendar first. Some leaders call these appointments their "big rocks." A high percentage of my big rocks carry the name "Janet" or the names of my two daughters or grandbabies.

In the early days, if I told my wife I would come home for dinner, but then somebody called me at the office, I would take the appointment and often not even call Janet to tell her I would come home late. One day, I realized I would never do that to anyone else, and that my wife is the dearest person to me on earth. I also realized that when someone calls, my assistant can rightfully say, "He has an appointment," and it's none of the caller's business who I'm meeting with. I make appointments with my wife and family and put them first.

Nonfamily relationships also matter, but some relationships rank higher than others. What are your top priority relationships? Nearly everything I do with others is based on relationship. Most places I go, my activities are all tied in with some relationship. Make your closest relationships your top priority.

2. Keep yourself free of resentment and anger.

Resentment and anger degrade your relationship with Jesus. Your relationship with God deteriorates when you don't like people, which is why God instructs us to love people.

The truth, of course, is that we don't like everybody to the same degree. In Jesus' name we love them, but I'm not going on vacation with them. If I have a free night, I'm not asking them over for dinner and a movie. You don't either, so quit acting so spiritual.

Nevertheless, I work hard to make sure that none of my relationships are broken to such a point that we can't talk about it or make it right. Romans 12:18 says, "If it is possible, as much as depends on you, live peaceably with all men." I've found that, most of the time, it is possible. When I become aware of a broken relationship and God deals with me about it, I usually come to understand that both of us contributed to the break. Rarely is a broken relationship 100 percent the fault of just one person.

The Christian way to handle this, I believe—and I know some individuals struggle with my approach—is to go to them and say, "I want you to know our trouble is absolutely 100 percent my fault. I want to ask you to forgive me. I've asked God to forgive me. I want us to bury the hatchet." I can hear the objections already: "How can you say that you take full responsibility, when you know it's *not* your full responsibility?"

I can do so because I've been reading about a person in the Bible— you've probably heard of Him, His name is Jesus. He went to the cross and took all of the blame although none of it was His. A good part of that blame was mine. I believe that we're to forgive as He forgave. And so, I offer to take all the blame for my fractured relationships.

Things often don't turn out how you might think.

When I'm at home and I say to my wife, "I really got to thinking about what I said to you last night. I was wrong in the way I said it and what I said. I've asked God to forgive me, and I want you to forgive me."

"No," she often replies. "I really couldn't sleep last night. I was wrong and I've asked God to forgive me, and now I ask you to forgive me. It's my fault."

How grateful I am that the Spirit of God has a way of bringing truth to bear on everything.

3. Don't be surprised if you occasionally suffer in your relationships.

What kind of an old person do you want to be? Growing older is a gift from God. You've already seen me quote Proverbs 19:20 a few times but read it again: "Listen to counsel and receive instruction, that you may be wise in your latter days." I want to be wiser in my latter days, not crankier.

For many years I've spoken at large, senior adult conferences. I do one in Gatlinburg, one in Myrtle Beach, and one in Branson. I'll be at some table signing one of my devotional books and an attendee will come by and say, "Pastor Johnny, would you pray for me? My grandchildren haven't been to my house in three years."

Wow, I'll think, but I'll keep writing and talking. Just a few moments later, the person starts grumbling and griping about this or that, and even as I continue to write I think, *If I were your grandchildren, I wouldn't come to see you, either.*

I've made up my mind that I don't want to be like that. I will *not* be like that.

When my granddaughter was seventeen years old, she called me one day and said, "Papa, when are you going to be home again? I want to come and spend some time with you." I thought it was because she loved me, but my wife said it was because she wanted something from me. Now, I don't know which was true, but I don't really care, so long as she keeps wanting to visit me.

4. Be alert.

Be alert to unhealthy forms of authority, which easily creep into relationships. If you're secure, you lead through relationships. People love you and respect you and you serve together. If you're insecure, you try to lead by authority.

I've heard staff members say, "I'm in charge of that department. If I told him to do it, don't you think he ought to do it?" They're leading through authority, and we could all see they had no significant relationship. "Have you ever seen him and his team together at lunch?" we might ask each other. "They never seem to do anything together."

Here's a bit of advice: Do less public speaking and more people development. Spend time with your people.

5. Search for possible kernels of truth in any criticism directed at you.

The founder of the Navigators, Dawson Trotman, was deeply admired by Billy Graham, who tried everything he could do to hire him, without success. Trotman died in 1956 while trying to rescue a swimmer at a lake in upstate New York. Graham preached his funeral, where he said he believed Trotman had personally touched more lives for Christ than anyone else he had known. Trotman is credited with saying, "There is a kernel of truth in every criticism. Look for it, and when you find it, rejoice in its value."[39]

I've received hurtful letters, unsigned letters, vicious emails. What do you do with them? I take them and put them in my study Bible, where I do my devotions. I meet with the Lord at home in the exact same place every morning. I let the note sit there for two or three days and then I get on my knees and read it aloud to the Lord. "Lord Jesus," I say, "I don't think this is true, but You know better than me. May the Spirit of God shine a light in my soul, and if any of this is true, would You show it to me?"

I promise you that God will answer a prayer like that! He may not show me all my fault, praise the Lord, but He will show me some of it. When He does, I draft a letter in which I might say, "I want to thank you for feeling at liberty to write to me. I've been praying over what you said, and God really did speak to me about a couple of things you mentioned. I've asked God to forgive me, and I would appreciate it if you'd pray for me, because I really desire to be what Jesus died for me to be. Thanks for caring." The writer may not have cared at all, but I still want to say "thanks for caring."

Just for the record's sake, how should we respond when somebody leaves the organization we lead, says something ugly about it on Facebook, and takes people with him? How should you deal with them? I write them a letter too. I thank them for all the years they served. I write of everything I remember about the way God used them to bless me. And then, every time, I write, "If you're half the blessing to your next leader as you were to me, he's a fortunate man to have you. God bless you."

Most of these folks circle back in about five or six years, apologizing for their bad behavior and wanting to make amends.

6. Be quick to say four things (and do so with sincerity).

Never hesitate to say, "Thank you," "I'm sorry," "Well done," and "I forgive you."

7. Move people first with prayer.

Some big things need to happen for many people, so pray for them earnestly. Pray that God would move in their life and move in. It's amazing what He can do! And then, pray that God would move *them*. A lot of times, He moves the boulders in our own hearts before He moves the rocks in theirs.

8. Return to the cross regularly and refresh your conversion and loyalty to Jesus.

All your relationships, as a Christian leader, begin with your relationship to Christ.

There must be times where God calls you to Himself in some public way. When He does this in my life, you'd better give me a clear line to respond. Tell me the way to the barn and I'm there.

An Unexpected Encounter

We all have a past. I have a past, you have a past, your people all have pasts. Those personal histories differ from one another, oftentimes radically so. Some people struggle in life more than others, others go off on wild tangents, but that doesn't make them lesser candidates for God's grace—or for your care or attention as a leader.

It amazes me how some of us are so harsh on some offenses and not so harsh on others. We so quickly decide who can be useful to us and who can't be, who is worth our attention and who isn't, and even who God might change and who He won't.

Years ago, I had the privilege to lead a famous fisherman to Christ, a delightful man named Orlando Wilson. At that time, Orlando had a celebrated television program called *Fishin' with Orlando Wilson* that had been running for eleven years. He eventually connected me with Ted Turner, the founder of WTBS and CNN. I shared the gospel with one of Ted's girlfriends and led her to Christ. We baptized her in Ted's private lake and then I spent an afternoon reasoning with Ted, at his request, regarding how he could be born again.

You never know where God may put you and what may happen because of where He has led. Will you be ready when God does something unexpected in your life as a leader? Do you have the people skills necessary to navigate whatever the opportunity or challenge may be, or to relate in a winsome way to someone whose lifestyle, choices, or behavior may repel you?

When I shared the gospel with Ted Turner, he told me that when he was nineteen years old, he helped set up chairs under a big tent in Chattanooga for a Billy Graham crusade. "At that time in my life," he told me, "I felt God was calling me to be a missionary."

Who would have imagined such a thing? You never know someone's backstory.

Orlando Wilson and Ted had become best friends, often going fishing and hunting together. Orlando told me, "I've never seen him listen to anyone like he's listened to you. Bob Hope was here recently, and he didn't give Bob Hope the time he gave you."

You may remember that Ted Turner was married and divorced three times and once famously declared that Christianity is a religion for losers. His outrageous comment made national and international news, but when he made them, he was drunk and receiving the Humanist of the Year Award.

When he first called my office, he said, "I know you've influenced my girlfriend." She piloted his private plane and oversaw new programming at CNN. "What would you recommend I do," he asked, "because I'm very sorry that I said what I did." He told me that he had bought the CNN building from Tom Cousins, whom he described as "a very godly man." Tom is one of the wealthiest businessmen in the Atlanta area, a real estate developer and philanthropist and indeed, a very godly man. Tom has shared his Christian testimony in various media outlets.

I was a lot younger in those days and I told Ted, "If you come to our church, I'll let you stand up and repent."

"I wouldn't recommend you have me in your church," he replied, "because I'm so big in media. There'll be hundreds of media people from all over the world who will show up. Let's come up with some other idea."

We did so and fixed up the fellowship hall so I could bring him there. He was very kind. "Do I have your permission to bring in one CNN camera and a feed so it'll go worldwide?" he asked.

"Yeah," I said, "we can do that."

Before he came, I took time off work to fast and pray. We anointed with oil every piece of furniture in the building where Ted and the media people would walk (I admit that I'm a bit of a Baptecostal). We prayed that God would be all over that place. Ted's best friends told me, "We've never seen him so nervous in all of his life."

The day of the event, Ted stood up and said, "I'm genuinely sorry for what I said and I deserve to go to hell." He then sat down beside me. I shared with him the story of the cross and the gospel and how he didn't have to go to hell because of what Jesus did for him.

You wouldn't believe the things he started trying to do for me after that day. Our people at Woodstock really got excited because the whole episode got splashed all over the media and traveled around the world. Janet and I had to leave our house for a while because so many media people desperately wanted to get a story from us. Some of our Woodstock folk said, "Man, we saw the other day that he's worth $8 billion. What if you lead him to the Lord and he joins our church and he tithes?" I thought I'd have a little fun with that one.

"That's rather humorous," I told the church, "because you believe that if Ted Turner gets saved, he'll tithe—and most of you don't."

All of that happened many years ago. Ted revealed in 2018 that he suffers from Lewy body dementia, a progressive disease resulting from protein deposits (called Lewy bodies) in the brain's nerve cells. The disease is incurable and affects movement, thinking skills, mood, memory, and behavior. Treatment focuses only on relieving symptoms.

I have no idea what may or may not have taken place in Ted Turner's heart, and that isn't the point of this story. The real question is this: Have you developed your people skills, your EQ, to effectively deal with whoever God sends your way? You may not like their politics, their faith (or lack of it), their taste or their language or their worldview. You may disapprove of the way they dress or how they spend their money. You might not like the way they smell. But...so what?

As a Christian leader, God asks you to love people, to care for them, to discover their needs and try to meet those needs. Who knows who He might send your way?

Are you ready?

Make Sure You Connect

A locomotive can go faster and farther by itself, but when it does so, it cannot accomplish the purpose for which it was created. A useful locomotive attaches itself to as many cars as it can pull and brings them along with it.

That's what leadership is all about, isn't it? We help as many as we possibly can—but how can we help them if we don't first connect with them?

PART THREE

PERSONAL **CONVICTIONS** OF A CHRISTIAN LEADER

9

Dedicated to Investing in Young Leaders

The ultimate blessing of your leadership influence occurs when God uses you to help others succeed. Come alongside young leaders, hold their hand, lift up Christ with whatever platform God has given you. Influencing them touches both you and your organization. Once you influence them for good, your influence reaches far beyond you and your little sphere to all those they will ever influence.

Mentoring young leaders means empowering them to make a difference in areas you'll never personally touch. And how do you mentor them? You don't just give them a little time. You give them a piece of your life.

If we say we're kingdom leaders, don't we want everyone to win? It's easier to preach about the kingdom life than to live the kingdom life, of course, but I really do want to be a kingdom believer. I want to invest in others. I want to grab a piece of the action everywhere I can. And I know that doing this increases the ability of others without decreasing myself.

Influence helps hopes become realities. Many young leaders wonder what's next for them. I try to walk with them through that uncertainty. "I'm there with you," I'll say. "I'll help you. I'll stand with you."

A Profound Influence that Lasts

While many leaders influenced me over the years, I had four primary mentors, all of whom have passed on. But their profound influence will never leave me.

I was in Kenya when Manley Beasley died. There had been a great move of God in East Africa among the fiercest warriors in Africa's history, the Masai. God had just opened their hearts and hundreds of thousands were swept into the kingdom of God. We baptized 5,000 one afternoon. There were 400 of us, all busy baptizing.

Manley Beasley had a huge influence on my life. I was much younger then, but his family asked if I would share a few words by way of telephone. He had influenced my life and my family in an incredible way—and now he was gone.

Maybe the most notable funeral in my life occurred after the death of my primary mentor, Adrian Rogers. I remember exactly where I sat and how the shepherd's stick had been placed across the casket. I had a direct line of sight to the person who had so greatly influenced me and encouraged my life.

Adrian influenced me profoundly by the way he carried himself and by the way he loved people. He was always one of the last to leave the building after a service. He was the single greatest spiritual influence in my life, by far.

Several years ago, I was honored to preach Freddie Gage's funeral. He was the one who said to me, "I know you're a pastor." He instructed me, "Never forget to tell the people that eternity is too long to be wrong." He taught me never to try to talk somebody into believing they're saved if they're not sure. He told me, "I'd rather have it on my record when I got to heaven that I prayed twice and didn't need to, than I prayed once and I needed two."

Janet and I felt deeply honored to be two of the 2,300 who attended Billy Graham's funeral in 2018. You couldn't find a dry eye in the place. It was one thing to watch the service on television, but to be there and catch it in person—I'm impressed that the US president and vice president both showed up. That's a mark of his enormous influence.

Billy Graham spoke eyeball to eyeball with 216 million people, more than anybody in history. Only God knows how many people he spoke to by way of television and radio. The other night, I went to my bedroom and used my iPad to listen to seven hours of stories and preaching of Billy Graham. I wanted to spend some time remembering him and thanking God for him. What a powerful man of God!

What if you could mentor a young leader who had the potential to exceed the influence of *your* greatest hero?

Ask Many Questions

The greatest men I've ever known in my life, as well as the most influential men in my life, were always asking questions. Great leaders are always asking questions.

One of my former mentees asked to fly down to Atlanta to meet with me. In just a few years, he helped grow his church to more than 3,000 in attendance. He had seen some phenomenal numerical growth but he wanted to come down to Atlanta to ask questions. "Man, I don't know what to do next," he said. "I want to learn from you guys who have been out there longer than me. What can I do?"

He told me, "I'm taking my wife off for a little rendezvous. I would like to come to Atlanta and worship with you that Sunday night."

"Great!" I replied.

"We're going to get a hotel," he told me.

"No," I said, "come spend the night with me."

The morning after he and his wife arrived, I got up early because I had a lot to do. I didn't know he would get up early, too, so I got him some coffee. For the next three hours, he engaged me with questions. He asked great questions.

So many leaders are great speakers but poor listeners. I don't know that I'm a great speaker but I do try to listen carefully. After I turned sixty, I called something like fifteen leaders. "Hey, I'd like to spend two days with y'all," I said.

"Why?" they wanted to know.

"Well, I'm sixty," I replied, "and you are right at that age, or a couple years older. I would like to talk to you about transitioning, just to get it on the back burner. I'd like to talk about how you're thinking about your leadership, going forward."

I had a lot of questions for them, and they were generous with their answers.

What to Look For

If you have a desire to influence young leaders, carefully select and intentionally train them. Remember how Moses' father-in-law Jethro instructed Moses to "select from all the people able men, God-fearing, trustworthy, and hating bribes. Place them over the people as commanders of thousands, hundreds, fifties, and tens" (Exodus 18:21 HCSB). Moses searched for young influencers who had the three major characteristics of leadership: morality, honesty, and integrity.

While it's been said that leaders know leaders, many of us need to make a change to seek out new blood. When you identify and begin calling to action those who display these three building blocks of leadership, you'll have people who are easy to train and able to help you take things to the next level.

Part of a leader's role is being a teacher, and that takes time. It takes discernment. It takes noticing what others need and what they need to hear. Jethro told Moses to teach the people "the way to live" (verse 20 HCSB).

Keep in mind the importance of character. That's because being in a leadership role makes a person's character more apparent. When you put a potential leader on a platform or stage, what happens to their behavior? Does it change? Do they go from humble and self-effacing to proud and boastful? Leadership magnifies an individual's character, for good or ill, so when you look for young leaders to mentor, prioritize character.

What Mentoring Looks Like

When I choose someone to mentor, I'll often have the person spend a year with me. He'll attend staff meetings, go on divisional retreats, accompany me to events of various kinds. I'll have him get involved with Timothy+Barnabas. He will have only a certain amount of money budgeted for that year and must keep track of it. I teach him how to manage the money in that account.

If I am to truly influence him, I must deal with my own insecurities. He needs to feel secure in his own skin around me so that he can talk to me about anything and everything. Fears must be replaced with faith. Dreads must be replaced with dreams. Self-preservation must be replaced with strength. We work through all those things.

I periodically teach mentees leadership lessons that God has taught me. I make sure they attend whenever I speak to staff about something God has clearly laid on my heart. I also hardly ever do anything alone.

I invite young leaders to travel with me. It becomes an opportunity to find out more about what God is doing in their life and how they can be more effectively developed. I once took a talented young man on a trip, thinking he must be about eighteen. He turned out to be twenty-two. I knew something about how his father had hurt his family, but despite that pain, he had become one of the most vibrant witnesses for Jesus in our entire church. I was impressed by his heart to share the gospel and to be a leader. He really blessed me, so I let him travel with me.

A few years ago, on a trip to Cuba, I took a young leader in whom I'd invested a good chunk of time. He had already given me great return on my investment and the trip helped him grow even more. Traveling together is a great way to wield influence.

Carrying On the Legacy

I have no son. I'm one of those preachers who would like to have a boy to carry on my legacy in preaching, but I went back three generations and all I could find was bootleggers. So, I quit looking.

But now I have a grandson, a young man named John Carson. He loves his Papa and he listens to his Papa. I take every opportunity to speak into his life. He still thinks I'm cool.

I have no son, but I do have a few prospective leaders who are like Alex. One Sunday night, I led an Indonesian diplomat to Jesus while preaching in Missouri. His name is Alex. He was in Missouri as a representative of the Prime Minister of Indonesia. Somebody knew him, brought him to a state Baptist convention, and God spoke to his heart.

Afterwards, Alex told me he was a Muslim from a Muslim family. We lost touch for a while. The next time I heard from him, he was a student at Midwestern Baptist Theological Seminary. He has since graduated, his family has disowned him, and he believes with all his heart that God has called him to be an indigenous missionary back in his hometown.

We decided to mentor him and sent him on several trips back to Indonesia. On one visit, he was arrested and remained under house arrest for weeks before the town's leadership finally released him. He met an Indonesian girl, a Christian, and wanted to get married. I met her for the first time one Sunday night. A lay leader who worked with me at Woodstock eventually adopted him. Alex calls him his father.

When I speak with Alex, I touch only one; but what if Alex touches thousands? How important is the stewardship of influence?

Another young leader called and said, "I'm going to be in town. I would stay over for days to spend time with you." I didn't know him well, but if I could influence his life for good, I wanted to make the effort. He joined several of us for dinner that Sunday night.

I once took my children to the wedding of one of my mentees. They were then fourteen, thirteen, and eight. They spent the night with me at a hotel before I officiated the next day at the marriage ceremony. My children all knew my mentee, loved him, and wanted to see him get married.

I have been mentoring for twenty-seven years, which means my kids got to watch what I did. My grandkids now have literally fallen in love with the guys I'm mentoring. And isn't that who I want my children and grandchildren to love, some godly young leaders?

Do you believe God may want you to mentor a young leader, but you've put it on hold? You've basically said, "This isn't a good season. I believe God wants me to do this, but I'll do it when my kids graduate from high school and they're out of the house." Listen, if God has told you to do it, it might be good to do it now. Be careful about postponing things for which God puts a passion in your heart, when maybe now is the time to do it!

Most of the young men I've mentored have since gone on to leadership roles in various settings, most of them in the pastorate. One became a scholar and is teaching at Oxford. Oh, that was *definitely* my influence on his life, that he's teaching Hebrew and Greek at Oxford. Ha!

From Maintenance to Multiplication

The best way to grow an organization or a movement is to grow a leader. And the best way to grow a leader is through the positive influence of a more seasoned leader.

Too many leaders, however, never understand that their organizations struggle because they have never taken the time to raise up younger leaders. The younger leaders therefore muddle through their leadership assignments, often getting stuck at some point or other because they have not been taught how to grow. They get stuck on one of five levels identified by John Maxwell in his book *Becoming a Person of Influence*.[40] The five outline points below come from Maxwell, and I've summarized his principles.

1. Scramble

According to Maxwell, leaders on Level 1 spend most of their time scrambling to find people to replace the ones they lost. They aren't thinking ahead and creating new leaders. If you see yourself here, what will it take to get you to move?

2. Survival

Maxwell says many companies do nothing to develop their upcoming leaders. They are able to keep their staff, but people aren't thriving. Rather, they are just hanging on.

3. Siphon

At this level, people are being trained, but those who do the training don't really build relationships with the upcoming leaders. While this is a step in the right direction, it doesn't go nearly far enough. I don't want merely to develop the young leaders I identify; I want to connect with them and so help them to grow into the leaders Jesus wants them to become so that they aren't siphoned off by another company.

4. Synergy

Not until a company makes an effort to truly develop their upcoming leaders do they empower them to achieve their potential. At this level, the company creates a good synergy that leads to growth and momentum.

5. Significance

Only a very few leaders reach this level. They know how to reproduce leaders who can achieve maximum results and will, in turn, help train up new leaders. It is at this level that leaders have a truly powerful and lasting influence on the world.

On what level would you place yourself? If you feel dissatisfied with your current position, what are you willing to change? What would it take for you to move up a level or two?

Three Tips for Developing Young Leaders

In addition to the ideas I've already suggested, permit me to give you three more tips on how to develop the young leaders in your sphere of influence.

1. Create opportunities to invest in them.

Sometimes a young leader will see me preparing for some event—maybe a wedding or a funeral—and ask me what I'm doing. "I'm officiating," I'll reply. "Why don't you go with me? Maybe you'll learn something." I invite promising young leaders to attend conferences with us, I give them speaking opportunities, and occasionally I suggest they lead conferences. I ask them to help with research, inquire how they would deal with current organizational issues, and periodically allow them to make consequential decisions.

Just as Jesus sent out the disciples two by two, so you need to send out your young leaders. A talented young staff member called me one day and said, "Would you help me to find a couple of people I can bring on my staff?"

I told him I would go one better than that. "I'm going to pray for you, that you bring me the people you believe God would have you add to your staff," I said. And he did exactly that.

Empower these young leaders to make their own decisions. Be willing to teach and mentor them. If God is using you in your leadership role, freely share your knowledge.

For the last thirty or more years, I've crisscrossed the country and the world, training young leaders and staying in touch with those who are making a big difference. Once I was having lunch in Turkey and joined some young men and women sitting at a table. "I was an architect in Tehran," one woman said, "and my husband was a movie actor."

"Gosh," I said. The couple had become believers in Christ, were persecuted for their faith, and had to flee Iran. They had landed in Turkey, waiting to see what would come next.

"What are you doing now?" I asked.

"I am part of a project translating the Bible into Farsi," she said, "and I'm also translating a commentary into Farsi."

"Whose commentary are you translating?" I asked.

"Danny Akin's *A Theology for the Church*," she replied. I immediately thought, *A Woodstock project!* Our church had paid for it.

So, there I sat at a table halfway around the world, speaking to a leader involved in a project funded by the church I pastored. You never know where your influence will show up when you believe in people, empower them, and pour into them—especially young leaders.

2. Network young leaders with successful older leaders.

You're never better as a leader than when you're helping younger leaders become their best selves. If I were to describe the stewardship of influence, it's using whatever influence God gives you to help others succeed. And part of that influence is wielded by leaders you already know. What joy I feel when I can connect a young leader with a friend who's been leading successfully for many years.

God has allowed me to know some great men of God over my career, and one who stands out is Dr. Charles Stanley. When I asked Dr. Stanley to speak into the life of the pastors whom God had brought around me through the years, he offered to let us use his new studio for a day; he would come and speak and then take any questions from any pastor there. He also had lunch with us, did a photo-op, and gave free signed copies of his book to more than one hundred pastors, who came from as far away as New York and California. I will never forget that day or Dr. Stanley's generosity. Charles Stanley is eighty-eight years old and in 2020 announced he would step down as pastor of First Baptist Atlanta, although he continues to lead In Touch Ministries, the outreach organization he founded in 1977. The Lord allowed me to do a similar event with Dr. John Edmund Haggai, who is now in the presence of Jesus.

We can summarize the stewardship of influence in one statement: Using what God has given you to enable others to succeed. Only heaven will reveal what these wonderful men of God have meant to me in my special one-on-one times with them. I am forever grateful.

3. Provide good challenges that enable people to grow.

Leaders are in the people business. Any leader worth his salt craves a good challenge! We're not at our best perched at the summit. We are climbers and are at our best when the way is steep.

The kind of challenges you give your young leaders will vary depending on their gifts, interests, maturity, and readiness. A stiff challenge for one leader may seem elementary to another. When you get to know the young people whom you especially want to influence, you'll know what kind of challenge will suit them and help them grow. You'll know, because you're a leader, and that's what leaders do.

Big Red Flags

None of the behaviors listed below should characterize a leader. If you see any of these behaviors in your young leaders, it's your responsibility to lovingly but firmly correct them. If you see several of these behaviors in a potential mentee, you might reconsider whether you should identify the person as a leader at all, regardless of talent.

1. Excusing Personal Faults

"Hey, friend, how's work going?"

"I'll just be honest, man, our division isn't doing well, but I'm just a humble little servant." What's humble about *that*? Deconstruct that excuse: "It's just who I am, so accept it and get over it."

Jesus Christ doesn't see us for who we are. If He did, He'd send us to hell and be over with it. Jesus Christ sees us for who we can become. Some of us want to see ourselves for who we are and almost excuse ourselves for it. We're basically saying, "This is the way I am, and I do not intend to grow in that area of my life."

2. Blaming Others

When problems arise, a true leader always looks in the mirror to see whether the problem might reside within, before looking out the window.

3. Claiming Undeserved Credit

No leader is solely responsible for an organization's success. When someone says, "Wow, you have done an amazing job to get this place running so well," you ought to reply, "Thanks, but give me a break. Come over sometime while we're having a staff meeting and I'll show you the team God has assembled to get us where we are. It's been a team effort." Understand that the word *ego* forms an acrostic: Edging God Out.

4. Speaking Sarcastically

Sarcasm can be clever, funny, memorable, and perceptive, but when it's directed at another human being, it is catastrophically demotivating. Any leader who uses it like a club is no leader at all.

5. Micromanaging

Nothing exposes a leader's distrust of people like micromanaging. I typically meet most of our new staff members for the first time when they get introduced to the organization. I trust my people who make most of our hires and I want them to know it.

6. Running over Others

We've all met them, so-called leaders who use people like rungs to climb some ladder—leaders eager to throw others under the bus, especially if it relieves them of blame. These are leaders who drop their friends as soon as they can make more powerful friends, leaders quick to flatter and even quicker to abandon. When they cross your path, run—or risk being run over!

Practice Positive Behaviors

All the positive, motivating behaviors that follow should characterize your treatment of mentees, as well as their behavior toward others. Some of them need no commentary.

1. Give Proper Recognition

Woodstock has a great prayer ministry that grew over the years, with little guidance from me. One night we held a special service of praise, worship, and prayer, led by four key laypeople. One of them was a far better prayer warrior than I am. Another could hardly walk or talk, but she needed to say something about prayer because she had so strongly championed it. I felt greatly honored to give credit where credit was due.

2. Always Express Gratitude

No one owes you anything. Never get to the point where you say, "If that person would just take time to recommend me, I could get that job." If you're not careful, you can begin to put your trust in people rather than in the God of the people.

3. Always Be Kind

Take the time to really care. Go the extra mile and show kindness. In doing so, you'll build relationships and trust.

4. Always Be Friendly

Have you ever started to read your own press releases or believe what your mother says about you? If you do, you can begin to think you're a bit too important to recognize "the little people" around you.

A few years after I arrived at Woodstock, our church began to grow. One night, a group of preachers I had always considered heroes had a special meeting during a convention—and they invited me. I couldn't believe it! Hardly anyone there knew me, the new kid on the block. After a while, one of my friends ushered me over to a well-known leader and said, "Hey, brother, meet Johnny Hunt. He's over at First Baptist Church Woodstock." The guy didn't even look at me.

My friend repeated, "Hey, won't you meet one of my buddies?" Without even turning around, the man said in a disinterested tone of voice, "Hi, John, how are you?" He never once looked me in the face.

Shortly afterward, a group of these men crowded together and started making a distinct buzz. I heard someone say, "Keep your eye on that young Hunt boy. He's over there at Woodstock, and the church has grown from 200 to 1,300. They're knocking it dead down there. The people are following him and you ought to see their facilities. It might be our next great church. Watch this one."

Moments later, the same man who had snubbed me walked over to me, all smiles, put out his hand and said, "Hey, brother Johnny, how are you?" I will remember that incident for as long as I live.

Always be friendly. Adrian Rogers used to tell me, "Johnny, treat them good on your way up, because you'll pass them on your way down." And then he would habitually add, "But I'm not coming down."

5. Be a Good Listener

Value what people say to you more than you cherish what you'd like to say to them.

6. Share Too Much Information

Withholding information is a form of distrust, especially with those on your leadership team (and those you're trying to mentor).

7. Ask for Forgiveness

Don't ever be too proud to ask for forgiveness. People need to know you are a person of integrity who genuinely cares about doing things right.

8. See the Ideas of Others as Possibilities

You're not the only one who has great ideas. The best ideas are yet to come! And who knows? One of your mentees might have one of them!

They Must Want It

Any young leader you want to influence must desire for themselves what you desire for them.

People often called me because of Woodstock's City of Refuge, a place where hurting or failed pastors can come for rest and restoration. "Pastor Johnny," they would say, "did you hear that Pastor Rick fell out of ministry?"

"Yes, I've heard."

"Please, take him in. I'll do *anything* if you will take him into your City of Refuge."

But that's not the way it works. *Rick* must have the desire to go even more than his friend wants him there. Never forget, the leaders you want to influence must desire for themselves what you desire for them.

When Mentees Become the Mentors

I jogged for many years. Today, I run a little every now and then, but mostly I speed walk, trying to stay healthy. Several years ago, my daughter Hollie wanted me to teach her to run. Our first time together, she wanted to take off and just sprint. In about five minutes, she felt dead and breathless. I then took her to Kennesaw Mountain to help build up her lungs.

Today, she runs half marathons and eight-minute miles. When she jogs with me, she says, "Dad, stay on this trail. I'll come back to meet you." I can barely see her, she's so far down the road. And so, the mentee became the mentor.

The first book I ever wrote, *The Building of a Spiritual Leader*, described my life story and some growth in my early days of ministry. Adrian Rogers wrote the foreword, which didn't hurt. I've always considered him my foremost mentor.

A few years before he died, he called me. "John," he said, "I have fifty years of experience and I want to use the rest of my life doing schools like your Timothy+Barnabas. Could you help me?" About every two weeks, he would call to ask, "How do you do your pricing? How about the guys who can't afford to come?"

"Underwrite it, Dr. Rogers," I would say. "Use some of your *Love Worth Finding* money. Scholarship them—it'll be a good investment." Dr. Rogers ended up doing two of his own conferences before he went home to be with the Lord.

How cool is that? In his latter days, my principal mentor looked back to me, one of his mentees, and *I* had begun mentoring *him*.

As a student at Gardner-Webb College, I had a professor named Logan Carson. He taught me Old Testament theology and he came to mean a lot to me. Dr. Carson was born blind. He often said he didn't want his sight back in this life because "the first thing I want to see is Jesus' face." He would walk into class every day, tapping around with his walking stick, find his desk, briefcase in hand, sit down, and say, "We're ready to begin." I can still see it all. He did it every single day.

After he retired from Gardner-Webb he continued to teach a bit at Southeastern Baptist Theological Seminary. He wrote me several years before his death in 2018 and said, "Johnny, I want to buy some of your material. I'm teaching preachers and I want to use your materials. Man, I heard your stuff on shepherds and sheep!"

Do you know what it's like to live long enough to see the people who taught you, now asking to use your material? He sent me a check and threatened me if I sent it back. The fact that he would even use my material was worth more than money!

If you live long enough, God sometimes allows your mentees to touch you, the mentor. And when your influence is exceeded by those you influenced, there's only one thing to do.

Celebrate!

10

Devoted to Peace

Ken Sande grew up on a ranch in Montana, worked as a mechanical engineer, and then led a team of highly competitive engineers at a California medical research and development company. What he saw happening in that environment, he said, triggered a lifelong interest in building relationships, conflict management, and creative problem solving.

He later returned to Montana to get a degree in law, hoping to apply his engineering experience to work in product liability litigation. But just one year after he graduated, God instead led him to pursue biblical peacemaking, and he founded the Christian Conciliation Service of Montana. Over the years, the service grew and morphed into Peacemaker Ministries, which exists "to transform relationships with the power of the gospel."[41] Through more than three decades of leading that organization, Sande helped mediate conflicts all over the world, ranging from personal disputes to church splits and thorny lawsuits. He also wrote *The Peacemaker*, which has sold more than half a million copies in at least twenty languages.

Not a bad start, right?

"What do you mean, *start?*" someone asks. I mean that in 2011, Sande perceived that God wanted him to go even further. "I sensed that God was calling me to shift my focus from *resolving conflict* to *preventing conflict* by building healthy relationships," he said. And so, he began to develop a system of biblically based teaching that he calls "relational wisdom." One year later, Sande founded a second organization called Relational Wisdom

360 (RW360), with a stated mission of equipping Christians "to develop strong, enduring and appealing relationships that display the love of Jesus Christ and the transforming power of his gospel."[42]

I love Sande's approach. While most organizations and groups focus on conflict management or resolution, he understands that the core issue is far larger and more comprehensive than that—and that the stakes are much higher. While as leaders we must help to resolve conflicts among our people and create an environment that effectively facilitates conflict resolution, as Christian leaders we want genuine, God-honoring peace, not merely the absence of discord. In this chapter, therefore, I will emphasize what it means to be a peacemaker, equipped with several valuable conflict resolution skills.

Expect Conflict

Conflict is a given in any organization filled with imperfect men and women. With so many individuals wanting so many differing things, it is inevitable that conflicts will arise. Regardless of the kind of organization you lead, conflict is coming and will cause problems for you if you don't address it quickly enough and in a satisfying way.

Some leaders wrongly see conflict as an opportunity to get rid of those who disagree with them. While some dissenters may choose to leave, instead learn to see conflict as your opportunity to develop and grow individuals who are not yet where they need to be in their own growth or understanding.

Conflicts arise for a huge variety of reasons. When people feel threatened, they lash out, sparking conflict. Personality differences cause conflict. Political differences cause conflict. Misunderstandings cause conflict. Disappointment causes conflict. Conflict of goals can occur, and not just between two desirable and yet incompatible goals, but between the goals of different people trying to fulfill the same vision. As the leader, you must deal with all of this. It is your responsibility to make sure these conflicts get resolved.

Working from God's Peace

Jesus told His followers, "Peace I leave with you, My peace I give you; not as the world gives do I give to you. Let not your heart be troubled, neither let it be afraid" (John 14:27). The world has its own version of peace, an external peace, but the Lord Jesus wants to do a work inwardly in our hearts. We can get people to put down their guns and stop shooting, but we can't get them to stop hating unless God does something on the inside.

The world's peace is really a truce; it's putting down your weapons long enough to reload. Society tries to put an end to yelling without doing anything about deep resentments. It endorses the attitude that says, "Let's go along to get along." The world often insists that the way to keep peace is to just keep quiet.

James 3:17 defines internal peacemakers and internal peacemaking. It calls wisdom from heaven "pure," which means truthful and peaceful. Any form of peace that doesn't issue from truth is merely a pretense of peace. God's way to peace is always through His holiness. We can never obtain true peace at the expense of righteousness.

When somebody says, "I don't care what the Bible says, I just want to get along," they may "get along" after a fashion, but that's not peace as God gives it. Hebrews 12:14 reminds us that one cannot divorce peace from holiness. We're to pursue peace *and* holiness, without which no one will see the Lord. When unbelievers observe Christians, they ought to see the peace of God ruling among them and within them.

Peace rules within our organizations when God's peace rules in our hearts. When we're at peace with God, we're at peace with ourselves, and therefore we're at peace with others.

The psalmist put it this way: "Mercy and truth have met together; righteousness and peace have kissed" (Psalm 85:10). God always brings peace, but He brings genuine peace in the context of truth. To be peacemakers, therefore, we must be both honest and truthful. Where we find true peace, we also find righteousness and holiness.

Trying to bring harmony by compromising righteousness forfeits both; you will have neither peace nor righteousness. The peace Jesus came to bring is not peace at any price. To be a peacemaker on God's terms means we must work toward harmony on the terms of truth and righteousness.

Jesus, Truth, and Peace

Jesus never evaded the issue of wrong or sinful behavior so that He could be a peacemaker. How He spoke to the woman at the well in Sychar (John 4) provides a perfect example for us.

Jesus intentionally went by that well because He loves to touch outcasts. I'm grateful to God that one day in heaven we will meet this lady. This sister from Sychar will tell us how the Lord Jesus Christ sought her out, when most of her neighbors wouldn't even talk to her. Jesus not only talked to her, He waited for that unpleasant hour in the middle of the day when the sun was both high and hot. Everyone else had left.

Jesus went there, ministered to the woman, and offered her great hope. But He did not offer that hope without first confronting her greatest need. He spoke to her about her multiple husbands and her sexual sin. He spoke about the right way to worship. But He did not hesitate to confront her godless life, because until she realized she was a sinner, she couldn't have peace with God.

Jesus wants to do the same thing in our lives, to bring us to that same place. The person who is unwilling to confront in the name of Jesus will find it difficult to be a biblical peacemaker.

What Is a Peacemaker?

"Blessed are the peacemakers, for they shall be called sons of God," Jesus said (Matthew 5:9). Peacemaking is a hallmark of God's children. "The fruit of righteousness is sown in peace by those who make peace," says James 3:18. God asks us, "Who is sowing righteousness?" and He answers, "Those who sow peace, the peacemakers."

Peacemakers have accepted the truth of God, have a heart to see people rightly related to God, are right in their own heart through faith in Christ, and right in their relationships with others. They've made all these things a priority.

Colossians 3:15 instructs us, "Let the peace of God rule in your hearts, to which also you were called." Notice that first word: *let*. Paul writes, "*Let* the peace of God rule." He means that we are to choose to allow the peace of God to act as an umpire. In every conflict of motives or contrary impulses, the peace of God must step in to decide which is to prevail.

When the peace of God rules, the child of God reigns. It's amazing what I can do as a Christian leader when the peace of God rules in my heart!

As Christian leaders, we're sons and daughters of God. Because a resemblance exists between us and our heavenly Father, I like the version of Matthew 5:9 that one translator created: "Blessed are the peacemakers, for they shall be doing a God-like work."[43] When we work to make peace, we don't merely manage conflict, we do a God-like work. When God sends a genuine peacemaker into an area of conflict, He is pleading through the person He sends, as though God Himself were imploring.

This is why, before we go into any spiritual battle, God tells us to put on His armor (Ephesians 6:10-18). It amazes me that the shoes He gives us are laced "with the preparation of the gospel of peace" (verse 15). God has prepared and equipped us with peace!

And what happens when we bring the peace of God to some nasty conflict? Psalm 133:1 paints a gorgeous picture: "Behold, how good and how pleasant it is for brethren to dwell together in unity!"

Christian Troublemakers

When Christians are at odds with each other, they are not peacemakers. Jesus cannot be glorified in them as He so desires to be. Believers out of the will of God can be troublemakers instead of peacemakers. Let me give you three brief examples.

I have no reason to believe that Lot was an unbeliever, but he brought great trouble to Abraham through his disobedience. He was out of the will of God when he moved into Sodom, but that was not the major problem. The biggest problem was that Sodom moved into him.

Our problem is not that we live in this world but that we let the world live in us. I'm grateful to God that even though I must be in this world by contact, I don't have to be in it by conduct.

When David got out of the will of God, he also became a troublemaker. He brought trouble on Israel, both when he committed adultery with Bathsheba and when he took a divinely disapproved census. What a difference from all the times when he let the peace of God rule in his heart!

When the peace of God rules in your heart, you reign in life. You were created to reign with Christ, to shine in your Christian walk. God wants you to be an overcomer—a peacemaker, not a troublemaker.

Jonah also was a believer, a mighty preacher. Biblical historians tell us that more people got saved in that revival in Nineveh than in any other revival recorded in the Word of God. Yet this leader got out of the will of God, and instead of being a peacemaker, he became a troublemaker.

Anyone who is not a peacemaker is either a disobedient Christian or not a Christian. So long as we live in unrighteous ways, we can't go into a conflict and make peace. In that case, we have separated ourselves from righteousness and truth, and therefore from the peace meant to rule in our hearts.

Four Principles for Peacemaking

I've been at odds with folks. I continue to pray through some relationships that still are not where I believe God would have them to be. I want to make sure that I've obeyed Romans 12:18, that as much as is possible, I try to be at peace with everyone. The following four principles give me a great deal of help.

1. Glorify God

This is the number one principle for every Christian peacemaker. Paul wrote, "Therefore, whether you eat or drink, or whatever you do, do all to the glory of God" (1 Corinthians 10:31). Biblical peacemaking is motivated and directed by a fundamental desire to please and honor God. Has it become a dominant force in your life? Do you so desire to please the Lord Jesus Christ and to glorify God that if conflict arises, you want to do everything possible within you, aided by the Spirit of God, to be at peace?

If you're a Christian leader, then God's interests, God's reputation, and God's commands should take precedence over everything else. You may say, "But this man causes trouble with everybody he's ever known!" What if God wants to use you to be the peacemaker? Maybe this man has endured so many disrupted relationships that he has never had a genuine friend. Perhaps he has never known a peacemaker. He may have had contact with many peace lovers and peacekeepers, but as yet he has never met a genuine peacemaker. Why don't you be the first one?

God may use you to set someone free who has gone from one sour relationship to another, leaving one organization after another the moment someone hurts him. Such a person can move to Africa and live more than 10,000 miles from home, and yet feel the pain in his heart. He can't get away from it without a peacemaker to help him.

2. Start with Yourself

Once you've identified someone in need of peace, what is the next step in this process? Come up with a plan to see him? No. The next step for every peacemaker is to first get the log out of his own eye. "First remove the plank from your own eye," Jesus said, "and then you will see clearly to remove the speck from your brother's eye" (Matthew 7:5).

Anytime I sense a disrupted relationship in my life, I know I need to draw closer to Jesus. I can't say, "I'm going in there to take care of it right now. I'll settle this thing, once and for all!" That's the flesh speaking. When the peace of God reigns in my heart, I draw closer to God, which may require me to get up an hour earlier to spend time in the Word of God.

I might say, "Lord, this relationship is not right, and I think I know what's wrong. But God, if I've done anything to offend You, or if You see where I have helped to sour this relationship, in the name of Jesus, would You show me?" Peacemaking requires us to face up to our own attitudes, to our own faults and responsibilities, before pointing out anything that others may have done wrong. Overlooking the minor offenses of others and honestly admitting our own faults will encourage similar responses from anyone watching us.

Before you confront anyone, first pray and remind yourself, "God, I am nothing without You." You can't successfully confront anything or anyone without first being right with God. We all need to depend on His wisdom and power. It takes a great work of grace in a leader's heart to come to the point where he realizes he is nothing. I suggest you ask God, "Please do three things in my heart: Help me to despise my sin. Help me to judge it. And then help me to forsake it."

3. Show Your Brother His Fault

"If your brother sins against you," Jesus said, "go and tell him his fault between you and him alone. If he hears you, you have gained your brother" (Matthew 18:15). Read on in Matthew 18 to see the whole process; it will tell you exactly what to do.

Peacemaking requires constructive confrontation. Some way or another, you must be willing to meet. I've left some such meetings saying,

"Thank God, that's exactly what I wanted to see happen." And I've left others in which nothing like it happened at all. Taking these steps doesn't guarantee success, but you won't find success without them.

4. Be Reconciled

"If you bring your gift to the altar, and there remember that your brother has something against you," Jesus said, "leave your gift there before the altar, and go your way. First be reconciled to your brother, and then come and offer your gift" (Matthew 5:23-24).

You'll never make things right until you offer the ultimate sacrifice, which is your obedience. Leave your gift there, whatever that gift might be, and go and be reconciled. People always come before activity.

Tips for Conflict Resolution

The first step toward effective conflict resolution is always to invite God into the process. James 1:5 says, "If any man of you lacks wisdom, let him ask of God," while James 3:17 calls the wisdom of God "peaceable."

You start with the Word of God. As you study the Word of God, you get the wisdom of God. When you get the wisdom of God, He will show you the will of God. When you see the will of God, you pray that God's will might be done in your life. And then you'll begin to see the works of God, peace being one of the greatest of those works.

Only then will you begin to see the wonder of it all.

A Short Lesson in Conflict Resolution

In the church at ancient Philippi, the apostle Paul had to deal with two feuding women named Euodia and Syntyche. We don't know what caused the conflict, but we do know Paul stepped into the middle of the fracas and said, "Let's end this. Let's bring God's peace to this situation." Here's what he wrote:

> I implore Euodia and I implore Syntyche to be of the same mind in the Lord. And I urge you also, true companion, help these women who labored with me in the gospel, with Clement also, and the rest of my fellow workers, whose names are in the Book of Life. Rejoice in the Lord always.

> Again I will say, rejoice! Let your gentleness be known to all
> men. The Lord is at hand (Philippians 4:2-5).

I see four potent principles in these verses that can help leaders to work with their people to deal successfully with the conflicts that inevitably occur in every organization.

1. Be of the Same Mind

Paul tells these women (and us), "Get to the place where you're of the same mind. Get your relationship right so that you can rejoice instead of grouse. Never forget that love and joy are eternally linked."

Whenever you get involved in conflict resolution, endeavor to find at least one point of agreement. God calls His people to contend without being contentious, to disagree without being disagreeable, and to confront without being abusive. When we confront, we are to "speak the truth in love" (Ephesians 4:15 NLT).

When peace reigns in your heart, you naturally look for points of agreement. But if conflict rages in your heart, you will look for points of difference.

Endeavor to find at least one point of agreement and be of the same mind about that one point.

2. Commit to Constant Reasonableness

Have you ever met someone who refused to reason with you? God help the person of whom it is said, "You cannot discuss anything with that jerk!" All of us probably have met such people—or been such people ourselves.

Paul took a different approach. What the apostle knew of God and what he had experienced in his life prompted him to commit to constant reasonableness. He wrote, "Let your moderation be known" (Philippians 4:5 KJV).

Moderation here means "reasonableness." Paul exhorted his friends to avoid any inflexible attitude that refused to bend or yield to another's opinion. Some translate this word "big heartedness." The word also can be rendered "graciousness," "forbearance," "yieldedness," "kindness," "consideration," "charitableness," "mildness," even "generosity." Notice that this single word incorporates all of the fruit of the Spirit. We could sum up all of Galatians 5:22-23 with one word: moderation.

My favorite translation of this verse goes, "Do not be unduly rigorous." Paul is saying to these warring women, "Do not get to the place where you cannot yield." I guarantee you that any marriage in which the partners refuse to yield will end up in divorce court.

In many disputes over the years, I have felt sure I was right. But I would rather be a Christian than to be unfailingly right. "What do you mean by that?" someone asks. Some leaders would rather be right than be Christian. It's a wonderful day under God when you don't have to be right!

There's a story about a woman who went deer hunting for the first time in her life. She had never even shot a rifle. But one day, she asked to go hunting with her husband and he reluctantly agreed. After a long time of waiting, she whispered to her husband, "Hold still, hold still! I see a deer. I can't believe it!" And she shot the animal.

She sprinted over to where the creature had fallen, and there she found a man, crying.

"I shot a deer, I shot a deer!" she exclaimed.

"Ma'am," the man said, "that's not a deer."

"It *is* a deer," she insisted. "That right *there* is a *deer*."

"Well, if it is," the man replied, "please let me get my saddle off him."

You may be the leader, but you don't always have to be right. All of us, leaders in particular, can become unduly rigorous. Instead, let's show big heartedness in dealing with our people. It's a great way to lay a foundation for resolving conflict. Paul would tell us, "Don't get carried away by an obsession about unimportant matters, to the point of fighting over nonessentials."

We know these two women feuded over nonessentials, because the Holy Spirit of God would never inspire the apostle to tell them to be of the same mind if even one of them believed something contrary to His Word. Had one of these women denied the deity of Christ, for example, Paul wouldn't say, "Be of the same mind," but rather, "Tell her to get her mind straight. She needs to repent." Repentance refers to a change of mind. So, we know these two women had a conflict over some nonessential issue.

Do you know that most of the things we fight over are nonessentials? We have some relationship that didn't turn out the way we had hoped. Conflict erupts and we lose our joy. We feel unsettled and great discontent fills our hearts because we insist on being right. When we refuse to yield in a relationship so that God might be glorified, we're really saying that we're smarter than God. No wonder Paul told Euodia and Syntyche, "Practice some moderation here." He would tell us the same thing.

3. Have a Willingness to Yield

Paul went a step farther. He said to his friends, "Let your graciousness be known *to everyone*" (verse 5 HCSB). You aren't genuinely gracious if you're unwilling to let everybody know it. Your people need to see that you have earned a reputation for moderation, for big heartedness. And one of the ways they know it is by hearing you own up to your faults when you get into conflicts.

How far should your confession go? Don't go into some secret place and say, "Um, by the way, I guess I sinned against you and have been talking about you behind your back. Please forgive me." No, tell everybody to whom you slandered that person. Your confession should be as broad as your offence.

The word *known* refers to knowledge gained by experience. Paul was saying, "I've been there. I'm not talking to you about something I've never dealt with. I haven't found a rule book and put my finger on rule number two, the one you broke. I've broken this rule myself. I want to find this kind of moderation in my own life, and I want everyone to know it."

4. Remember God's Presence

Paul ends his short passage on conflict resolution by reminding his readers, "The Lord is at hand" (verse 5). Wherever believers go, God is present. The Lord is near.

It's much harder to keep a conflict sizzling when you remember that God is present. Even in our troubles, Jesus is near. In fact, He lives in our hearts—and how can He get closer than that?

Psalm 119:151 says, "You are near, O LORD, and all your commandments are true." I often come to my heavenly Father, aware of some conflict in my heart. I talk to Him about it. And I remember the promise of James 4:8: "Draw near to God and He will draw near to you." When I draw near to God, He does not always improve the circumstances of my conflict, but I've never gone to the place of prayer where He did not change *me* and make *me* better. And in my restored position, I am far better able to address the conflict, whatever it may be.

If It Helps, Use It

It's no biblical secret that human beings get into conflicts with one another or that the proper handling of conflict can lead to many positive outcomes. In his book, *Conflict Resolution: Theory, Research, and Practice*, James A. Schellenberg wrote, "Conflict is so fully a part of all forms of society that we should appreciate its importance—for stimulating new thoughts, for promoting social change, for defining our group relationships, for helping us form our own sense of personal identity, and for many other things we take for granted in our everyday lives."[44]

A journal article about organizational culture noted, "The vision needed in organisations is that conflict can be healthy when undertaken with the right intention and when implemented in a culture that values the positive aspects of conflict."[45]

A mountain of information exists in secular literature about conflict management and resolution. I find much of this information helpful and practical, even though the authors often write from worldviews far distant from my own. Jeremy Pollack, for example, published a book titled *Conflict Resolution Playbook*. Despite the lack of any discernible Christian influence, Pollack offers a lot of good, practical counsel on how to deal effectively with conflict. I repeat, however, that absent a Christian worldview and biblical context, any counsel offered, as good as it may be, is only capable of moving the needle a bit. Without the Spirit of the living God transforming human hearts, the best we can hope for is a tad of improvement in our relationships.

Pollack urges his readers to get "a deeper appreciation for the basic human needs that drive conflict when unfulfilled" and endeavors to give them "a set of basic communication skills that are critical for conflict resolution."[46] To better understand how to resolve conflict, he advises us to "gain a better understanding of conflict itself, including where it comes from, why it cuts so deep, and how it can be valuable."[47]

Pollack defines a "peaceful" relationship as "one that satisfies our innate desire for trust" and says that "with trust comes peace, and with distrust comes avoidance and/or conflict." In his system, trust implies that one's "core needs" are supported, while distrust implies that those core needs are threatened. Conflict, then, occurs with "the existence or perception of an impediment to one's core needs, values, or goals."[48]

Pollack identifies six core psychological needs, including: identity (sense of self and purpose); safety (both physical and psychological); care (evidence of belonging); autonomy (the power to choose how to live); growth (the need to progress in life); and stimulation (through intrigue, challenge, entertainment, or interesting pursuits).[49]

In times of conflict, Pollack says we choose either to fight or to flee. Our emotions take over and we stop thinking rationally. While we can't prevent such a reaction, he says we can learn to manage it through various techniques (breathing, repeating mantras, self-soothing).

The crucial way to resolve conflict, Pollack says, is to build trust between people so that they will not "sabotage" meeting one another's needs.[50] While conflict resolution is ideal, conflict management is often more attainable, as it minimizes the negative effects of conflict.

Conflict can be useful, Pollack says, for it may lead to several benefits:

- Healthy debates about a problem can lead to more informed solutions.

- Arguments can bring to the surface underlying issues, resulting in greater mutual understanding and care.

- Conflict can lead to positive changes in the organization (e.g., establishing better operating procedures).

- Conflicts can clarify what does and doesn't work in an individual's life, creating a stronger sense of identity and confidence.[51]

The key, according to Pollack, is figuring out which core need is driving the conflict. Once you identify that core need (or needs), you can devise an appropriate response.

What Controls Your Hand?

Before he became king, David had a frightening, long-lasting conflict with Saul, the first king of Israel. For years, Saul tried to murder David. On two separate occasions, David had the chance to kill Saul before Saul could do the same to him. Why did David refuse to strike down Saul when he had the chance, even when his friends and associates urged him to do so?

David refused to kill his violent antagonist because he knew that Saul was the king, the Lord's anointed, regardless of how wicked Saul had become. It was God's role to remove Saul, not David's. And so, when David twice had the opportunity to take Saul out, he refused.

Let me give you one final principle: Because the peace of God controlled David's heart, the power of God controlled David's hand. And the same is true for you.

When the peace of God controls your heart, the power of God will control your hand.

11

Committed to Being Full *and* Content

A successful businessman friend of mine, Josh Dorminy, volunteered for thirteen years in various key positions at my former church. He also led our Timothy+Barnabas ministry for five years. At that time, he worked as a broker and managing member of a commercial real estate firm. One day I got a call from someone I didn't know.

"Can I come down and see you?" the man asked.

Who is this? I wondered. "Please tell me what you'd like to talk about," I said.

"I work for Coca-Cola," the man replied, identifying himself as Frank Harrison, the chairman and CEO of Coca-Cola Consolidated, the largest bottler of Coca-Cola in the United States. He said he wanted to talk to me about partnering in some pastor training in Kenya. He could fly down to Atlanta from Charlotte, North Carolina, he said, where his firm's corporate headquarters are located. I agreed and we set up an hour meeting.

Once Frank arrived in his private plane, my schedule quickly got busted. Frank and I spent four enjoyable hours together, becoming friends in the process, as Frank explained the work in Kenya and how he hoped I might be able to partner with him. We agreed to see how the partnership might work, and after Frank left, I brought in Josh to help set up the initiative and take care of all the details.

Although the pastor training in Kenya went exceptionally well, one thing in particular stood out to Frank: Josh's impressive ability to organize the whole event. He later told me that he believed Josh could help him decide how to effectively give away a pile of money. "I could really use Josh's assistance with a big corporate challenge," he said.

"The ultimate corporate giver we've found so far in the United States is Chick-fil-A," Frank continued, referring to the restaurant chain owned by the Cathy family, strong Christians. "They're leading the way, and so we're praying that God would help us to give even more than we have." Frank hoped he could talk to Josh about the challenge and I enthusiastically endorsed the idea. Today, Josh serves as Senior VP and Assistant to Frank at Coca-Cola Consolidated.

While soft drinks don't generally get me excited, perhaps you can better understand my enthusiasm when you read the mission statement of Frank's company: "Our Purpose is to honor God in all we do, serve others, pursue excellence and grow profitably."[52] How encouraging that the CEO of the largest bottler of Coca-Cola in the United States would say he had been challenged to expand his charitable work because of the work of another Christian! Frank is the kind of Christian leader I'd call "full," a man who wants to maximize the fullness God has given him.

What Does It Mean to Be Full?

Last night, I slept in a comfortable bed with clean sheets, complete with a warm blanket and a soft pillow. I had a sturdy roof over my head and strong walls around me that kept me safe from outside threats.

I don't generally eat much for breakfast, but come lunchtime I'll be ready, and I assure you that there will be more on the table than I can consume.

I have plenty of clothes, so I don't have to worry about going around naked this week.

My income (and the incomes of the vast majority of those of us who live in the US) makes us better off financially than most of the world's population.

By all worldly measurements, I'm "full." I have more than I need to live. And beyond such physical categories, God has given me access to countless areas of spiritual fullness as well, including:

- Joy (John 15:11; 16:24; Acts 2:28; 1 John 1:4)

- Faith, wisdom, and power (Acts 6:3,5,8; 11:24)

- Good works (Acts 9:36)

- Goodness (Romans 15:14)

- Blessing (Romans 15:29)

- Spiritual understanding (Colossians 2:2)

- Hope (Hebrews 6:11)

- Mercy and good fruits (James 3:17)

- Glory (1 Peter 1:8)

Finally, when I keep in step with Jesus, I'm also "full of the Holy Spirit" (Ephesians 5:18; see Acts 2:4; 4:8; 4:31; 6:3,5; 7:55; 11:24; 13:52, etc.), which deepens and enriches and enhances all these other areas of fullness. I am a blessed man!

If you are a Christian leader, chances are that you are "full" in these same ways. God has given you and me more than we need to live physically and far more than we deserve spiritually. In that sense, we have a great deal in common with the apostle Paul, who wrote: "Not that I speak in regard to need, for I have learned in whatever state I am, to be content: I know how to be abased, and I know how to abound. Everywhere and in all things I have learned both to be full and to be hungry, both to abound and to suffer need" (Philippians 4:11-12).

Like Paul, I'm full. But do you know there's a problem with being full, especially if you're a leader? Let me help you picture the challenge.

Go grab a decent-sized mug. Once you have it, fill it to the brim with water. Then try walking back to this book without spilling any of it.

Do you see the problem? It's hard to balance the cup when it's full. It's far more difficult to navigate with a full cup than with a half-full cup—and the same problem is true of your life and mine.

It's good to have a full life. It's a blessing. The best leaders are always full leaders. Have you ever tried to work with a leader who seemed only half-full? Few of us call it a pleasant experience.

Fullness, however, presents its own difficulties. And it might surprise you to hear about one of the most common problems related to fullness. I believe I can name the chief trouble in one word: contentment.

Are You Full *and* Content?

It may seem counterintuitive, but leaders who are full often struggle with contentment. In fact, times of prosperity and abundance can lead to the toughest temptations we face as leaders. The failure to properly handle fullness can pull our hearts away from God.

Leaders who gain material wealth through their hard work often feel compelled to gain even more, rather than learning how to live contentedly. It is often very difficult for a leader in a prosperous condition to live as though Jesus Christ is truly enough. Every Christian leader needs to learn a crucial lesson: Contentment is not the fulfillment of what you want, but rather a full appreciation for how much you already have.

Imagine being able to enjoy whatever you find most gratifying, with unbounded energy and passion, forever. Does that sound good? It does to me! So, how do we arrive at such a joyful destination?

Here's the secret: If God's pleasure in His Son becomes our pleasure as leaders, then the object of our greatest pleasure will be Jesus—and Jesus is an inexhaustible source of satisfaction, delight, and fulfillment. He will never become boring or disappointing or frustrating.

We may enjoy a great many things here on earth, but none of them last. Have you ever excitedly looked forward to some special trip, and while you really enjoyed the experience, you could hardly wait to get back home? Did you ever pull up into your driveway after a much-anticipated vacation, sigh, and say, "There's no place like home"? And yet, before you left, you couldn't wait to get there. You thought, *I've never been to this place. This is going to be* incredible! And you did enjoy it…just not as much as you thought you would. It didn't turn out to be everything you had made it out to be.

In this life, we lack the ability to enjoy almost anything with unbounded energy and passion forever. Why is that? Three things stand in the way of our complete contentment in this world.

1. Nothing has an intrinsic worth great enough to meet the deepest longings of our heart.

This world is not our home. While nobody will go on living here, everybody will go on living somewhere. C.S. Lewis wrote in *The Joyful Christian*, "Aim at Heaven and you will get Earth 'thrown in': aim at Earth and you will get neither."[53]

2. We lack the strength to savor the best treasures to their maximum potential.

Imagine that you go on a date with your spouse or schedule a special time with your closest friend. Before you go, you think, *I'm going to savor this for all it's worth!* And you do...until you find yourself tempted to respond to or occupy yourself with your smartphone.

3. Our joy here comes to an end.

I'm a very happily married man. Janet and I once went away for three days, just to rest and enjoy one another. After we returned home, I called her from work the next morning, just to tell her how much I enjoyed our trip. "Gosh, in just a few days we'll experience forty-six years of being married," I said. "I can't believe how much I still enjoy being with you!" I meant every word, but in this world, nothing lasts, not even our most cherished relationships.

Not long afterward, I said to Janet in a sweet moment, "I *love* being married to you! I'm glad we're saved. We're going to be together forever!"

"No," Janet immediately answered, "the Bible says there's no marrying or giving in marriage in heaven. You won't be my husband in heaven."

Her reply ticked me off. "You may not be married to me in heaven," I declared, "but you can't date anybody else."

Nothing here lasts. That relationship you've been looking for all your life? It doesn't last. That leadership post you've wanted for years? It doesn't last. Nothing of this world lasts.

Still, we can find lasting contentment. As spiritually mature leaders, we can model contentment to our peers, colleagues, employees, and associates. We can become examples of contentment as long as we remember that contentment is not the fulfillment of what we want, but a full appreciation for how much we already have.

Be careful about developing an entitlement attitude, even when you've worked hard in your leadership to achieve. You're wrong if you believe that everything you have is yours. Last time I checked, you're a steward of everything entrusted to you, not the owner of anything you currently have.

Your soul is trying to go somewhere special. You sense that, don't you? You may believe that the next thing you purchase, the next place you go, the next executive position you get, will be all you've been grasping for. But if you choose that route, you'll only end up with another fistful of wind (see Ecclesiastes 2:11).

It's time to start seeing what God might want you to do with what you already have. It's time to start learning how to be content, so that you can become a better leader than ever before.

Learn to Be Content

Even the apostle Paul, one of the greatest leaders in history, said he had to learn how to be content. Over time, Paul learned to model contentment when he was full and when he was hungry, when he "abounded" and when he lacked basic needs (see Philippians 4:12). As he walked with Christ through the years, he learned how to model for others glad obedience to God's command: "Let your conduct be without covetousness; be content with such things as you have" (Hebrews 13:5).

When the apostle said he "learned" to be content, he used a Greek term that means "to be initiated into a secret." It means that he reached that stage through trial and testing. Both poverty and prosperity initiated Paul into this wonderful secret of contentment.

In ancient times, Greek mystery religions used the word "contentment" to describe people who had worked their way up through various lower levels and had finally been admitted into full possession of the mystery. By using this term, Paul was saying, in essence, "I have made my way up through many degrees of progression. I am no slave to the things of this world, whether its comforts or its discomforts. Finally, I've reached maturity. I know the secret. Circumstances can never again touch me." Paul had learned this lesson, bit by bit, test by test, circumstance by circumstance. He had persevered through the lower degrees until, at last, he graduated and the secret was his.

Contentment does not come easily! The apostle purchased it at the price of exacting discipline. We know he learned the lesson well, because when he wrote the letter of Philippians (in which he says he learned contentment), he was sitting in a Roman prison. It had been about thirty years since he had first come to faith in Jesus. As he sat in jail, this amazing leader said, "I have all and abound. I am full, having received from Epaphroditus the things sent from you, a sweet-smelling aroma, an acceptable sacrifice, well pleasing to God" (Philippians 4:18). Did you notice how he described himself? "Full." He sat in jail, chained, and yet said, "I have all and abound." Amazing!

The Greek term translated *acceptable* was used when worshipers brought an animal to the temple for sacrifice. Paul called such a sacrifice "well pleasing" to God. Have you come to the place of spiritual maturity that you believe, when the Holy Spirit of God speaks to your heart and you obey Him, that you can take care of others because you're "full" and they are in great need? That is, after all, what mature Christian leaders do. It's also why Paul could then immediately write, "My God shall provide all your need according to His riches in glory by Christ Jesus" (verse 19). The Greek term translated *according to* means "out of a supply that is never depleted." When God meets a need, regardless of its size, He is no more impoverished than before He met the need. His resources are inexhaustible. Paul was saying to the Philippians (who were poor, by the way) that since they had been faithful and well-pleasing to God with what they had given him, God would supply all of their needs "according to His riches in glory."

When you're full, don't just sit around and enjoy that fullness for yourself. When you're full, be ready to give and willing to share. Don't ever tell someone, "My God shall supply all your needs," unless you've already allowed God to use you to supply another's needs. Too many of us like to quote Philippians 4:19 when we've done diddly-squat to help anyone.

I thank God for those in my life who were full but who knew their blessings weren't just for them. I thank God for those who, instead of holding their full cup and seeing if they could balance it without spilling, sensed the need to pour it out.

If today your belly is full, give away some of your fullness to fill someone else's belly. Too many leaders, the more they make, the more they keep. But giving it away is so much more fun. God wants to provide our needs, but He doesn't want us to live lavishly when our resources might be better used to promote His work throughout the world.

I have a remedy for you if your life is full: Pour out some of that full-ness. Your life will be far easier to balance when you learn to give. I still remember a great one-liner that the late financial advisor Ron Blue deliv-ered in a meeting I attended: "As God blesses you, the only antidote to materialism is generous giving."

Why Has God Blessed You?

If God has really blessed you, understand that He has a reason for doing so. Too many leaders try to find that purpose in money, posses-sions, power, prestige, relationships, jobs, or freedom from difficulty. Jer-emiah Burroughs wrote several centuries ago, "Christian contentment is that sweet, inward, quiet, gracious frame of spirit, which freely submits to and delights in God's wise and fatherly disposal in every condition."[54] In our own era, pastor and theologian John MacArthur has said, "Con-tentment is a highly prized, but elusive virtue."[55] Contentment depends on trusting God's sovereign, loving, purposeful providence. This means that God's richest blessing is not necessarily in attainment, but in contentment.

Do you think you would be happier if you just got more? Money doesn't get you to contentment; godliness does. So Paul wrote that "god-liness with contentment is great gain" (1 Timothy 6:6).

Not long ago I ran into an acquaintance from church whose business has really taken off. "I haven't seen you lately at church," I said to him.

"Nah," he stammered, "nah, uh, I haven't been much this year."

"Really?"

"Yeah, man, just pray for me. God is really blessing. I mean, He's just so blessing the business, it's kind of hard to get to church." What could I say?

It's often difficult for someone in a prosperous condition to live as though Christ is enough. I have met some leaders who seem to spend hours studying the Bible just to see if they can justify how cheap they can be. When I find leaders who are cheerful in their giving, it does something for my soul. What if we really understood how generosity has the capac-ity to transform us as leaders?

What if we defined "rich" or "wealthy" by how much we gave away, rather than by how much we make? What if we measured our wealth not by how much we have on the bottom line, but by how much we helped others with our resources? What if we considered Jesus as worthy of at least a good chunk of all our earthly possessions, because He has given us everything? I wonder if America doesn't believe it needs Jesus, because it doesn't see many Christian leaders who live dependent on Him? God asks us to be conveyer belts of His riches, not reservoirs.

Honey, Sweet but Sticky

Have you ever heard someone say, "I have a sweet job, a honey job"? The Bible speaks a lot about honey. My current favorite verse is Proverbs 25:16, which says, "Have you found honey? Eat only as much as you need, lest you be filled with it and vomit." Anytime you see that four-letter word in Scripture *lest*, it signals a warning. Here, the warning is "lest you be filled." That means, you're full. And if you eat too much of that fullness, too much of that honey, you will throw up.

Don't get me wrong: God gives you that honey. It's both sweet and delicious. But God didn't give you all of that honey just so you could eat it all by yourself. It's too sweet of a substance, too good of a commodity, to keep for yourself. You are to share that honey with others who need it.

The Johnny Hunt version of this verse might read, "Make a moderate use of all the enjoyments God gives you, but if you overindulge in worldly pleasures, you'll pay a stiff price." God warns against indulging in too much of a good thing. The Bible doesn't prohibit pleasure; it prohibits excess indulgence of pleasure. There is a point at which pleasure becomes pain. If pleasure is to remain pleasant, it must be enjoyed moderately and intermittently.

Scripture therefore lands upon the principle of benevolence: Enough for us, abundance for others (see 2 Corinthians 8:14; 9:11). Jeremiah Burroughs wrote, "It is the abundance of outward prosperity that is the undoing of most men."[56] Are Christian leaders exempt from such undoing? Hardly. Any quick Internet search will reveal name after name and tell story after story of this or that business leader, organizational head, ministry founder, or governmental office holder—all of them claiming to belong to Christ—who crashed and burned when they chased after riches, indulged in constant pleasures, and gorged themselves on honey.

There is a far better way.

Are You Rich Toward God?

A friend once wrote me a note in which he said, "Prosperity is a blessing from God. His Word makes that clear, but He also makes it clear that prosperity can kill you. Abundance brings with it the very real danger that we will forget God, the true source of it all."

Jesus once made practically the same point in Luke 12 when an unnamed crowd member shouted out, "Teacher, tell my brother to divide the inheritance with me." Jesus answered him, "Man, who made me a judge or an arbitrator over you?" Our Lord then turned to the crowd and said, "Take heed and beware of covetousness, for one's life does not consist in the abundance of things he possesses." He wove a story about a wealthy farmer who, instead of sharing his riches with those in need, decided to build bigger barns and larger warehouses where he could store his super-abundant crops.

The businessman in Jesus' story had a cup filled to the brim. To keep from spilling its contents, and in order to keep everything in the cup for himself, he decided to find some bigger cups. The cup is never big enough, you see. Never.

That wealthy man, probably a leader in his community, lived as though God didn't exist. But one day God spoke to the man, calling him a "fool." The world would have called this executive anything other than a fool. It would have said, "This dude is savvy," "This guy has a great business mind," "This man is blessed." But God said to him, "Fool! This night your soul will be required of you; then whose will those things be which you have provided?" (Luke 12:13-20).

That's chilling enough, but Jesus added a final, sobering comment: "So is he who lays up treasure for himself, and is not rich toward God" (verse 21).

Are you rich toward God? That is something money can't buy and death can't steal. Being rich toward God is the opposite of laying up earthly treasures for yourself. It's the opposite of treating the self as though it were made for things and not for God. It's the opposite of acting as if life consists in the abundance of possessions and not in the super-abundance of knowing God. Being rich toward God is your heart being drawn toward the Lord as your most precious treasure. Being rich toward God is having no treasure greater than Jesus.

Where do your riches lie? Do they lie in a dynamic relationship with God, who gives you an abundant, joyful life, regardless of how many years you might have left on this earth? Is He your most precious treasure? The best reward of the Christian life is not going to heaven, passing through its pearly gates or walking on its golden streets. The best reward of the Christian life is Jesus Himself. Being rich toward God means counting God as greater wealth than anything on earth. It means using your earthly riches to show how much you value God. Proverbs 11:24 says, "There is one who scatters, yet increases more; and there is one who withholds more than is right, but it leads to poverty." Do we withhold more than is right for a leader who wants to be godly, especially those of us with full cups?

Someone once asked me, "What if God chose a week or a month or a year to give you back ten times what you had given Him? How would that work out for you?" All of us naturally tend to withhold more than is right. In our inherited-from-Adam fallen state, we tend to keep, hold, and hoard more than we give, release, and scatter. Jesus tells us that to whom much is given, much will be required (Luke 12:48). All of us will stand one day before almighty God to give an account of what we've done with whatever He has given us.

If your life were to end today, would your greatest treasure stay down here or be waiting for you up there? Where is your greater treasure, here or beyond here?

American Christians tend to say, "When someone dies as a Christian, he or she departs to be with the Lord." Kenyans use a very different terminology. They say the believer has arrived, rather than departed. When the time comes for you to depart this world, will you depart from your treasure, or will you arrive at your treasure? What have you laid up on the other side? And yes, you *can* send it on ahead.

If I were to die today, I'd like to think that you would hear my wife say, "I'm going to miss my husband, but he lived for Jesus, valued Him above all, and right now he's better off than I am." I hope that I would be remembered as a leader who took seriously the life message of Paul when he wrote, "For to me, to live is Christ, and to die is gain" (Philippians 1:21).

Seven Principles About Being Both Full *and* Content

Some of us retire too early. We think, *I can't wait to get out of the work-force.* After about six months, however, we go stir crazy. And then we begin to think, *What else can I do?*

Instead, why don't we consider what we can do, starting right now? If your sea of honey is difficult to navigate safely, then how can you build some canals to channel some of that honey to otherwise dry places? In other words, if you are full, then how can you make sure you don't waste what God has put in your cup by needlessly spilling it as you walk through life? As a leader, how can you become an example to those you lead by giving them a model of Paul's coaching?

> Our desire is not that others might be relieved while you are hard pressed, but that there might be equality. At the present time your plenty will supply what they need, so that in turn their plenty will supply what you need. The goal is equality, as it is written: "The one who gathered much did not have too much, and the one who gathered little did not have too little" (2 Corinthians 8:13-15 NIV).

It's one thing to be full; it's another to be content at the same time. I offer the following seven tips to help you navigate the difficulty.

1. You can learn to be full, as Paul did.

You'll know you have learned to be full when you can answer the question, "How much is enough for me?" If you never determine how much is enough for you, you will never make significant gifts to others or to kingdom work, because you'll always "need" whatever you have, regardless of how much you actually own.

2. You have learned to be full when you can discern the best use of what you have.

How can you best distribute the fullness God has given you? And just for the record, if you desire to be who God wants you to be, and you press into Jesus, God will use you to challenge others in amazing ways that you never dreamed possible.

3. You have learned to be full when you can avoid the evils of the temptations that typically accompany fullness.

Proverbs 1:32 says very bluntly, "The prosperity of fools shall destroy them" (KJV). Prosperity has done more harm to many leaders than adversity ever could.

*4. You have learned to be full when what you have makes you a
good servant, not a miserable slave.*

Mature believers may have many possessions, but none of those possessions ever have them. If you have a hard time letting go of what you have, it's because your possessions have a hold on you.

*5. You have learned to be full when you allow your fullness to lead
you to the source of your fullness.*

You're full because God has made you full. And you become content when you recognize the source of your fullness, and that He owns everything you have.

*6. You have learned to be full when you spread out your fullness and
offer it to God for His use.*

As I write, I'm sixty-nine years old. In my mid to late thirties, I made up my mind to get debt-free so I could go anywhere God called me to go. That decision has given me far more choices and much greater freedom.

*7. You have learned to be full when you know your heart in the midst
of your abundance.*

I know what you're thinking: *No one can know his own heart.* While you may not be able to know it fully, you can know something about it. If you have trouble giving, for example, you can know that you have a heart problem.

One of the greatest joys of my life is to be able to bless others because God has been good to Janet and me. I'm a honey man. I'm full. And I'm content. God has given me gallons of honey, and I've discovered that if we'll just share that honey with those who desperately need it, we'll be far richer for it—and so will others.

12

Determined to Finish Well

The Lord gave me a wake-up call about a dozen years ago. Any time you hear the C word in the doctor's office, it doesn't feel right. Prostate cancer? *Me?* You learn to give thanks in it, but not for it. I thank the Lord that most men catch it in time.

But not everyone does.

Not long ago, we buried one of my friends, a great guy. He was my age and had the same kind of cancer as me at about the same time; he just approached treatment differently than I did. "What are you going to do, Pastor Johnny?" he asked.

"They told me they can treat it in me or take it out," I replied. "I told them, 'Take it out.'" And then I asked him, "What are you going to do?"

"I'm going to just watch mine," he replied.

I thought, *Watch cancer grow?* In the medical community, it's often called "watchful waiting" or "active surveillance." That's the strategy my friend chose. He watched it and waited.

After getting several good checkups he got a little sure of himself and missed some of the watching. Then one day he went in to see his doctor and they discovered the cancer had grown outside of the prostate, spreading into his bones. We had the funeral not long afterward.

This tragic episode made me think: *If I were to die today, what have I tried to accomplish with my life?* The question is not merely what did I accomplish with my life, but what did I hope to accomplish? Every Christian leader should ask this crucial question.

What life goals would you like to accomplish before you die? Have you ever thought about writing them out? It takes some time to do so; you can't finish it in fifteen minutes over a break. Also, don't write out your life goals in ink or print them out and put them in a frame—at least, not until after you've had a couple of months to meditate on them. They will almost certainly change from your initial answers. Let them marinate. Ponder what you really want to accomplish with your life, and then go from there.

I'm not talking here about a vision for your organization, but a vision for your life. What would you like to do with the days you have left? How can some specific goals based on your life vision help you to finish strong? Make those goals personal. Just as David could not fight in Saul's armor (1 Samuel 17:38-39), so you cannot lead effectively with personal goals handed to you by somebody else. Creating your own personal goals also keeps you from blaming others.

The Seven Priorities of My Life

I have identified seven priorities for my life. All of them are subject to change, depending on what God may call me to do in the future; but for now, these seven priorities help me to order my life and lead effectively.

1. I want to better equip the church in the crucial areas of evangelism and leadership.

After thirty-three years of pastoring the First Baptist Church of Woodstock, I resigned my position there in late 2018 and at the beginning of 2019 began full-time work as the Senior VP of Evangelism and Leadership at the North American Mission Board of the Southern Baptist Convention. That's the greatest platform I have right now, with the potential of touching hundreds of thousands of lives all over the world.

I always thought I'd retire at Woodstock, but when God unexpectedly opened this exciting new door, in time I saw how I could have a bigger impact for Jesus in my latter years than ever before. I believe that building a culture of evangelism in the church begins with the pastor. I also believe that pastors who know how to lead effectively, and who train their people in evangelism, can have an outsized influence on our world. That's why I made the switch—although I don't mind telling you, it felt agonizing to leave Woodstock. But when you believe God has called you somewhere, you go.

2. I want to mentor young men whom God has called to preach the gospel.

I've personally mentored around fifty such young men, the vast majority of whom have fanned out over the world to serve the Lord. It concerns me that many of those who go to seminary don't end up in a church, and far fewer of them spend their entire careers serving in a church. I want to continuing mentoring these godly young men so long as I can do so.

3. I want to encourage and train those who are presently pastors.

When I left Woodstock, I offered to give the Timothy+Barnabas ministry to NAMB; it then created the Timothy+Barnabas Institute. What we used to do on a smaller scale for pastors located mostly in the South, we are doing on a larger scale for pastors around the country. We are currently training 200 young pastors in groups of about ten. These pastors meet twice a year at NAMB for mentoring by veteran pastors, staying with those mentors for two years.

Not long ago, God let me stand elbow to elbow with 3,770 leaders, over twelve months, to encourage them in their work and to give them tools to be more effective. How could I do that with everything else I'm doing? It's a priority.

I urge you to find a way to train young, high potential leaders. Invest in the future by mentoring gifted and godly young men and women.

4. I want to touch poverty.

Since I came out of poverty, I want to give back in that area. We have a special needs granddaughter, Hope, who has cerebral palsy. One day, God put it in my heart to build a medical clinic, named after Hope, in the poorest country in the Western Hemisphere. When the facility opened, we flew our whole family to Haiti to dedicate the Hope Center.

I never walk in that clinic without seeing Hope's picture on the wall. I cannot go in there without crying. Haitians would survive a lot of the things that now kill them if they just had the right pills. We got them some of those pills, because I want to touch poverty.

My wife and I support three Haitian children. Our support gives them something to eat, maybe the only meal they get all day. We clothe them in neat khaki pants and cute yellow checkered shirts. We buy the material and let Haitians themselves make the clothing, so they can earn a wage. We want to bless the nation's economy.

We dig a well for every church we plant, and guess who the village elder is? It's the pastor. The water is kept under lock and key to protect its purity, and the people come to the pastor to get their water. While the well serves the church, the church also runs a school. The day we open these schools, they're full. I started supporting my first Haitian child about a decade ago. We saw her on the street, stopped, and asked our host, "Who's this little girl?" He speaks Creole and learned her name was Rose.

"Is Rose in the school?" we asked. She's as cute as could be.

"No," he replied." Once we got Rose in school, we discovered she had two brothers who also wanted to go to school. Rose got saved in school and I later baptized her. I may be one of the first child sponsors to baptize his own sponsored child! Now, Rose has a chance. How absolutely glorious!

Many of these kids have serious potential, and so the church sends them to college. In the past thirty-five years, some of these children have grown up to become Christian lawyers and teachers and other professionals, and many of them have returned to help the school. Isn't that called making disciples?

Since we want to touch poverty, one day we thought, *Wouldn't it be cool if we could feed all of the kids in those schools?* How many would that be? About 9,000?

I called my friend Sonny Perdue, the former US Secretary of Agriculture from 2017-2021. "Sonny," I said, "I have a burden I'd like to share with you." I'd never asked him for anything, although he attended Woodstock for eight years. "Is there any way I could enlist you to feed children in Haiti?"

"Funny you'd ask that," he said. "Did you know that we were feeding thousands of hungry people in Haiti before the corrupt government came in and started selling what we gave them on the black market?"

"How about *now*, Sonny?" I pressed. "Did you know they have a better government now?"

"Yes, and we're ready to reengage them," he said. "What's your request?"

"Would you feed 9,000 schoolkids for me?"

That's stewardship of influence. My relationship with Sonny accomplished it. I can't feed 9,000 kids a day by myself, but if I make myself available for God to use the influence He has built into my life, maybe I can feed 9,000 Haitian kids a day.

Could it be that God wants to do so much more through you than you're believing Him for? What might God want to accomplish through you and your leadership?

5. I want to train college and seminary students.

When a college calls me to ask if I'll come and speak to its students, I make it a priority. I want to influence students with what I've learned over four decades of pastoring and leading. I also visit seminaries to teach, getting the ears of talented men and women in their twenties, thirties, and forties. At one seminary, the campus shuts down during my visit and students spend about six hours with me to discuss leadership. It's incredible, the largest single investment in the student body that the school has. I'm cheap to hire, I invest in students, and I give them gifts. What's not to like?

6. I want to plant churches.

I want to plant churches in underserved areas. About nineteen million people live in L.A. County, with just a handful of churches there, most of them attracting maybe twenty or twenty-five attenders each week. Montreal is 99.5 percent unevangelized—but we have four young preachers up there, each about thirty-five years old, who are averaging almost 2,000 in attendance. One night not long ago, they baptized fifty-five individuals, gave the gospel at the baptism, and sixty-five millennials came to faith in Jesus. I want to join a work like that!

Where do you see God at work in your area of interest? How could you join Him there? Be creative.

7. I want to model generosity.

I want to be known as a generous giver, especially since I came out of poverty.

Modeling generosity has really worked with my family, as all my children are very generous. My son-in-law is a fantastic giver and has been since his early thirties. He came to me one time and said, "When I dated your daughter, I saw you read your Bible and then put in a generous offering, on top of your tithe. I couldn't believe that you'd give away that much money! It spoke to me and got into my heart."

Those are my seven priorities. I don't know what yours might be, but I know you have some. These are the priorities that drive me. May I tell you how these seven priorities help shape what I do and how I spend my time—always, of course, with finishing well in mind?

A Lens to Narrow My Focus

When I get an invitation to do something or speak somewhere, my main question is, "Does it fall within my seven life priorities?" These priorities act like a powerful lens, enabling me to narrow my focus and decide what I'm going to do with the rest of my life.

As I've said, training leaders is one of my priorities. We trained 180 leaders in Ho Chi Minh City a few years ago, and later went back to establish the first evangelical seminary in that communist country. And guess who gave us approval to establish it? The Communist Party. We had planned to establish the school secretly and train leaders at night. As it turned out, that wasn't necessary.

Life is so glorious!

What can you do that no one else can do? Go ahead and do it. At my stage of maturity, I don't have to do certain things I used to do. I can think of nothing I won't do, but some things don't make the best use of my time, as perhaps they once did.

No one in my organization can be me. No one in your organization can be you. Populate your days, weeks, months, and years with the many things that only you can do.

Moses knew that his father-in-law Jethro spoke truth when he advised Moses to have his assigned judges "bring you every important case" (Exodus 18:22 HCSB). Moses couldn't be everything to everybody, but God had called him alone to handle the major matters of national leadership. Such a call requires focus, priority, and simplicity. God doesn't call you to do everything, not because you're too good to do these things, but because it takes all you have to do well the few things that only you can do.

The Traits of Those Who Have Finished Well

However long I live and serve, I want to finish with my testimony intact. Solomon says the day that you die is to be celebrated more than the day you were born (see Ecclesiastes 7:1-2). When someone passes, we call it a "celebration of life," a greater day than any birthday. But the only way that remains true is to die with one's testimony intact. We're all suspect until then.

What does it mean to lead yourself well? What does it mean to train yourself to be a godly leader? Let's consider some observable characteristics in the lives of God's people who finished well, so that when our life comes to an end, we will also be able to say, "We finished well." Chuck Lawless at Southeastern Baptist Theological Seminary suggested these categories for strong finishers to me many years ago.

1. They oozed humility.

On only one occasion did Jesus ever address a characteristic of His own life. Jesus never said, "I am love"; it was John who said, "God is love" (1 John 4:8). Jesus never said, "I am holy"; it was Peter who said, "God is holy, so you be holy" (1 Peter 1:15). But Jesus did say, "I am meek and lowly" (Matthew 11:29 KJV). He used the word for "humble" and told us, "Learn from Me" (verse 29).

How significant is it that Jesus, the greatest leader in history, spotlighted only one aspect of His personal character? I desire to be the best leader I can be. I think about it often. I don't want to be better than anyone else, I simply want to be the best me I can be.

I want to do a great work for God. I have only one life, and I refuse to spend it in a dogfight with those who claim to follow the same Bible I read and who will spend eternity in the same place I will. I'm dogmatic about leading because I really do believe I'll give an account to Christ for my leadership. We must not forget that our work in leadership is not about us, but about Jesus, which makes it really humbling.

2. They always knew they could be one step away from a fall.

"Hey, did you hear what so-and-so did?"

"I did."

"I tell you what, I've done some stupid things, but I'd never do *that*."

You might want to read your Bible before you say anything like that. First Corinthians 10:12 says, "Let him who thinks he stands take heed lest he fall." Since when did your stupid become less stupid than their stupid?

We tend to justify our sin because we think our sin is not as bad as their sin. Even though it was sin that nailed Jesus to the cross, we like to put sins in categories: "I've done some foolish things, but never would I do *that*."

The Proverbs are full of encouragement, but also warnings. Proverbs 6:26 tells us that sin not only pursues us but is setting an ambush for us. As a leader, you're a special target for the enemy. If he can bring you down, he will hurt a whole lot more people than just you. Honestly recognizing that you could fall should make you ever alert and prayerful for God's protection.

3. The thought of failing Jesus filled them with horror.

The godly men and women of the Bible who ended well all passionately loved Jesus. Serving Him meant more to them than anything else in life. I dread the thought of doing some wicked thing that would disqualify me from doing what I love doing. I do what I do not because I can't do anything else, but because I don't want to do anything else. For those biblical characters who finished strong, even the thought of dishonoring Christ broke their hearts.

4. They planned to finish well.

In my book *Demolishing Strongholds*, I tell the story of a man who took his own life. Some months before he committed suicide, he and I had a straightforward conversation about getting rid of habits or behaviors that would prevent him from finishing well. I'll never forget that evening.

I later wrote a sermon titled "The Devil Desires to Have You." I remember taking a sheet of paper and drawing a line down the middle. On one side I wrote down the benefits of living in a right relationship with the Lord, and on the other side I wrote down what it costs you if you decide not to.

Sometimes people say, "I didn't know what I had until I lost it." Maybe you ought to think about what it would cost beforehand. When you consider the staggering price tag, you might realize it's far too high a price to pay.

Great leaders don't end well by accident. At some point, they make a commitment to finish well each day, and soon the faithful days became faithful months, and then years, and then decades. And then they are gone.

5. They remained firmly committed to their families.

They adored their spouses and children, and everybody knew it. Early on in my ministry at Woodstock, Janet and I cut up a lot. One Sunday, she met with the sound people before a Sunday service and they gave her a microphone. I knew nothing about it.

In the middle of me telling some story about the two of us, she came walking up the aisle, carrying the microphone. I thought, *What are you up to?* She said into the mic, "How many of you would like to hear my side of the story?"

I expected to hear a few cheers from the women, but all the guys started whistling. Everyone wanted to hear from my wife. And I thought, *I'm in bad trouble and this is not going to end well.* By the time she finished, I was toast.

One person e-mailed me afterward and said, "I came to church to hear about the Lord, not about y'all." But I think our people ought to know that I'm committed to my spouse and that I love her and our children.

Leaders who end well adore their spouse and their children, and everybody knows it. For them, serving God means building their homes first. If you can be a good Christian at home, then you can be a good Christian anywhere. And if you're not a good Christian at home, then you can't be a good Christian anywhere.

If your spouse, children, and grandchildren can't believe the message of Jesus because of the way you live and act at home, then you're a total failure as a leader. You need to repent and get right with God, and then you can get back on the winning side. You're not right with God until you're right at home.

A godly leader should want to go both home and to work. I hate to think that some leaders get stuck in busy traffic every day, detesting the day's work ahead. If that's what they're doing, then they're going to the wrong job. Great leaders love going to work and love going home.

6. They made sure to stay in a mentoring relationship.

Every leader needs a mentor. Think in a fifty-mile radius of where you live. Who has retired as a godly leader, who lives around you and who you could visit? In recent years, I had two different mentors. One had a major surgery at age 93, but before the operation, he was still as sharp as a tack.

After the surgery, he lost nearly all his memory. I still miss what he used to pour into my life.

Every leader ought to have a mentor. These aren't always formal mentoring relationships, but they are very intentional. The leaders I've known who finish well always had somebody walking with them and encouraging them. Who is that person in your life? Who can you talk to about the issues in your life?

7. They lived in the Word and on their knees.

Whatever you do, learn to have an unhurried quiet time. I give myself enough time every day to read the Word, to think through and pray and spend quality time with God. I'm in no hurry. Henry Blackaby once invited me to accompany him as he taught a room full of Fortune 500 leaders. After he spoke about how to have a fresh encounter with God, he took questions. "Help me, Mr. Blackaby," one man said. "I already get up at 4 a.m. How am I going to have a quiet time in the morning?"

"Get up at three," Henry replied. "Is there another question?"

If the man had something important enough to get him up at 4 a.m., then he should ask himself, "Is Jesus a priority for me?" If He is, then either he's going to reevaluate how he spends his early morning hours, or he's going to find that extra time.

Successful Christian leaders live in the Word; I don't know how else to say it. When you read the Bible, God talks to you. And when you pray, you have an opportunity to respond and talk to God. Bible reading and prayer are not mere ritual but a vital piece of a dynamic relationship with God. I want deeper intimacy with God. My leadership suffers without it.

8. They were committed to integrity.

Integrity means that you're clean all the way through. Your yes means yes and your no, no. Never for long did anyone question the truthfulness of either the lives or the words of the Bible heroes who finished well. Why not? They were committed to integrity.

9. They evangelized regularly.

When David asked God to restore him after his sin with Bathsheba, he said, "Then I will teach transgressors Your ways" (Psalm 51:13). There ought to be times when Christian leaders share the gospel. Do you remember the last time you intentionally shared the gospel, as a leader? When did you last lead somebody to faith in Christ?

Great Christian leaders evangelize regularly. While this characteristic may surprise you, we can't deny what we see in the lives of godly Christian leaders who ended well. Godly leaders want others to know about Jesus, that their world is first and foremost about Him.

10. Their greatest ambition was to please Jesus.

An overriding ambition to please Jesus profoundly affects how all strong-finishing Christian leaders do their work. In all that I do, my core ambition is to please Jesus, and Jesus called me to lead. I'll give an account to Him one day of what I did with my call to lead and with the resources and gifts He gave me.

If you are a Christian leader, God has gifted you and called you to serve in that role. He didn't stick you out there on your own and say, "Go and do the best you can." He sovereignly and supernaturally gave you what you need. Take it and use it.

Claim the God-given freedom you need to be free to be who the Lord created you to be. You have only one life. No one has the right to take away your calling to lead.

I have not reached the place where I am because I'm a pushover for somebody trying to usurp the leadership role God has given to me. Most of the time, when a man tries to tell you what your organization should do, he is doing so because he hasn't found anyplace else where he can tell someone what to do. He's not in charge at work, his wife kicks his butt at home, and his children don't obey them, so he thinks, *Put me in that group, I'll take charge there.* Don't let him!

At one church I pastored, a guy said to me, "I don't want you to take it personally, but I'm going to vote against everything you bring to the deacons."

"You are?" I replied. "Why would you do that?"

"I just feel it's my calling," he replied. "I feel as though everybody tries to let the preacher have his way, and I believe the Lord placed me here to be the 'no.'"

Ultimately, we shouldn't concern ourselves with what people think about us or how they respond to us.

As a Christian leader one thing should be far more important for you than hearing the accolades and applause of men. After you cross the finish line, you want to hear from the Lord, "Well done, good and faithful servant; you were faithful over a few things, I will make you ruler over many things. Enter into the joy of your lord" (Matthew 25:21).

Finish Well!

I pray that you finish well. If you're married, talk over this crucial issue with your spouse. If you have children, speak to them about it. Discuss it with your colleagues at work or in your organization or church. Consider carefully with them how you can finish well as you work hard to nurture a healthy organization.

I want to be a healthy man, a healthy husband, a healthy father, a healthy grandfather. I want to be good friends with a lot of people, but I don't ever want to compromise the position of leadership to which God has called me. I don't want to disqualify myself and so get put on the shelf as someone the Lord can't use.

You have only so much life. You have only so much time. You have only so much treasure. How are you going to steward what God has entrusted to you? I believe that the judgment seat of Christ won't be about sin because our sin already has been judged at the cross. With all my heart, I believe that at the judgment seat of Christ we will give an account for what God has given us and invested in us. To whom much has been given, much will be required.

I wrote my first book, *Building Your Spiritual Resumé*, in 1999. Right at the beginning, I say, "If you ever lose your testimony, you'll be fortunate to live long enough to re-establish it."

Let's make a new commitment to one another, to our spouse and to the Lord Jesus, that more than anything else, we will commit to finishing well.

APPENDIXES

Appendix A

Survey Results

n June 2021 I sent out an eight-question survey asking about leadership to more than 5,000 leaders—pastors, business owners, organizational heads, etc. We created the survey to help focus the content of *How to Become a More Effective Leader* so that in the book I could take care to address the key problems facing Christian leaders today. In other words, I wanted to scratch where they itch.

We received responses from 255 leaders, for a response rate of about 5 percent—fairly typical for surveys of this type. Since not all respondents answered every question, in this appendix I report percentages rather than raw numbers. For the open-ended questions, I report actual number of respondents whose responses fit in each category.

The survey we sent out looked like this:

1. *I feel very frustrated about some aspects of leading my organization.*

1	2	3	4	5	6	7	8	9	10
Strongly agree		Agree		Neutral		Disagree		Strongly Disagree	

2. *I do not struggle in any area of my leadership.*

1	2	3	4	5	6	7	8	9	10
Strongly agree		Agree		Neutral		Disagree		Strongly Disagree	

3. *The people in my organization follow my lead without hesitation.*

1	2	3	4	5	6	7	8	9	10
Strongly agree		Agree		Neutral		Disagree		Strongly Disagree	

4. *I need outside help to troubleshoot some key leadership issues in my organization.*

1	2	3	4	5	6	7	8	9	10
Strongly agree		Agree		Neutral		Disagree		Strongly Disagree	

5. *I could use a mentor to help me improve my leadership.*

1	2	3	4	5	6	7	8	9	10
Strongly agree		Agree		Neutral		Disagree		Strongly Disagree	

Open-ended questions:

6. *Where do you think you most need to grow in your leadership? Why?*

7. *What one thing would best equip you to become a more effective leader?*

8. *What is the most difficult leadership task you face?*

Results

Question 1: "I feel very frustrated about some aspects of leading my organization."

Strongly agree: 14.1%

Agree: 57.6%

Neutral: 13.7%

Disagree: 13.3%

Strongly disagree: 1.1%

Of the 255 respondents, a whopping 71.7 percent feel a lot of frustration about some aspects of leading their churches/organizations.

Question 2: "I do not struggle in any area of my leadership."

> Strongly agree: 1.9%
>
> Agree: 3.5%
>
> Neutral: 6.3%
>
> Disagree: 60.3%
>
> Strongly disagree: 27.7%

This yielded even stronger results than the first question. Again, while only 5.4 percent of respondents said they don't struggle with leadership in their organizations, a mammoth 88 percent said they did struggle with some areas of leadership.

Question 3: "The people in my organization follow my lead without hesitation."

> Strongly agree: 3.5%
>
> Agree: 39.6%
>
> Neutral: 30.1%
>
> Disagree: 25.4%
>
> Strongly disagree: 1.1%

It's striking that only 3.5 percent of respondents could say strongly that their people followed their lead without hesitation. While it's good that 39.6 percent said their people followed their lead without hesitation, the fact that less than half (43.1 percent) could say their people followed them without hesitation is troubling.

The fact that 56.6 percent either had ambivalent followers or non-followers also seems troubling, although it's good that only 1.1 percent strongly disagreed with the statement.

Question 4: "I need outside help to troubleshoot some key leadership issues in my organization."

> Strongly agree: 12.6%
>
> Agree: 48%
>
> Neutral: 24.8%
>
> Disagree: 13.3%
>
> Strongly disagree: 1.1%

No surprise that a majority of respondents said they could use some trouble-shooting help (60.6 percent), but 32 respondents said they "strongly agreed" that they needed such help (12.6 percent). And only 14.4 percent said they didn't really need such help. That seems to speak to a pretty big need.

Question 5: "I could use a mentor to help me improve my leadership."

> Strongly agree: 26.4%
>
> Agree: 60%
>
> Neutral: 10.2%
>
> Disagree: 2.7%
>
> Strongly disagree: .4%

An overwhelming 86.4 percent say they could use a leadership mentor, and over a quarter of respondents said they strongly agreed they could use a mentor. Only 2.7 percent disagreed with the statement, and only .4 percent (1 respondent) strongly disagreed.

Takeaway

The biggest hits we got on this quantitative side of the survey both got 152 votes out of 255 responses. A total of 152 respondents said they could use a leadership mentor, and another 152 respondents disagreed with the statement, "I do not struggle in any area of my leadership."

Open-Ended Question 1

"Where do you think you most need to grow in your leadership? Why?"

Personnel development/leader development/discipleship (39); vision (37); personal development (29); delegation (17); administration (16); conflict resolution (12); improved relationship skills (12); leading through change (12); time management (12); communication (10); following God/trust in God (9); evangelism (4); counseling (3); planning/strategy (2); other (19)

Personnel development/leader development/discipling (39 comments)

(Note: From here onward, some comments edited lightly for clarity)

> I need to know how to prepare a leadership team to take over my company when I leave.

TRAINING

I have a hard time with the concept of authoritarian leadership. I believe that the leadership of the church should be a plurality of elders. With that said, it is hard to get elders on board with this idea. Most of my past elders stepped down because they felt I should be making the majority of decisions and instituting things. So, my problem, I guess, is leading the "leaders" and trying to get them to own their leadership position.

STAFF

- How to develop the next phase (split middle and high school) and how to develop my leaders in youth ministry; I do okay but want to improve
- Leading volunteers to follow through on commitments
- Investing in the right key leaders for growth and unity
- Events and opportunities for leaders to put their heads and hands on the Great Commission; let the Holy Spirit guide them with small groups besides the congregational regular events
- Better at discipling individuals within the church

- I need to do a better job of equipping the saints, so they are discipling others
- Training leaders
- The ability to develop other leaders
- Developing new leaders
- Implementation and motivation of lay people
- Getting volunteers to serve
- Shepherding
- Leading staff
- Not having the time and resources to mentor key leaders for ministry
- Discipling, time restraints, bivocational pastor
- Equipping and empowering
- How to recruit and develop leaders; it is hard to identify possible candidates
- Discipleship and evangelism
- Learning to equip other leaders; I am the one who takes things on and makes it my job to accomplish it instead of recruiting others to assist
- Leadership development
- I am constantly having to remind myself that I did not mature overnight and will have expectations of others to grow faster; at the same time I feel our culture has discouraged so many believers from maturing as believers that I feel an urgency to be more discerning as how to bring believers "up to speed"
- Engaging and developing young adults
- More effectively discipling my leaders
- Dealing with youth
- Leadership development: being more intentional with my time in developing leaders inside the church
- Developing other leaders: finding the balance of not adequately equipping others for the task at hand versus micromanagement

- Transforming doers into leaders
- Sending out independent leaders
- Recruiting other leaders to oversee and lead in areas outside my giftedness
- How to attract youth/younger generation
- Developing others to lead and grow
- Enabling staff and key leaders to take hold of their roles with consistency
- Developing and deploying people to serve and lead
- Leadership of paid staff, particularly in regard to supervision
- Continuing to develop leaders

Vision (37 comments)

- Pushing out the vision I have of ministry
- Casting vision and having others buy in
- In casting the vision, many times I become afraid I will miss God in leading
- Knowing clearly what God's vision is for the church; if I am not clear, then the congregation will not know where we are going
- Vision casting, delegation, and leadership development in an established setting; my skills were sharpened in these areas in a planting environment, and I find they are dull in the current environment
- Communicating my vision with my team
- Vision casting and having training for equipping leaders; also, just with dealing with the hard stuff—I too often wait when I need to act; maybe need encouragement in these areas; feeling greater stress these days, as I know others are
- Probably in the area of logistics and making our vision clearer to everyday people
- Vision casting
- How to get needs and vision to the senior pastor and get his dreams and visions in order to implement them

- Learning to lead people and getting them to catch the vision God has given me
- Vision casting and administration
- We are in a good place now. But overall, throughout my ministry I have struggled with getting the people to fully buy into the vision I sought to cast
- Clarity of vision and tenacity to follow through and getting people to buy in and take ownership
- Vision and inspiration; it seems harder to motivate people
- The ability to clearly define the end goal
- Casting vision and leading through it; charting direction and determining next steps is not as difficult as constantly keeping the vision in front of the people and leading them through it
- Communication of the overall vision
- Casting vision that motivates people to give and volunteer
- Visioneering, planning, organizing, motivating, leading as a whole
- In prioritization and future planning
- Casting a vision
- I believe I need to grow in how to cast vision for people
- Communicating vision in a way that engages people to join the work for the long-haul
- Casting vision: I am more tactical in my thinking and would benefit from learning to be more strategic
- Casting vision and equipping leaders
- I need to be better at articulating the vision for the future that builds excitement and not the fear of changes
- Casting vision they will follow
- Vision
- Inspiring confidence in my ability to lead; articulating my vision; I was Student Pastor at my church for over a decade before becoming Senior Pastor. It seems a lot of folks will always only see me as the "youth guy"

- Future vision casting
- Vision casting: I know where I want to lead our church to go, but I have a difficult time getting certain members to buy into the vision and potential for ministry
- I could do better in casting vision; I love to teach and deal with people but casting vision for the future is something I struggle with
- Engaging others to help translate vision into reality
- Vision: I need help in casting a vision and helping God's people to see it too
- Confidence and direction or vision
- Getting the vision from inside myself to outside for others to see

Personal development (29 comments)

- I am in my fifties and some look upon me as out of touch; I disagree but am willing to make changes
- Finishing tasks I have started
- Being more bold in leading; I often just go with the flow, when I perceive another flow might be a better trip
- Be more grounded/decisive
- I need growth in the area of creativity (finding ways to get our people involved in outreach)
- Patience and patience
- To be more assertive without being a jerk; to be kind always
- Self-leadership; there always seems to be too much work and not enough time for leading those who are set in their ways
- I need more confidence in myself and ability to lead
- I need to negotiate more clearly and strongly; I say yes to ideas too quickly; I need to take more time to pray before making decisions
- Developing creative, out-of-the-box ideas that will lead to momentum in disciple making
- Thinking through the problem before making a decision; getting all the facts to make a godly decision

- Patience: I want to see things happen now! I know it is not my timing but His; the other is getting past all the traditionalism—it stifles growth
- Personal growth and organizational growth
- Pastoral leadership
- Courage and conviction to lead those in my charge where and how I believe the Lord is directing me
- Becoming more confident in myself
- Be more assertive as to the difference in the spiritual and business side of the church
- I lack confidence and fear being shut down when presenting new ideas (because "new" seems to scare a lot of the older generation and they shoot them down before we even finish explaining)
- Overcoming fear of what others think, as it has at times kept me from doing what I know needs to be done
- Being bold when holding people accountable
- Being more loving and merciful
- Discernment
- Faith to move into risky areas and change the norm
- Decision making: I have the desire to make faster well-informed decisions but don't always have the luxury of waiting for all the details
- Leading with confidence
- Discipline: I need more discipline in my life
- Confidence in the leadership role God has placed me
- Making tough decisions

Delegation (17 comments)

- Delegation: I feel that if I do it, it will be done like I wish for it to be done; it is hard to let go
- Delegating responsibilities

- Delegation: trusting the team around me to do their work with excellence with limited involvement from myself

- Knowing what to delegate and what to keep; I'm single full-time staff and rest are part-time or bivocational—day-to-day duties often fall on me

- Been leading 49 years; need help letting it go

- Delegating as well as empowering/entrusting others to do the work of ministry, and practicing the fact that God can use other people too

- Delegation: I find myself doing what others could do because it's easier to do it myself and I do have a little control issue here as well; I can't wait for tomorrow when I can do it today—Lol

- Letting go

- Not trying to do it all on my own; trusting that it will get done

- Releasing individuals to use their God-given talents and abilities; I tend to just jump in and do it myself

- Delegation and organization

- I need help on delegation, building a team, and building forward motion with that team

- To be about delegating to others to allow them to lead and to free me up; also, to have regular training opportunities for new leaders to help them be a spiritual leader

- Delegation training: training others to independently function and carry out tasks—often I have volunteers, yet they are not independent operators; they need the dreaded micromanagement—they will follow but do not embrace making decisions

- Delegation

- I wish I could remember who said it, but this quote pretty much sums it up: "Be a developer, not a doer"—I need to work on delegating and developing others rather than just getting it done myself

- Delegation

Administration (16 comments)

- Changing computer systems, media, administration
- Overseeing the financial accounting; forcing myself to oversee the details
- Organization
- Sunday school administration, youth program
- Administration
- Administration
- Organizing
- Administrative tasks; getting people to follow through
- Administration/Vision casting; why? That is a good question!
- Administration and learning how to be an "ex-officio" on committees and still be effective. It all stems around building relationships, but some committee members are only interested in maintaining power/control. At times, this attitude has been hard for me to handle. It has a tendency to put me on the defensive and takes my focus away from leading. If I'm not careful, I find myself trying to "win" the wrong prize (control) and not the right prize (knowing Jesus and leading others to know Him too!). Truth is, the hardest nuts can always be cracked. I know God wants me to search His heart to find His tool for the job. Sometimes I just want to smash the nut and be done with it; but He reminds me He didn't do that with me!
- Administration: This is an area I'm not gifted in and struggle to lead in because of lack of training, experience, and knowledge
- Organization, advance planning
- Infrastructure: I lead an established church that was previously run by a few families. I have a strong group of people ready to lead and serve but no pipeline to assimilate, identify, and raise up leaders
- Leadership/Administration is not my spiritual gift, yet good, solid leadership is indispensable within the church
- Business
- Structure and systems to facilitate growth

Conflict resolution (12 comments)

- Having difficult conversations and giving feedback to others around me; it is unnatural to me to do this
- Being tough on people who are purposefully sabotaging
- I don't even know how to answer, if I'm honest; I'm frustrated and know God has called me here, but the people are often so unloving toward the pastor and family
- Dealing with those who are former members, who are supposed to be Christians, talking about me and the church
- Conflict resolution: Though it's not an everyday occurrence, when it happens, I struggle to meet the expectations of the multigenerational congregation
- Dealing with leadership that is more carnal than spiritual; some have been in leadership so long that they are not wanting change
- Compassion for those who either do not want to follow or are just flat out antagonistic—and not getting consumed by the opposition
- Confronting people in areas of sin in their lives
- Dealing with people when trying to change the direction of the church; longtime members bow up against new ideas or passively resist the changes, even when they are biblical
- Conflict resolution: Sometimes I will move too fast on something while dealing with a staff member and at other times too slow
- Respect: There have been so many occasions where members of my leadership team do not show up or show no interest in what we are trying to accomplish. They are more worried about their own corner of ministry rather than the vision of the pastor and kingdom ministry
- Conflict resolution

Improved relationship skills (12 comments)

- Relationship building/influence; getting the uninvolved involved
- Understanding others' thoughts and thought processes

- Stronger interpersonal relationships and follow up on assignment of tasks—sometimes I confide more than I should. This leads to failure in fully accomplishing set goals
- Gentleness, because I'm often too forceful
- Relationships: I long for more of a family connect with my staff and church and they do as well—comradeship is missing; I fall way short in this area
- Listening: I need to understand before being understood
- Emotional intelligence
- Becoming a better listener
- Emotional intelligence, control over emotions, and connection with others
- Making regular contact with members and nonmembers outside of church—I have three jobs beyond being pastor of a church so sometimes I think about church at church
- I need help in trusting in the process of leading people. Impatience is my biggest struggle. I've seen my impatience come out in conversations with my people. And I don't want to do anything that could harm the unseen things God is doing in hearts that I'm not aware of because of impatience
- Motivation of people

Leading through change (12 comments)

- New directions; the uncertainties of where we are going as a society
- Moving quicker through each transition or introducing new things quicker
- Regaining influence: Following COVID, I feel like I'm starting over in regaining the influence I had pre-pandemic. Many decisions were made in the midst of the pandemic and some church members disagreed at various points and lost confidence in me as a leader
- I need to grow in pastoring people through change; my first inclination is to make the "right" decision and move on without working with the naysayers

- Breaking out of COVID and getting us into the community
- Dealing with the issues of modern society, such as living together without marriage and the gay agenda
- Knowing when and when not to speak to popular issues that affect our mission
- Learning how to lead post-COVID would be good
- Pushing through this COVID culture with the Great Commission
- Leading an established congregation through the changes of methods and thought processes with a rural congregation
- How to navigate the new normal. These have been incredible months during the pandemic. Leaders have had to reinvent themselves and we were not prepared for many aspects of ministry. Technology is an area where we need a better grasp
- Leading in a post-COVID world

Time management (12 comments)

- I think time is what I need in my church more than anything; I never seem to have the time to plan and act. I am a bivocational pastor and have good people around me but can't seem to manage my time
- Time management
- Time management, busy on a lot of things, need to prioritize my time
- Getting the best use of my time, so I am not stretched so thin
- Time management, vision focuses
- Learning how to balance time as a fulltime police officer and pastor. Sometimes gets overwhelming as I believe some don't understand. Even fulltime pastors don't or can't understand the dynamics of pastoring and still working fulltime
- Time management and prioritization
- Time management
- Better understanding how to manage time

- Time management: I don't know how to say no
- Time management: I think I should be able to get more accomplished in the time that I have
- Finding one specific thing to tackle at a time…too many wildfires; trying to lead my congregation in one thing we do well at a time

Communication (10 comments)

- Communication
- Communicating adequately to staff and vice versa, and communicating effectively to congregation. A glaring deficiency in our church is communication between senior pastor and administrative pastor (I am the admin)
- Communication
- Communication
- Communication in time with the followers
- I need to continue to communicate and organize a little more
- Clarity: better communicator
- My ability to communicate: It seems everyone wants it in writing
- Clarity of message and making the necessary time allotments to sell it properly
- Better communication

Following God/trust in God (9 comments)

- I am constantly aware that God has placed me as the pastor of His church. I need to stay out of His way and depend solely on Him for my leadership keys
- Clear direction of the Lord: I struggle with seeing things run smoothly in other organizations and attempting to emulate others' behaviors and outcomes rather than focusing on the Lord's direction for His ministry in my life
- Trust in the Holy Spirit and allowing Him more control and influence in my life. I need more of His power and guidance and less of secular leadership strategies

- My own personal walk with God—sometimes I get so busy doing I neglect hearing from God
- Listening to the Holy Spirit in prayer and in reading God's Word
- Stronger relationship with the Lord
- Spiritual maturity
- Time with God to listen for His wisdom
- Following God's will

Evangelism (4 comments)

- Evangelism
- Leading others to evangelize!
- How to motivate people to see the urgency and necessity to share the gospel
- Community: I don't doubt my leadership here at the church; it's in God's hands, no doubt. I want to be more courageous in my community and be as outspoken there as I am here!

Counseling (3 comments)

- Counseling: So many people have so many difficult issues they are confronted with, I struggle with advice to give at times. At times, it is my first encounter with a specific issue and I find it hard to believe, not to mention hard to address
- Marriage counseling, because I still don't have that experience
- Pastoral counseling

Mentoring (2 comments)

- Experience and wisdom from experienced leaders
- Coaching

Planning/strategy (2 comments)

- Strategy
- Planning: Often when the results do not match my expectations,

I can see where better planning and recruiting of the right persons to lead an activity could have made the outcome better

Other (19 comments)

- Accepting the limitations of leading a volunteer organization where participants oftentimes have individual priorities which are outside of the organization. I get frustrated when I need to rely on people who are already overburdened (10 percent of the people do 90 percent of the work)

- I don't think it's one particular area; I think I can always improve in all areas of the ministry God has called me to

- Timing on decision making

- Healthy pace

- Passion for the people I lead over what we do

- Problem solving concerning parents and their children

- The struggle is people our own age

- Addressing an increased culture of excellence

- Endurance: People give up too easily

- Be able to give people "want to" versus "get to"—you lead by example, but it takes a lot of encouraging for people to follow and to be disciples of Jesus Christ

- All aspects of leadership

- I'm consistently pushed outside the limits God has set for my spiritual gifts, time, energy, and more. It's dangerous and exhausting to work outside of these limits and I want to make adjustments to solve this problem. I need to be in a position that allows me to use my spiritual gifts and allows me to fulfill the other areas of ministry God has entrusted to me, areas outside of the responsibilities I have at church

- Succession

- In the Latin churches it is difficult to be a good leader, because the people are unpunctual; they have a lot of roots from the country they come from that do not change, like gossip and jealousy between brothers. That is something very difficult to change when there is a lot of diversity of nationalities in a church and most are older people

- To get pastors not to be lone rangers
- Timing
- Spiritual challenges, because of the diversity of the Association
- For me, growing as a leader is a never-ending process, so just having reminders of how important leadership is in the spiritual as well as the secular world
- Influence, understanding others' giftedness

Open-Ended Question 2

"What one thing would best equip you to become a more effective leader?"

Mentors/seasoned counsel (63); personal development (36); spiritual practices/resources (33); additional human resources (17); don't know/ unsure (13); leadership training (13); time management (11); helpful tools (8); planning (6); rest/physical health/tangible resources (5); accountability (4); encouragement (4)

Mentors/seasoned counsel (63 comments)

- I have tried to mentor young men in my life but have never really had a mentor
- Experienced mentorship with my concern about succession
- Having a seasoned leader to seek advice and counsel from
- A mentor/coach from a successful (emphasis on successful) established church our size (1,500 or a little larger)
- Mentor
- A motivator/encourager to continue to push me when I get bogged down
- Mentor
- A Timothy
- Mentoring
- A mentor
- More (any) open and confidential discussions with fellow ministers away from our church area
- A mentor
- Mentor—a model I can talk to
- Mentors
- A personal mentor would have been helpful
- To be around more leaders

- Someone who would listen to my culture story for our church and then point out what is going well first and then point out some areas for change or adjustment
- Good advice from seasoned pastors
- Seeing how someone in a similar context dealt with similar issues and observing the results
- A stronger leader leading and discipling me
- A mentor
- A mentor
- Perhaps finding a mentor myself—someone who has been where I've been and with the Lord's help, taken the church and his leadership to the next level
- Hearing from successful leaders that I can glean ideas and practices from
- In my ministry, it's being around other godly leaders and learning from them
- Interview with seasoned/veteran pastor that has served faithfully
- Coaching that I can afford
- Having someone in my corner who doesn't look to me for leadership
- Seeing working models
- Mentors
- Mentorship
- Having a successful model to follow
- A mentor that has been in a similar situation to help lessen mistakes and show me what is needed and what can be overlooked
- Being able to get helpful insight and learn from someone who has been in similar circumstances
- Mentorship
- Having a mentor
- Honest mentorship

- Mentor
- Regular coaching and mentoring
- I would love to have a mentor (even though I'm 50 years old)
- Learning to invest in younger leaders without losing a sense of personal identity
- Mentor
- Mentor
- Support from a mentor
- Someone to coach me through the process
- Practical examples
- Another pastor's wife who is older and wiser to share and grow under
- Mentor that has been in my shoes
- Mentor
- Mentor
- Networking with other pastors or mentors
- I need a model of how to take a church from where we are at and grow it
- Structure and systems coach
- Mentoring
- A mentor
- Having a mentor
- Having a mentor that holds me accountable; it's hard to find one in the small town because everyone knows everyone. Most importantly, I need someone that doesn't know the people, and can give you objective truths that help you in ministry
- A mentor to bounce ideas off of and kick me in the rear when needed
- I have been blessed to have mentors. I think personal mentoring is the biggest help
- Mentor/accountability

- Good mentorship
- A mentor
- Good mentorship

Personal development (36 comments, especially confidence and courage/boldness)

- Confidence
- Leading with boldness and assurance
- Consistency
- Being organized
- Be more organized in my approach to evangelism
- Confidence
- I need to be more detailed; I am a big-picture person and sometimes the details fall through the cracks
- More leadership experience as far as dealing with difficult people
- Confidence in self
- To be better able to convince others of the potentials I see in them, that they do not see themselves; I would like to be able to get them to *stay* on a path I have directed them to, for them to exploit their potentials
- How to develop influence in the first five years of becoming the pastor
- Patience
- Being more sociable, and therefore relational
- Increase my influence
- Confidence
- Knowing, understanding the psychology of people to be able to infect them with the desire to be disciples
- Better listening
- Knowing how to use my leadership type to bring others along in leadership

- Patience
- Better listening
- Confidence in my calling
- Being better at sharing vision and getting others to buy in and participate, to share in that vision
- Listen to myself more than others who talk me out of what I think God is saying and wants to do in His church
- Become more of an encourager
- Greater boldness when needed
- Being able to see problems/opportunities before they materialize
- Continuing to lead by example
- Accuracy—meaning getting things right the first time
- Discernment: I need to identify the most important things
- Become less of a people pleaser
- Experience
- Learning to invest the time in more people to help them in their own personal growth as a believer; I try hard at it but don't feel like I'm as effective as I should be
- Time and hands on experience
- Opportunity for more growth and experience
- Invitational improvement—more dynamic
- Developing my own courage and vision to lead

Spiritual practices/resources (33 comments, 15 on prayer)

- Holiness
- Trust God when I'm not sure what to do next
- Prayer
- A better spiritual relationship with God
- Prayer
- Empowering of the Holy Ghost
- More effective prayer life

- Getting along with God; seeking Him
- Wisdom
- The prayers of my brothers and sisters
- The Holy Spirit
- Prayer
- More Word and more prayer
- Prayer
- Wisdom
- The Holy Spirit
- Prayer and mentoring
- James 1:5: I ask daily, and still need more wisdom
- God's grace in abundant fashion!
- Following the leading of the Holy Spirit
- The Bible
- Divine guidance
- More prayer
- Empowerment: help of the Holy Spirit
- More study!
- To always focus on being with God over doing things for God; my walk with Him and being with Him has to be top priority
- The simple act of knowing others are praying and care about my ministry
- More devotion to prayer; also, more seminary training (PhD)
- What I am doing now; discipline in the Word of God
- Prayer
- Prayer
- Prayer and the help of a pastor who has been there
- More people praying for me

Additional human resources (17 comments)

- Bringing energy to my tired volunteers
- Followers
- Extra staff
- Someone to share the leadership responsibilities with
- Followers
- Delegating
- More leaders to share the load
- Having a like-minded team around me to help with the ministry
- More people willing to help with the mission of the gospel
- Someone helping lead in the trench with me
- Having a ministry staff of at least three people that are willing to go over and above in ministry
- Learning how to trust others to do the task assigned to them
- People I trust
- More aggressive and team-minded pastors
- Administrative and logistical help
- Delegating assignments
- Building effective, intentional teams

Don't know/not sure (13 comments)

- I really don't know
- I don't know
- Nothing I can think of
- I don't know
- I am not sure
- Don't know
- Not sure
- Not sure
- Not sure

- Not sure
- I guess to know the answer to this question…I don't know what I don't know
- Not sure
- Unsure

Leadership training for staff/volunteers (13 comments)

- Training men to be leaders
- Teamwork abilities
- Trust more but follow up on work assignments
- Training on a more consistent basis
- Seminars
- More in-depth training
- Administrative training
- One-on-one discipleship
- A group that has love, compassion and a lot of patience and is trained for that job
- Practical leadership training tailored toward small church, single staff/bivocational pastors
- More leadership training in my area of ministry
- Outside of God giving me that gift, training; I do read on leadership
- Online seminars on using technology

Time management (11 comments)

- Better grasp on managing time
- Being a bivocational pastor it sometimes is very difficult to lead the church in a fulltime capacity. It makes it very hard to put in the time that is needed to make the programs that are important to proper leadership successful
- More time
- Prioritization

- Time management
- The time to personally invest in becoming a more effective leader
- Time
- Time management and organizational skills
- Time management
- Knowing how to prioritize issues and time
- Better time management skills

Effective tools (8 comments)

- Tools
- Ready-made tools, etc., that don't require time and energy to develop
- Onboarding systems that work to bring people from guest to committed
- Give me something that works
- Personal feedback
- Good helps
- Supervision techniques for ministerial staff
- Daily growth or daily devotional stating the purpose of leadership from a biblical perspective and using and understanding that our Savior did not come to be served but to serve

Better planning (6 comments)

- Planning
- Planning
- More time set aside for planning and calendaring and having fewer last-minute changes to the church calendar
- Focus on goals
- A schedule
- A more organized plan for leading our church after construction of our new building

Rest/physical health/tangible resources (5 comments)

- A sabbatical
- Better health
- Money
- Truthfully, more days off (fulltime bivocational pastor)
- Time off for preparation

Accountability (4 comments)

- Accountability
- Accountability
- Leadership accountability
- Accountability

Encouragement (4 comments)

- Encouragement
- Encouragement
- I think some encouragement from my pastor would be welcome
- I love the Monday morning encouragement from Johnny; things like that are very helpful

Other (19 comments)

- The discipline to give feedback to other staff and volunteer leaders
- There is no one thing
- Healthy church DNA
- A better understanding of where we're going in the next four years in America
- More up-to-date info and commentary
- Clarity regarding deacon role expectations
- Just doing what I already know needs to be done; working with busy volunteers!

- More opportunity to lead!
- A more open channel of communication and also consistency; consistent response to email, etc.
- Learning how to find the community's needs
- Compromise
- Communication with other leaders and volunteers
- Organization
- Practical examples/applications of leadership principles: Sometimes I struggle with finding practical ways to apply a principle, or a good quote, so then I don't and it just becomes a cool quote on the quote board in my office. So, practical applications would be huge
- Develop a clear vision for ministry and make sure that everything that we do builds toward that vision
- For everyone to work like the guy in my head lol; we've been shut down for over a year, so probably focus going back into it
- Focus
- Communication
- Better examples from our SBC leadership, not BLM pleasers

Open-Ended Question 3

"What is the most difficult leadership task you face?"

Personal challenges (42); motivating people (31); the daily grind (31); handling conflict (29); building an effective team (27); challenging times (25); moving toward the vision (19); staff issues/hiring and firing (15); SBC issues (4); other (7)

Personal challenges (42 comments)

- Being a servant shepherd
- Managing time
- Relying on myself, my experience, my knowledge, and my power of persuasion
- Time management
- Being the example I need to be
- Leading my spouse to love my ministry as much as I do
- Balancing time
- Leading with confidence; I often feel less of myself
- Decision making
- My own gaps in consistency to be obedient to God's Word about my call to being a pastor for His church
- Being expected to give equal time toward personnel, facilities, and office management and preaching/studying
- Frustration as to why Christians aren't in the church
- Staying on task; so many distractions
- Discerning and leading through realistic and unrealistic expectations; learning which methods are most effective in mass communication
- Finding time to reenforce my leadership skills by reading, attending seminars, etc.

- Burnout
- Patience
- Time; I'm bivocational
- Delegation, time management, and mentoring
- Finding time to spend on general pastoral care without causing other areas to suffer
- Being faithful to God's vision while constantly being attacked
- Influence
- Leading *me*!
- Balancing my life and giving my family my best time
- Frustration over not being able to accomplish more because I cannot personally accomplish all I would desire to do
- Leading those who don't want to be led
- Balancing time
- Not knowing how to handle a situation, asking the question, then not getting a response for a greater than necessary length of time; in the meantime, someone else is waiting on a response from me
- Leading myself to be disciplined
- Personal clarity and health of mind and emotions
- Decision fatigue: making decisions for all areas of ministry that could be delegated to other leaders
- Influence of others
- Resources on being a better communicator
- Trying to do it all
- Dealing with issues within the church and the discouragement of leading
- I cannot compromise. We're faced with that decision every day.
- Making sure I'm doing the right things
- Saying no to people
- People talking without ever addressing the issue with me

- Effectively handing off leadership
- Slowing down
- Telling people no

Motivating people (31 comments)

- Leading people to maintain their relationship with Jesus; preaching the Word but it's falling on unconcerned people
- Motivating members to use their spiritual giftedness
- Getting involvement
- Getting people to buy in
- Leading when the congregation is apathetic
- Energizing and organizing the staff around evangelism, missions, and discipleship; they are willing, but they have never walked these paths
- Motivating my congregation to take that next step in their sanctification
- Keeping people engaged past Sunday morning
- Motivating people to serve
- Getting people back on track after COVID
- Get people to bring friends enthusiastically
- Getting a church member to see that church is not a spectator sport, that we must be willing to get involved and do more than just show up and tithe
- Helping people see the necessity of ongoing discipleship and spiritual growth
- To push forward those who don't care to grow in ministry and excellence
- Getting people to show up
- Changing minds
- Those in the church who don't seem to want to grow as a believer
- Leading older people that have not followed God's Word for most of their lives

- Motivating people to have an outward look—reaching out; sharing the gospel, inviting people to church
- Motivating people to do the work of the ministry
- Getting people to commit to ministry
- Motivating membership to do what God has called them to do
- Motivating people
- Motivating people to serve
- Getting the congregation to have high expectations for the service and ministry we do for God
- Keeping younger parents interested and focused on leading their families in Christ; to come to church, to give, to be involved in missions—soooo many busy schedules
- Getting others involved and passionate about serving
- Leading those who don't seem to want to go any further than they are
- Getting people to do things God's way
- Lack of commitment from young adults
- Inspiring the unmotivated

The daily grind (31 comments)

- Ongoing demands of preaching and teaching
- Dealing with the same people who always need my attention
- Giving feedback
- Communication
- Administration tasks
- Staying out of the rut of ministry and pretending all is well, when it's not; loneliness and emptiness tend to fill my calendar too often!
- Planning
- Keeping the church pure and educating people with little education
- Administrative responsibilities
- Administrative help
- Time and task management

- People's personal feelings/preferences
- Finances
- Interacting with a diverse group of people
- Administration
- Planning
- Visiting the lost and the sick
- Details, management, etc.
- Holding people accountable
- Status quo
- Surrender of the ones following with strict obedience to the truth of God's Word
- Time management: the battle between getting done what needs to get done to "keep the machine running," but then also setting aside time to dream and plan for the future, or even just researching and developing ideas for small improvements/changes. I find myself often getting caught up in the day-to-day "fires," and then another week goes by without looking ahead; vision-planning
- Organization
- Time is a challenge, being bivocational. I am a "serve in there with you" person, not a task-assigner. My precious people are tired
- Time management
- Time management
- Visitation
- Individual soul care
- The daily pressures of pastoring a church
- Managing the building and grounds of the church; I'd much rather focus on ministry

Handling conflict (29 comments)

- Not saying what I want/need to say to those who go against what I ask
- Saying no to some good ideas, over accepting only the *best* ideas

- Confronting those who do not do what I ask
- Removing someone who is not following the vision that had been cast
- Administration and confrontation; being sure I'm hearing from God
- Confrontation of others
- Dealing with negative people
- Mean, powerful people
- Church discipline
- To get others to utilize my open-door policy and talk to me before they take "drastic" steps like leaving the church
- When there are fights among members
- Working with strong personalities on the deacon board
- Leading people who aren't on board with the mission
- Removing the ungodly influences of antagonistic people in leadership positions
- Dealing with unruly people who agree with me, then do what they want to do
- Problem solving among members who are at odds with each other and then turning it against the pastor when trying to resolve issues; fickleness of men
- Resolving longstanding conflicts in the organizational leadership
- Handling conflict and church discipline
- Disruptive people
- Discipline of church members
- When the people want to do things their way
- Training/re-training deacons who are established and set in their ways
- Confronting leaders who are off the path
- Getting people to believe what the Bible says about leadership in the church; from what they think a deacon's duties are to the finance committee (that they don't call the shots on God's money)

- Confrontation when truly needed
- Dealing with conflict
- Dealing with difficult people
- Conflict resolution seems to always be a challenge
- Confrontation

Building an effective team (27 comments)

- Working with and building a team
- Putting key people in place
- Helping my team see the big picture and long-term journey to get there
- Instructing volunteers on how to overcome failures without discouraging them
- Encouraging volunteers to find satisfaction in their work
- Developing other leaders
- Recruiting people to whom I can delegate
- Discipleship
- Leading my lay leaders
- Discovering those who can and want to come alongside as co-laborers
- Training leaders
- Volunteers
- Growing functional leadership in the church
- Delegation
- Recruiting and training volunteers
- Lack of leaders
- Convincing workers of the importance of ministry growth
- Empowering others to do the work
- Getting all discipleship leaders on the same page in our Sunday school ministry
- I wish I had more people to help

- Discipling other lay leaders within the church
- Leading and working with volunteers that are not connected to the day-to-day function and execution of the mission
- The most difficult task recently is seeing pastors all over social media have a staff, and I don't. In my mind, I'm not being effective like I should. I've learned that God has surrounded me with people that can help get effective work done. And a mindset that "it's all about the kingdom" has help me to be filled with joy for those that do have a full staff. A chapter discussing how to work through this would be helpful for a lot of pastors.
- Leading volunteers who are crazy busy already
- Gaining and keeping the respect and support of my team
- Tired leaders
- Consistent and faithful commitment on behalf of the leaders I lead

Challenging times (25 comments)

- Dealing with families that have experienced a loss or death
- Influencing needed change
- Coming into a new church and hearing how good the former pastor was
- Addressing necessary change
- Juggling responsibilities within a church that is transitioning between sizes that demand different leadership structure
- Age difference in my church; I think the members find it hard to trust the leadership of a younger pastor
- Dealing with the current societal deficiencies in the Word of God
- Changing existing traditions or getting people to trust me and communicate with me what is going on
- Trying to change tradition
- Reimagining what our leadership structure needs to look like post-COVID
- I am not able to use my gifts to benefit other believers. I serve as an associate pastor, supposedly at an executive level. I have little time

to use the gifts God has given me to help someone through a difficult time, develop staff or build a ministry. Instead, I will be organizing a last-minute event for kids. This task is important, but it should not be my task to complete. It will take all of my strength and energy to complete this task because I don't think God has equipped me for this work. So, today, the task is a kid's event

- COVID culture
- Leading the lions
- Dealing with established norms that have been passively accepted for generations but are not necessarily practical or biblical
- I inherited elders and deacons who are loving, caring individuals and have been saved an average of twenty-five years, but never matured past being a baby in Christ
- Reshaping an ineffective culture
- Breaking traditions
- Paying off a $2 million dollar mortgage on the church that I inherited when I became pastor
- Financial issues and bringing us back to health in that area
- When COVID hit, many small Spanish-speaking churches closed. We launched on March 1, 2020. We decided to ride the wave and continue with the vision to plant the new church. Because we were opened and starting something fresh with a clear vision, it brought people from different churches. The task of putting everyone on the same page has been overwhelming. The biggest challenge has been to make sure people don't try to do things the way they did it before
- Changing the norm
- Keep going in times of desert
- The unknown right now
- Dealing with change

Moving toward the vision (19 comments)

- I would say it is my confidence in my ability to put forth a plan for the direction for our church to be its best version of what God wants

- Accomplishing tasks, executing vision, while seeking competent volunteers, where, in the past, volunteer standards have been nonexistent
- As a whole, we are a busy church but do not have the people to carry out the busy. We do not do a good job churchwide of training up folks and casting vision to help people see the *why* behind the ask
- Carrying out new ideas and getting volunteers
- Leading into the new future
- Vision casting effectively
- Leading the church in revitalization
- Determining the exact goal
- Church growth
- Clearly communicating the vision of "what we're going for"
- Evangelism
- Communicating a compelling vision
- Casting a compelling vision for our future
- Buy-in
- A clear, concise vision
- Building consensus around an inspiring vision
- Knowing how frequently to cast a fresh vision
- Getting everybody on the same page! Leadership means a lot of different things to people. To a businessman, it means to take charge and go ahead. To most other people in the church, it can't be done that way. Finding the balance is difficult for me
- Follow through of a good vision—both with consistency on my end and the help of others

Staff issues/hiring and firing (15 issues)

- Hiring and firing
- Confronting staff about problems

- Staff
- Internal communication (organizational communication)
- New staff
- Overseeing staff
- Letting staff go and all that involves
- Leading my staff
- Termination of staff
- Personnel
- Staff development
- Firing staff members while at the same time trying to not hurt the church in a negative way
- Creating a positive and effective staff culture
- Personnel
- Correcting ministerial staff personnel

SBC issues (4 comments)

- SBC problems within deacon body
- Supporting SBC leadership and leading my church to support and not focus on the negative publicity
- Navigating SBC issues with our constituents
- Communicating with churches about the Association and our partnership

Other (7 comments)

- Having a sounding board or like-minded people to bounce ideas off of
- Being the pastor to pastors; I serve as an associational missionary
- Decisive people
- Replication and multiplication
- Structure and systems that facilitate growth

- Moving our congregation toward identifying more with our community
- Leading God's people who have numerous years of spiritual/ministry experience in the latter season of their lives, while at the same time caring for/loving God's people who are in the early season of their spiritual journey; doing both of these with love and bringing the two together for the glory of God

Rhetorical Vision in a Time of Drought

A Case Study in Applying Symbolic Convergence Theory to the Evangelical Church

A high percentage of local US church leaders report that they struggle not only with creating a motivating vision for their church, but also with how to present that vision in compelling ways to get buy-in from their congregation.

This appendix, originally written as an academic paper for a PhD program in communication, is adapted for How to Become a More Effective Leader *to help church leaders think more deeply about how vision works on a human level, as well as how to effectively convey that vision to congregations in ways that encourage congregants to clearly understand it, enthusiastically accept it, and energetically work to bring the vision to reality.*

A string of books, studies, polls, and articles in the past several years all have chronicled the shrinking church in America. "It's no secret that the percentage of Americans in church on any given Sunday is dropping fast," wrote Julia Duin, former religion editor for the *Washington Times* (11). But while mainline Protestant churches in the past half century have suffered dramatic declines in attendance—the Episcopal Church and Presbyterian Church USA have lost over half their former memberships— "in the past decade, it's the evangelical churches that are losing ground"

(Duin 13). And why does church attendance remain flat or continue to shrink? "My research suggested that people are simply not being pastored," Duin writes. "Often ministers are out of touch with what's happening on the ground, as they are surrounded by a wall of secretaries and voice mail. Congregants have to wait up to a month for an appointment, if they can get in at all" (22). And she observes, "One of the top reasons people give for their leaving church is loneliness: the feeling—especially in large congregations that no one knows or cares whether they are there" (50).

In addition, many believers see church as "irrelevant," according to *Faith in the Halls of Power*, a book based on in-depth interviews with 360 influential evangelicals. These Christians lost interest in church "because they consider it a waste of their time. These influential people had written off committee meetings that focus on minutiae, incompetent leadership, and inefficient projects. They thought in business terms—long-term planning, strategies, vision, bottom-line performance and progress" (Duin 31).

Kinnaman and Lyons took three years to interview "outsiders" about why they stayed away from church. The authors summarized their main findings by quoting a man from Mississippi: "Christianity has become bloated with blind followers who would rather repeat slogans than actually feel true compassion and care. Christianity has become marketed and streamlined into a juggernaut of fearmongering that has lost its own heart" (Kinnaman and Lyons, 15).

Such accounts fault evangelical leadership with a lack of "big picture perspective" and a drought of compassion and care. Novelist Gabriel Garcia Marquez memorably wrote of *Love in the Time of Cholera*; can the evangelical church develop an effective Rhetorical Vision in a Time of Drought?

Somewhat surprisingly, Symbolic Convergence Theory (SCT) rarely has been applied in church contexts, despite clear promise in that arena. Cragan, who along with Bormann and Shields was instrumental in developing SCT, stated in a personal email, "not a lot of SCT work has been done on religion." And in another personal email, Shields spoke of a friend in the early 1980s who used SCT to create a new vision for his Midwest church. Although the friend reported good results, "He wasn't a scholar, so no one ever wrote it up."

One published study from 1975 used SCT to analyze the rhetoric of the Disciples of Christ (DOC) denomination in the nineteenth century (Hensley). In almost half a century of SCT scholarship, Hensley's study is one of only a handful of published applications of the theory to the church. This appendix presents an overview of Redeemer Church, an evangelical congregation in moderate decline*; summarizes key components of SCT; and applies SCT to Redeemer's situation to suggest how the church might develop a new rhetorical vision with the power to unite and energize its congregation.

A Struggling Church

Redeemer Church once enjoyed an average weekly attendance at Sunday worship of 2,620. Every year since that time, attendance and membership has declined. Eight years after its highest reported attendance, it registered an average weekly Sunday attendance of 2,063—a drop of more than 21 percent in seven years. In the fall of that year, at the church's annual meeting, leaders reported another 3 percent attendance drop.

Redeemer attempted to reverse the trend by trying several new initiatives, none of which halted the numerical decline. Alterations to worship services, changes in administrative structure, job reshuffling, staffing adjustments, modified ministry focus, revisions to the church mission statement (at least four in ten years), and various program shifts did not significantly slow the church's declining numbers. In response, the congregation's elder board organized several task forces to investigate the problems it deemed most critical. Several streams of information helped to influence the board's activity, including two professionally conducted congregational surveys, three focus group sessions, and an independent qualitative study that asked ten former member/attenders why they left the church. This section of the appendix summarizes the findings of these inquiries.

Results reported from the first survey indicated that while Redeemer enjoyed strong member participation in small groups, the church did "not appear to have a strong outreach to new congregants" and showed "very low levels of inviting non-Christians to church." Survey participants reported low satisfaction with church-provided opportunities to serve in

---

* Redeemer is a pseudonym for the actual church used in this study.

general, as well as low participation in serving under-resourced individuals. A full 26 percent of respondents agreed with the questionnaire statement, "I sometimes consider leaving/will likely leave the church." In fact, every demographic segment of Redeemer was more likely to leave the church than their counterparts in similar churches (Reveal).

Another survey two years later reported that 13 percent of respondents felt dissatisfied with Redeemer, and 18 percent had hesitations about inviting others to church. Twenty-three percent of individuals who had been attending Redeemer for twenty or more years reported feeling dissatisfied with the church; 24 percent of those who identified themselves as "stalled" in their spiritual growth reported such dissatisfaction; and 29 percent of individuals sixty years old and above reported feeling dissatisfied with Redeemer's worship and music. Forty-five percent of "very dissatisfied" attendees were not involved in any group connected with the church.

Dissatisfied participants used the open-ended portion of the survey questionnaire to record several complaints, the most typical including: "Redeemer is being run more like a business not a community." "The church is adrift, losing older members and failing to attract younger." "No real excitement in Christ [the term "lack of energy" also appeared, as did "tired"] and making a difference in the community." "I have dropped my attendance in the past year, yet nobody really seems to notice that I don't attend." (The words "lonely" and "alone" also often appeared.) "Watching my friends leave in droves has definitely made me wonder about the future of the church." "My husband calls the service a 'show' with too many theatrics so he doesn't like to go." "I'd like more depth, more challenging messages directly from Scripture." "I feel the church needs to improve feeding the flock."

In tandem with the later survey, Redeemer organized three focus groups, one of which discussed dissatisfaction with the church (Focus Group). This panel attracted seven individuals, ranging in age from thirty-five to eighty-three, including single, married, and divorced persons. Three of the seven attended care groups, and at one time all were involved in some ministry. Typical comments included the following: "The messages used to be more biblical and applicable to life." "It seems like we don't know what we want to be." "Very difficult to make relationships in church. I sit alone, and no one sits next to me. I am very lonely."

"We offered to host a care group and never got a response. We dubbed Redeemer 'The Church of the Pretty People,' and we decided we must not be pretty enough." "No connection to the pastoral staff." "It seems that we've lost the importance of relationships in the church." "Maybe it's about shepherding."

An independent qualitative study of former Redeemer members and regular attenders, produced the same year as the second survey, identified four major reasons why those interviewed said they left the church after many years of active participation: (a) a commitment to performance, stage, and spectacle over authenticity, heartfelt expression, and solid truth; (b) the absence of some Big Idea with the power to unify the whole congregation and energize it for effective service; (c) an acute lack of pastoral care provided by senior staff, resulting in the widespread conviction that church leadership desires to hand off all congregational care to specialists and volunteer care groups; and (d) a serious deficiency in managerial leadership (Halliday). Comments from participants in this study closely paralleled statements made by current Redeemer members and attenders, as reflected in the second survey questionnaire and focus groups.

Two attempts to reorganize the church's ministry preceded the investigations just summarized. The first occurred about five years before the first survey, when leaders decided to restructure church management and programs to reflect principles in the book *Doing Church as a Team*. Senior staff became part of a "Management Team" and began to have less regular contact with subordinates. Shortly thereafter, some junior staff members began commenting that they felt cut off from various ministries of the church and no longer knew Redeemer's direction. Although the restructuring was meant to encourage team building, attract additional lay volunteers to join modified outreaches, and create a more relational environment within the church, the effort did not halt Redeemer's attendance decline.

A second major effort to rehabilitate the church's sagging fortunes took place just before and after the first survey, when the church underwent a "realignment" process. A board memo from that time laid out the major objectives for this effort. It included "understanding the problem and admitting we need to change," "casting a vision in order to change," developing strategic initiatives organized around the new vision, and developing tactics "in order to live out strategic initiatives." The church's stated mission, "connecting people to Jesus through relevance, discipleship and authenticity," was to be fleshed out through five strategic initiatives: 1) create an externally focused culture; 2) create a culture of authentic relationships and spiritual reproduction; 3) expand inspired, genuine, heartfelt (God-connecting) worship; 4) develop superior communication; 5) integrate and simplify. The phrase "For the greater good" became the Big Idea around which all of this new alignment was to be built.

A year and a half later, a "strategic plan update" listed several "completed items" from the earlier memo, including the reconstruction of Sunday programs to make them "culturally relevant and inviting to seekers," instituting small group and evangelism training, and clarifying the mission of Redeemer. It also listed several "new initiatives," which included growing Redeemer by 10 percent in "traditional metrics of church-health." It called for developing a culture of outreach, organizing church-wide efforts to serve a local public school, and other efforts designed to nurture an evangelistic ethos. In addition, the update listed several initiatives targeting discipleship, "next generation," "authenticity" (including "develop healthy and productive Management Team"), and several others aimed at organizational effectiveness.

Seventeen months later, Redeemer's board found itself once again addressing multiple familiar issues. A "strategic planning report" asked, "What went wrong the last time we did strategic planning and how can we correct it this time so the same thing doesn't happen?" It reported agreement among board members "that the overarching issue was a lack of trust between team members that [. . .] essentially derailed the process." It also reported agreement "to set aside three critical components of clarity as to who we want to be as a church: community, relational, intergenerational." And it reported "broad agreement" that a key solution "would be to identify a crystal-clear vision for the church and the team that would unify efforts."

Redeemer's board said it believed it had identified not only some major causes of the church's prolonged struggles, but also several significant characteristics of a new future it desired to nurture. Yet Redeemer never did appear to develop a "rhetorical vision" or an "organizational saga" (see "Overview of SCT" for definitions) to guide, nurture, and sustain group cohesion. This appendix contends that Symbolic Convergence Theory may offer significant assistance in creating, raising, and sustaining the kind of rhetorical vision that can help turn the desired future described by Redeemer's leadership into a reality.

(While the following overview of SCT will help readers to understand how the theory is designed to work, some readers may want to skip to the next section, "SCT Applied to Redeemer," to get a quicker sense of how this communication theory can be practically applied to church contexts.)

Overview of SCT

SCT is a general communications theory that "helps explain broad aspects of interpersonal, small group, public, organizational, mass, and intercultural communication" (Bormann et. al. 2001, 271). SCT attempts to account for "those dramatizing, communicative processes that create and sustain a community" and seeks to explain the development of shared dramatizing themes "that coalesce into a rhetorical vision (the shared symbolic ground exhibited by a vision's participants)" (Bormann et. al. 2001, 273). SCT makes use of several technical concepts grouped in six categories. Each of the major technical concepts is briefly described below.

Basic Concepts

A *dramatizing theme* "depicts characters engaged in action in a setting that accounts for and explains human experience," especially in regard to confusing or disturbing events; it is a "creative [. . .] interpretation of events which fulfills a psychological or rhetorical need" (Bormann et. al., 2001, 282). A *symbolic cue* is a shorthand notation or code that represents a dramatizing theme, such a sign, symbol, or inside joke (e.g., New Deal, Manifest Destiny, glasnost, etc.). A *dramatic type* is a "stock scenario used to explain new events in a well-known, dramatic form" (e.g., Watergate); it has been called "the workhorse of rhetorical visions" (Bormann et. al. 2001, 284). A *saga* is "a detailed account of the achievements in the life of a person, group, community, organization, or nation" that "typically represents the symbolic consciousness of an organization as culture" (Bormann et. al., 2001, 284). Without an organizational saga, "both the members' commitment to the organization and their ability to create a cooperative communicative climate will be slight" (Bormann, 53).

Message Structure Concepts

A *rhetorical vision* is "a composite drama that catches up large groups of people in a symbolic reality" (Bormann et. al. 2001, 285). It contains many dramatizing themes that depict heroes and villains (*dramatis personae*) in dramatic action (plot lines) within a scene (setting). In addition, some outside or overarching authority (sanctioning agent) gives legitimacy to the rhetorical vision. "Within a group such a vision establishes identity, cohesion, and culture" (Shields). Rhetorical visions exist on various continua, including flexible to inflexible, intense to passive, secretive to proselytizing, pure to mixed, and healthy to paranoid.

Dynamic Structure Concepts

Rhetorical visions may be of *righteous*, *social*, or *pragmatic* character, referred to as master analogues. Righteous master analogues emphasize the "right" way of doing things and so stress correctness and morality. Social master analogues are concerned primarily with social relations, humaneness, brotherhood, family and the like. Pragmatic master analogues emphasize expediency, practicality, utility, and "whatever it takes to get the job done" (Bormann 1996, 4).

Communicator Concepts

Dramatizers are individuals who share in and sustain a rhetorical vision, while *rhetorical community* describes the cohesive group that shares a common rhetorical vision.

Medium Structure Concepts

SCT functions best in environments that foster group and public sharing. "The moments when communicators are caught up in the sympathetic participation of a common drama" may be called *dramatic chains* (Bormann, 51). *Dramatic sharing* is the expression of a dramatized message that prompts the distribution of group dramatic themes. *Group sharing* occurs when chained dramatic themes get embellished, reconfigured, and reworked in such a way that group members gain a stake in their symbolic construction. *Public sharing* occurs when the dramatic themes that begin in small groups get transported into the public arena (often through speeches picked up by the mass media).

Evaluative Concepts

The idea of *dramatizing theme artistry* concerns the rhetorical creativity, novelty, and competitive advantage of dramatizing themes, symbolic cues, fantasy types, rhetorical visions, and sagas (Bormann et. al., 2001, 291). Effective dramatizing themes must have enough rhetorical power to bring about a desired effect. Compare, for example, Horace Greeley's famous advice on Manifest Destiny—"Go West young man"—to the message shouted by a New Jersey politician on the campaign trail: "Make way, I say, for the young Buffalo. He has not yet got land enough" (Blum et. al., 261). In addition, a dramatizing theme "should fit its rhetorical community and be consistent with other [dramatizing themes] of the rhetorical vision" (Bormann et. al., 2001, 292). *Shared group consciousness* reminds researchers to check for the presence of symbolic convergence. *Rhetorical vision reality-links* "tie rhetorical visions and dramatic themes to the objective reality of the public record and material facts" (Bormann 2001, 293).

Bormann claims that all rhetorical visions have a discernible life cycle. They develop, mature, and decline in largely distinguishable phases. The first phase is *consciousness creating*, in which shared dramatic themes create new symbolic ground for a specific community. In this phase, "speakers dramatize new formulations, and others share them until group and community [dramatic themes] explain the unfolding experience in novel ways" (Bormann 1996, 3). Three rhetorical principles guide this stage.

The *principle of novelty* asserts that when established visions fail to adequately explain current conditions, they often fail to attract younger members of the inheriting groups; rhetoricians must therefore develop innovative dramas to regain lost allegiance (Bormann 1996, 3). The *principle of explanatory power* asserts that when events become confusing and disturbing, individuals begin to share dramatic themes that seem to explain the situation in a credible and satisfying way. The *principle of imitation* asserts that when individuals grow bored with or confused by old visions, they begin to share dramatic themes that rehabilitate and reinvigorate the old dramas.

In the second phase, *consciousness raising*, the activity of proselytizing "leads inquirers and newcomers to share the [dramatic themes] of a rhetorical vision in such a way that they become converts and members of the rhetorical community" (Bormann 1996, 10). Two principles guide this stage, the *principle of critical mass* and the *principle of dedication*. Five key factors allow a rhetorical vision to reach critical mass: (a) a sizeable number of potential converts judge that the new dramatic themes do a good job of making sense of a confusing time; (b) the personal problems of many individuals echo one another, giving the individuals a common predisposition to share the dramatic themes that characterize the new vision; (c) the vision attracts rhetoricians with the artistry required to develop messages that make the new dramas compelling and attractive; (d) the vision attracts administrative and rhetorical staff with the ability to sustain the vision; (e) evangelists of the vision have adequate means and channels of communication to reach many people. The principle of dedication asserts that rhetoricians can raise consciousness by planning events calculated to inspire people to act in line with key emotions of the vision's rhetoric. "Members of rhetorical communities often plan their consciousness raising efforts so that they end with the new converts taking some action that publicly testifies to their conversion" (Bormann 1996, 12).

The third phase, *consciousness sustaining*, is aimed at stoking the commitment fires of those who have embraced the rhetorical vision. Three principles come into play at this stage. The *principle of shielding* describes an effort to block counter messages in both formal and informal channels of communication. The *principle of rededication* describes how criticism or planned, positive dramatizations may keep the vision fresh and vital. The *principle of reiteration* asserts that visions are "sustained by restating the key [dramatizing themes] and types in new patterns that encapsulate the dramatic structure of the vision in artistic symbolic cues" (Bormann 1996, 17).

All rhetorical visions eventually come to an end. In the *decline stage*, three rhetorical principles are at work: (a) *explanatory deficiency* asserts that visions wane as they lose their sense-making power (Bormann 1996, 19); (b) *exploding free speech* asserts that, after a significant period of sustained censorship, a sudden increase of counter-rhetoric in informal channels often ensues (Bormann 1996, 20); (c) *resurfacing competitive rhetorical visions* asserts that, with reopened channels of communication, the natural competition of alternative visions resumes (Bormann 1996, 21). A further principle, that of *rapid implosion*, asserts that, "an inflexible, righteous rhetorical vision tends not to decay incrementally but to implode on itself when an accumulation of problems, triteness, inability to explain rapidly changing events, and contradictory motivations become too great for the vision to accommodate" (Bormann 1996, 24). Many churches discover the truth of this principle only after the tragedy of an implosion.

Seven of the twelve preceding principles apply to all rhetorical visions: novelty, explanatory power, imitation, critical mass, dedication, rededication, and reiteration (Bormann 1996, 25). These seven principles, along with the evaluative concepts of dramatizing theme artistry and rhetorical vision reality-links, may provide a basic framework for building a template for churches that desire to bring a new or reinvigorated rhetorical vision to their congregations.

SCT Applied to Redeemer

SCT can be and has been used to help shape a desired organizational rhetorical vision. Cragan and Shields, for example, used it to guide a corporate strategic planning intervention to bring "unity of focus to corporate positioning, market segmentation, sales story and advertising creation" (1992, 199). Their intervention concerned "the death and rebirth of a corporate symbolic reality" (206); new ownership triggered the implosion of an old corporate vision, resulting in reorganized departments, the firing of long-term personnel, uncertainty spawned by rumors of financial instability, and fears about job security.

While new groups tend to coalesce around the rhetorical vision articulated by the group's founders—followers come because of the vision, and no extant group exists to offer competing rhetorical visions—established groups operate according to a different dynamic. New rhetorical visions cannot simply be imposed from above on an established group, since competing rhetorical visions normally exist; and when an established group's primary rhetorical vision falters, the principles of exploding free speech and resurfacing competitive rhetorical visions normally come into play. In Redeemer's case, attempts by leaders to impose the *Doing Church as a Team* paradigm, and later the Big Idea of "For the greater good," failed at least in part because they did not resonate with large portions of the congregation.

SCT suggests that leaders who want to create a new rhetorical vision, or reanimate a flagging one, must encourage the stated needs of the rank and file to bubble up from below even as the stated desires of leadership trickle down from above, purposefully creating a new mix that incorporates elements from both below and above. Then begins the process of finding compelling terms to express this new mix, rhetoricians to articulate it, channels to convey it, events to celebrate it, and so on. In other words, leaders must design dramatizing themes congruent with established visions.

The remainder of this section of the appendix briefly applies SCT principles to Redeemer to suggest how such a process might begin there.

To start, we must identify a few critical concerns/needs voiced by members of the congregation. Survey, focus group, and independent study data consistently identified at least three issues named by significant portions of the congregation: (a) no discernible Big Idea generates congregational excitement, leading to concern about a "church adrift"; (b) an environment lacking in caring relationships leads to feelings of loneliness and rejection; and (c) a lack of relevant, biblical, spiritually deep teaching leads to a shallow, performance-oriented "show."

Next, it is necessary to identify the core desires expressed by Redeemer's leadership. The church board's strategic planning report identified three "critical components of who we want to be as a church": (a) community (referring to church outreach to the local public); (b) relational (referring to the encouragement and strengthening of transformative relationships); and (c) intergenerational (referring to the facilitation of widespread and significant mentoring friendships between congregants of differing ages).

A key question therefore becomes, what sort of big idea could mesh the expressed concerns of the congregation with the stated desires of its leadership? In Redeemer's case, such a big idea might take the shape of biblically-informed, intergenerational relationships that transform individuals in such profound ways that outsiders feel a powerful desire to experience such relationships for themselves. A rhetorical vision that encompasses such a Big Idea would be categorized as a social master analogue.*

Novelty

The principle of novelty asserts that rhetoricians must develop innovative dramas, or dramatizing themes, to regain the allegiance of group

---

* A scriptural text that might effectively provide a theological foundation for such a big idea is John 13:35, where Jesus said, "By this all men will know that you are my disciples, if you love one another."

members disaffected by a fading rhetorical vision. First, Redeemer's leadership could look for compelling stories within the congregation that highlight the kind of transformative, intergenerational relationships it wants to encourage, and then use those stories to communicate the declared rhetorical vision in an energetic way.

Jackson and Esse explained how a British firm used storytelling to "lay the foundations for a sustainable, profitable future" (26). In 2001 the company lost nearly £200 million; after two restructurings, it broke even in 2005. The company wanted to communicate a shift in priorities—"from now on it would be about building a great business and achieving our goal of being the UK's most trusted worldwide express carrier"—and it wanted a "relative and memorable way of making the strategy relevant to our colleagues" that would "generate energy and ownership in order to make progress" (27). It used storytelling to "create a process through which our strategy or corporate 'story' could be brought to life." It solicited and used real-life stories and "storytelling evangelists" to communicate the company message; the best stories told at a grass roots level were fed back to the executive board and used throughout the company. The firm learned that for storytelling to work, it required high levels of commitment from leadership. By 2005-2006, the company exceeded its profit target by £1 million and surveys of employee satisfaction rose to their highest-ever level, with 70 percent saying they enjoyed working for the company (28).

Second, Redeemer could emphasize how significant intergenerational relationships can give the church's youth the rare tools they need to grow up emotionally and spiritually healthy, even in a desperately unhealthy culture; at the same time, it could emphasize how intergenerational relationships can give adults an open door to energetic experts who grasp the vast technological and cultural shifts taking place in the world. In other words, the older help the younger, and the younger help the older.

Explanatory Power

This principle asserts that in confusing and disturbing times, individuals look for and begin to share dramatic themes that appear to supply a satisfying explanation for their troubles. First, Redeemer might consider highlighting various biblical explanations for dysfunctional relationships (in general, alienation from God and living apart from divine guidelines for healthy relationships) as well as the Bible's response to these dysfunctions (honesty, humility, concern, presence and other biblical strategies for creating true community). This principle also could find expression in an expanded adult education effort.

Second, Redeemer might more carefully define what it means by "relevance," since its public statements and actions do not make it clear whether it conceives of relevance primarily as mirroring certain elements of the dominant culture, or as addressing human needs within the dominant culture.

Imitation

This principle asserts that when old visions begin to bore or confuse group members, individuals begin to share dramatic themes that rehabilitate and reinvigorate old dramas. What "old dramas" could serve this function at Redeemer? What accounts from its growth years, community outreaches, youth ministry, short-term mission trips, or other tales from its remembered history could be "imitated"? What "big successes" from the church's past could be resurfaced to support the new rhetorical vision?

Critical Mass

This principle states that five key factors permit a rhetorical vision to reach critical mass and therefore begin to sustain a group: (a) A significant number of individuals agree that the new dramatic themes do indeed make sense of a confusing time. Which demographic groups at Redeemer are most likely to resonate with the new rhetorical vision? What can the church do to inform and energize these groups? How can the church foster positive interaction between these groups and those that are less likely to quickly resonate with the new vision? (b) many individuals in the group experience similar problems, predisposing those individuals to share the dramatic themes of the new vision. What groups at Redeemer may fit this profile? Two possibilities may be those suffering through divorce or marital difficulties, and those struggling with finding employment in a difficult economy. A rhetorical vision that championed healthy, deep, intergenerational friendships might find special resonance with such individuals, who naturally tend to feel isolated and disenfranchised; (c) rhetoricians with the artistry required to develop compelling and attractive messages adopt the rhetorical vision. Redeemer already has a "preaching team" of talented teachers; it also has in its membership a number of other gifted and trained public speakers who periodically teach classes or speak in group settings. Redeemer might consider organizing a training seminar for these individuals in which the new rhetorical vision is laid out in a logical, compelling form, and invite input from these speakers on how to make public presentations regarding the vision as attractive as possible. It could especially solicit input on compelling, succinct ways to verbalize the rhetorical vision; (d) the vision attracts administrative and rhetorical staff with the ability to sustain the vision. First, Redeemer might take whatever steps it can to ensure that staff members responsible for publicly expressing the new rhetorical vision—once it is developed and artfully framed—do their best to convey it with enthusiasm and heartfelt excitement. Dutiful or rote presentations of a rhetorical vision do not assist in its eager acceptance by the rhetorical group. Second, Redeemer might consider organizing a series of smaller, more intimate sessions with support staff and key volunteers, designed to present a thorough explication of the rhetorical vision, its implications, and the activities required to build and perpetuate it. Question and answer segments might be especially important, with follow-up sessions scheduled over a designated period. Third, it might be helpful to designate a small number of easy-to-access authorities on Redeemer's rhetorical vision who could answer questions about various aspects of the vision, its related dramatizing themes, and the church's strategy to develop and sustain the whole effort; and (e) adequate means and channels of communication exist for vision evangelists to reach a wide audience. Redeemer might consider using not only its current channels of communication to broadcast the vision—worship services, streaming events, classes, small groups, website, newsletters, meetings, social functions—but also creating special channels for additional opportunities to distribute key information.

Gothard reported how health care giant Aetna turned around its ailing business, in part by creating new communication channels. To build business literacy and make sure its employees understood the company's competitive business environment, Aetna used executive messaging, video communication (a five-part video series featured senior leaders fielding questions from employees), a special business plan website, and direct mail. Aetna annually prepared a printed document that reinforced the company's values and business goals, each year emphasizing different overarching themes that highlighted company priorities. It also produced four "knowledge maps" designed to strengthen employee understanding of marketplace issues, and how the firm planned to respond to them (Gothard 28). The company used the maps when it brought together small groups of employees from different functions and business units, "in sessions that were fun and engaging. Participants were challenged to think about Aetna's business, the impact of industry trends and how they could help the company achieve success. Not a typical class or lecture, these sessions created an open learning environment for people to explore concepts and come to their own conclusions" (Gothard 29).

Dedication

This principle asserts that rhetoricians can raise consciousness by planning events calculated to inspire individuals to act in line with key emotions of the vision's rhetoric. For example, a slumping Reuters recorded losses of almost £500 million in 2002, prompting its CEO to describe the company as "fighting for survival." Only one year later, it recorded profits of almost £500 million. "Communication was at the heart of this remarkable recovery," wrote a company executive (Bell 18). Reuters designed and executed a special one-day event that included all its offices in more than 140 countries. The event involved live video feeds, Q&A sessions, a special website, toolkits, teasers prior to the event, and locally organized social activities after the event. "Feedback from employees both on and following the day was overwhelmingly positive. Even the CEO described it as 'the day the company turned the corner'" (Bell 21).

Rededication

This principle asserts that both severe criticism and planned, positive dramatizations may help to keep the vision fresh and vital. Bormann discusses how congressional anticommunist hearings utilized this principle during the Cold War, and how "freedom crusades" in multiple forms were used at various times to "sustain the committed in their dedication to the Cold War vision" (Bormann 1996, 16).

Reiteration

This principle holds that restating key dramatizing themes and types in new patterns encapsulates the dramatic structure of the vision in artistic symbolic cues, thus helping to sustain visions. Redeemer might consider identifying and refining several key dramatizing themes and then brainstorm multiple ways to use them in various contexts.

Dramatizing Theme Artistry

This evaluative concept uses rhetorical creativity, novelty, and competitive advantage to present various dramatizing themes. One SCT study described how voters in Iowa were more persuaded by an artistically presented campaign that glorified riverboat gambling's romantic connections with Mark Twain-era scenes, rather than a competing righteous master analogue that emphasized the moral evils of gambling. The study strongly implied that an organization can increase its rhetorical success by developing and skillfully using artistic dramatizing themes (Duffy, 291 ff). While this appendix does not endorse gambling, the story does emphasize how the skillful use of story can have a much more powerful effect than simple moralizing.

In the past, Redeemer tapped into its large creative community to produce innovative and popular local offerings, particularly in music and drama. It might consider inviting these communities to reengage, with a view toward helping church leadership frame key dramatizing themes in artistically compelling ways. In addition, Redeemer might consider bringing more innovation and native creativity to its public worship services, thus more fully utilizing the demographic range of members and attenders available to it. If Redeemer wants to encourage intergenerational ministry, then it might consider the idea that bringing special focus to youth does not require the church to minimize the appearance on stage of more mature believers. Finally, Redeemer might bring more artistry to its communication of dramatizing themes in large group meetings by experimenting with what might be called a continuum of presentational variety. If rhetorical visions themselves exist on a continuum (e.g., from flexible to inflexible), then the presentation of those visions also may benefit from a continuum of portrayal. Redeemer could consider several such continua of presentational variety: traditional to innovative; planned to spontaneous; clear to mysterious; hard to soft; direct to indirect; frequent to occasional. Thinking in such categories may help to improve dramatizing theme artistry by encouraging creativity, novelty, and competitive advantage.

Rhetorical Vision Reality-Links

A final evaluative concept ties rhetorical visions to "real-world" events and circumstances. Redeemer might consider how to continually and publicly connect its chosen dramatizing themes to current events, local realities, and immediate congregational concerns. An emphasis on telling "real life" stories, grounded in contemporary situations, might be one good way to begin accomplishing this.

Conclusion and Recommendations

Because Redeemer struggles with many issues that researchers say have hampered the growth of evangelical churches nationwide, it may serve as a good case study for other congregations that find themselves mired in outdated, moribund, or irrelevant rhetorical visions. SCT may provide such churches with both a good diagnostic tool to analyze their current rhetorical situations, as well as with an effective grid for constructing or reconstructing a more viable rhetorical vision appropriate to their current contexts and in line with a God-inspired vision.

This essay has only scratched the surface of how SCT might be utilized in church ministry. Researchers might also investigate whether theories similar or comparable to SCT—such as Pearce and Cronen's Coordinated Management of Meaning, or Gerbner's Cultivation Theory—might serve as viable candidates to help churches diagnose and ameliorate, or even help cure, their current stagnation ills.

Notes

1. Ken Blanchard, as cited in Michelle Braden, "In Leadership, Influence Is Not a Given," *Forbes*, June 15, 2018, https://www.forbes.com/sites/forbescoachescouncil/2018/06/15/in-leadership-influence-is-not-a-given/?sh=122121dc6797.

2. John C. Maxwell, "7 Factors that Influence Influence," *John C. Maxwell*, July 8, 2013, https://www.johnmaxwell.com/blog/7-factors-that-influence-influence/.

3. John C. Maxwell, *The 21 Irrefutable Laws of Leadership* (Nashville, TN: Thomas Nelson, 2007), 252.

4. Ralph Waldo Emerson, as cited in *Thoughts on the Business Life*, Forbes, https://www.forbes.com/quotes/7810/#:~:text=Quotes%20Thoughts%20On%20The%20Business%20Of%20Life&text=It%20is%20one%20of%20the%20most%20beautiful%20compensations%20of%20this,help%20another%20without%20helping%20himself.

5. Martin Luther, as cited by Steve Perisho, *Liber Locorum Communium*, July 12, 2016, http://liberlocorumcommunium.blogspot.com/2016/07/i-have-held-many-things-in-my-hands-and.html.

6. These three strategies can be found on the Center for Creative Leadership website at "Influencing: Learn How to Use the Skill of Persuasion," *Center for Creative Leadership*, https://www.ccl.org/articles/white-papers/learn-persuasion-skills/.

7. Daniel Harkavy, *The 7 Perspectives of Effective Leaders* (Grand Rapids, MI: Baker Books, 2020), front matter.

8. Harkavy, *The 7 Perspectives of Effective Leaders*, front matter.

9. Brian Tracy, *The Power of Self-Confidence* (Hoboken, NJ: John Wiley & Sons, 2012).

10. Lynn Matti, *5 Weeks to Self-Confidence* (Emeryville, CA: Rockridge Press, 2019).

11. Barrie Davenport, *Confidence Hacks* (CreateSpace, 2014).

12. For example: Stamp out negativity, know how others perceive you, have an accurate opinion of yourself, eat well, exercise, meditate, sleep, stop comparing yourself to others, surround yourself with positive people, give yourself positive self-talk, face your fears, after failing try it differently and so build resilience, show others how to treat you, don't "should" yourself, gain some perspective, prepare well, focus on things you can control, get regular feedback, remind yourself of your achievements, identify your strengths and work in them, know your role, create good goals, build

a support network, review your recent successes, accept your limitations, try something new, accept compliments, visualize yourself performing well.

13. Harkavy, *The 7 Perspectives of Effective Leaders*, 14.

14. Chip Heath and Dan Heath, *Decisive* (New York: Crown Business, 2013).

15. As cited by Jessica Peng, "Steve Jobs' Last Words," *Columbia Computer Science*, April 28, 2019, https://blogs.cuit.columbia.edu/jp3864/2019/04/28/steve-jobs-last-words/.

16. "The Mission," *Museum of the Bible*, https://www.museumofthebible.org/the-mission.

17. C.H. Spurgeon, *An All-Round Ministry* (Carlisle, PA: The Banner of Truth Trust, 1978), 191.

18. Ken Camp, "'Chaplain of Bourbon Street' dies at 89," *Baptist Standard*, July 6, 2017, https://www.baptiststandard.com/news/baptists/chaplain-of-bourbon-street-dies-at-89/.

19. Camp, "Chaplain of Bourbon Street."

20. Spurgeon, Pray Without Ceasing," *The Metropolitan Tabernacle Pulpit*, vol. 18 (1872), from the C.H. Spurgeon Collection.

21. Accessed from author's personal files.

22. Max DePree, *Leadership Is an Art* (New York: Currency, 2004), 11.

23. Winston Churchill, as cited in Steven F. Hayward, *Churchill on Leadership* (New York: Three Rivers Press, 1998), 68-69.

24. Larry Bossidy and Ram Charan, *Execution* (New York: Crown Business, 2009), ix.

25. Peter Salovey and John D. Mayer, "Emotional Intelligence," *Imagination, Cognition, and Personality*, vol. 9, no. 3, March 1, 1990.

26. Daniel Goleman, *Emotional Intelligence* (New York: Bantam Books, 1995).

27. "The Meaning of Emotional Intelligence," *Institute for Health and Human Potential*, https://www.ihhp.com/meaning-of-emotional-intelligence/.

28. Christopher D. Connors, *Emotional Intelligence for the Modern Leader* (Emeryville, CA: Rockridge Press, 2020), xi.

29. Connors, *Emotional Intelligence for the Modern Leader*, xi.

30. Connors, *Emotional Intelligence for the Modern Leader*, 1.

31. Connors, *Emotional Intelligence for the Modern Leader*, 5.

32. Connors, *Emotional Intelligence for the Modern Leader*, 6.

33. Connors, *Emotional Intelligence for the Modern Leader*, 7.

34. Connors, *Emotional Intelligence for the Modern Leader*, 8.

35. Connors, *Emotional Intelligence for the Modern Leader*, 9.

36. Connors, *Emotional Intelligence for the Modern Leader*, 16.

37. Connors, *Emotional Intelligence for the Modern Leader*, 34.

38. Connors, *Emotional Intelligence for the Modern Leader*, 36.

39. As cited by Harold Lawrence Myra and Marshall Shelley in *The Leadership Secrets of Billy Graham* (Grand Rapids, MI: Zondervan, 2005), 89.

40. John C. Maxwell, *Becoming a Person of Influence* (Nashville, TN: Thomas Nelson, 1997).

41. "Meet Ken Sande," *RW360*, https://rw360.org/meet-ken-sande-2/.

42. "About," *RW360*, https://rw360.org/meet-ken-sande-2/.

43. This is not an official translation but a paraphrase by William Barclay (see https://www.precept austin.org/matthew, 59.

44. James A. Schellenberg, *Conflict Resolution: Theory, Research, and Practice,* (Albany, NY: State University of New York Press, 1996), 9.

45. Enyonam Kudonoo, Kathy Schroeder, and Sheila Boysen-Rotelli, "An Olympic Transformation: Creating an Organizational Culture That Promotes Healthy Conflict." *Organization Development Journal*, 30, no. 2 (2012): 51.

46. Jeremy Pollack, *Conflict Resolution Playbook* (Emeryville, CA: Rockridge Press, 2020), 1.

47. Pollack, *Conflict Resolution Playbook*, 2.

48. Pollack, *Conflict Resolution Playbook*, 3.

49. Pollack, *Conflict Resolution Playbook*, 4.

50. Pollack, *Conflict Resolution Playbook*, 8.

51. Pollack, *Conflict Resolution Playbook*, 10-11.

52. "Investor Relations," *Coca-Cola Consolidated*, February 12, 2021, https://investor.cokecon solidated.com/news-releases/news-release-details/coca-cola-consolidated-inc-release-fourth -quarter-2020-and.

53. C.S. Lewis, *The Joyful Christian* (New York: Touchstone, 1977), 138

54. Jeremiah Burroughs, *The Rare Jewel of Christian Contentment* (London: Peter Cole, 1655), 4.

55. John MacArthur, *The MacArthur New Testament Commentary Philippians* (Chicago, IL: Moody, 2001), 296.

56. Jeremiah Burroughs, *Contentment, Prosperity, and God's Glory*, ed. Phillip L. Simpson (Grand Rapids, MI: Reformation Heritage Books, 2013), https://www.google.com/books/edition/Content ment_Prosperity_and_God_s_Glory/4jMSEAAAQBAJ?hl=en&gbpv=1&dq=%E2%80%9Cth e+undoing+of+most+men%22&pg=PT32&printsec=frontcover.

References

Bell, Anne Marie. (2005). Inspiring organizational change at Reuters. *Strategic Communication Management*. Aug/Sep (9)5; 18-22.

Blum, J.M., Catton, B., Morgan, E.S., Schlesinger, A.M., Stampp, K.M., & Woodward, C.V. (1963). *The national experience: A history of the United States.* New York: Harcourt, Brace, & World.

Bormann, Ernest G. (1982). The Symbolic Convergence Theory of Communication: Application and Implications for Teachers and Consultants. *Journal of Applied Communication* Research. (10)1, 50-61.

Bormann, Ernest G., Cragan, John F., & Shields, Donald C. (2003). Defending Symbolic Convergence Theory from an Imaginary Gunn. *Quarterly Journal of Speech*. (89)4, 366–372.

_____. (2001) Three Decades of Developing, Grounding, and Using Symbolic Convergence Theory (SCT). In *Communication Yearbook 25*, ed. William B. Gudykunst. Mahwah, New Jersey: Lawrence Erlbaum Associates, 271-313.

_____. (1996). An Expansion of the Rhetorical Vision Component of the Symbolic Convergence Theory: The Cold War Paradigm Case. *Communication Monographs*. (63)1, 1-29.

Bormann, E.G., Howell, W.S., Nichols, R.G., & Shapiro, G.L. (1982). *Interpersonal communication in the modern organization* (2nd ed.). Englewood Cliffs, NJ: Prentice-Hall.

Bormann, Ernest G., Knutson, Roxann L., & Musolf, Karen. (1997). Why do people share dramatic themes? An empirical investigation of a basic tenet of the symbolic convergence communication theory. *Communication Studies*, (48)3, 254-276.

Cragan, J.F., & Shields, D.C. (1994). *Advancing symbolic convergence theory: A paper in honor of Ernest G. Bormann.* Paper presented at the University of Minnesota, Minneapolis.

Cragan, John F., & Shields, Donald C. (1992). The Use of Symbolic Convergence Theory in Corporate Strategic Planning: A Case Study. *Journal of Applied Communication Research.* (20)2, 199-218.

Duin, Julia. (2008). *Quitting Church: Why the Faithful Are Fleeing and What to Do About It.* Grand Rapids, MI: Baker Books.

Focus Group: Dissatisfied with Redeemer. 8 July 2009. Church resource.

Fuller, Linda K. (1998). Saving Stories: A Goal of the Cultural Environment Movement. *International Communication Gazette.* (60)2, 139-153.

Gothard, Ann Marie. (2005). Improving business literacy and profitability at Aetna. *Strategic Communication Management.* June/July, (9)4, 26-29.

Halliday, Steven W. (2009). A Church Love Affair Gone Sour: Former Attenders Tell Why They Tearfully Left. Unpublished paper, Regent University.

Hensley, Carl Wayne. (1975). Rhetorical Vision and the Persuasion of a Historical Movement: The Disciples of Christ in Nineteenth Century American Culture. *Quarterly Journal of Speech.* (61)3, 250-265.

Jackson, Susan, & Esse, Alison. (2006). Making a difference through storytelling at Parcelforce. *Strategic Communication Management.* (10)3, 26-29.

Key Findings and Statistics on Religion in America. http://religions.perforum.org /reports. Web. 2 December 2009.

Kinnaman, David, & Lyons, Gabe. (2007). *Unchristian: What a New Generation Really Thinks About Christianity.* Grand Rapids, MI: Baker Books.

New Statistics on Church Attendance and Avoidance. www.barna.org. Web. 2 December 2009.

Newport, Frank. No Evidence Bad Times Are Boosting Church Attendance. www.gallup.com. Web. 2 December 2009.

Redeemer attendance figures. Church resource. n.d. Print.

Reveal Spiritual Life Survey. Survey taken May 2007, findings reported 30 October 2007.

Shields, Donald C. "Symbolic convergence theory." www.blackwellreference.com. Web. 3 December 2009.

Bible Notifications

All Scripture quotations are taken from the New King James Version®. Copyright © 1982 by Thomas Nelson, Inc. Used by permission. All rights reserved.

Verses marked KJV are taken from the King James Version of the Bible.

Verses marked HCSB have been taken from the Holman Christian Standard Bible®, Copyright © 1999, 2000, 2002, 2003, 2009 by Holman Bible Publishers. Used by permission. Holman Christian Standard Bible®, Holman CSB®, and HCSB® are federally registered trademarks of Holman Bible Publishers.

Verses marked ESV are taken from The ESV® Bible (The Holy Bible, English Standard Version®), copyright © 2001 by Crossway, a publishing ministry of Good News Publishers. Used by permission. All rights reserved.

Scripture quotations marked NLT are taken from the Holy Bible, New Living Translation, copyright © 1996, 2004, 2015 by Tyndale House Foundation. Used by permission of Tyndale House Publishers, Inc., Carol Stream, Illinois 60188. All rights reserved.

Verses marked NIV are taken from the Holy Bible, New International Version®, NIV®. Copyright © 1973, 1978, 1984, 2011 by Biblica, Inc.® Used by permission of Zondervan. All rights reserved worldwide. www.zondervan.com. The "NIV" and "New International Version" are trademarks registered in the United States Patent and Trademark Office by Biblica, Inc.®

More Great Harvest House Books by Johnny Hunt

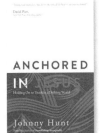

Join Johnny Hunt on an exploration of what it means to have a *living* relationship with Christ—the kind that allows Him to work in you so that you reflect His character more and more. Anchor yourself in Jesus…and let Him transform you!

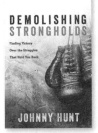

Ever wonder how to be victorious in the trenches of life? Pastor Johnny Hunt offers biblical encouragement and guidance to help you break spiritual strongholds so you can move forward in God's will and become the kind of man you've always wanted to be.

With sensitivity and clarity, Johnny Hunt addresses some of the things men find most difficult to talk about. Discover how the temptations you face can become opportunities to grow your faith so you can love God and your family well.

You are not alone in this battle, and you were not created to be a prisoner of shame. This growth and study guide will help you face your struggles and draw strength from God and other believers. Be amazed by how the power of God can work in your life!

To learn more about Harvest House books and
to read sample chapters, visit our website:

www.HarvestHousePublishers.com

HARVEST HOUSE PUBLISHERS
EUGENE, OREGON